That's All

✧ Reference Series ✧

1 **ALL TOGETHER NOW**
The First Complete Beatles Discography, 1961-1975
by Harry Castleman & Walter J. Podrazik

2 **THE BEATLES AGAIN**
[Sequel to *All Together Now*]
by Harry Castleman & Walter J. Podrazik

3 **A DAY IN THE LIFE**
The Beatles Day-By-Day, 1960-1970
by Tom Schultheiss

4 **THINGS WE SAID TODAY**
The Complete Lyrics and a Concordance to The Beatles Songs, 1962-1970
by Colin Campbell & Allan Murphy

5 **YOU CAN'T DO THAT**
Beatles Bootlegs & Novelty Records, 1963-1980
by Charles Reinhart

6 **SURF'S UP!**
The Beach Boys On Record, 1961-1981
by Brad Elliott

7 **COLLECTING THE BEATLES**
An Introduction & Price Guide to Fab Four Collectibles, Records & Memorabilia
by Barbara Fenick

8 **JAILHOUSE ROCK**
The Bootleg Records of Elvis Presley, 1970-1983
by Lee Cotten & Howard DeWitt

9 **THE LITERARY LENNON: A COMEDY OF LETTERS**
The First Study of All the Major and Minor Writings of John Lennon
by Dr. James Sauceda

10 **THE END OF THE BEATLES?**
[Sequel to *The Beatles Again* and *All Together Now*]
by Harry Castleman & Walter J. Podrazik

11 **HERE, THERE & EVERYWHERE**
The First International Beatles Bibliography, 1962-1982
by Carol D. Terry

12 **CHUCK BERRY--ROCK 'N' ROLL MUSIC**
Second Edition, Revised
by Howard A. DeWitt

13 **ALL SHOOK UP**
Elvis Day-By-Day, 1954-1977
by Lee Cotten

14 **WHO'S NEW WAVE IN MUSIC**
An Illustrated Encyclopedia, 1976-1982
by David Bianco

15 **THE ILLUSTRATED DISCOGRAPHY OF SURF MUSIC, 1961-1965**
Second Edition, Revised
by John Blair

16 **COLLECTING THE BEATLES, VOLUME 2**
An Introduction & Price Guide to Fab Four Collectibles, Records & Memorabilia
by Barbara Fenick

17 **HEART OF STONE**
The Definitive Rolling Stones Discography, 1962-1983
by Felix Aeppli

18 **BEATLEFAN**
The Authoritative Publication of Record For Fans of the Beatles, Volumes 1 & 2
Reprint Edition, With Additions

19 **YESTERDAY'S PAPERS**
The Rolling Stones In Print, 1963-1984
by Jessica MacPhail

20 **EVERY LITTLE THING**
The Definitive Guide To Beatles Recording Variations, Rare Mixes & Other Musical Oddities, 1958-1986
by William McCoy & Mitchell McGeary

21 **STRANGE DAYS**
The Music Of John, Paul, George & Ringo Twenty Years On
by Walter J. Podrazik

22 **SEQUINS & SHADES**
The Michael Jackson Reference Guide
by Carol D. Terry

23 **WILD & INNOCENT**
The Recordings of Bruce Springsteen, 1973-1985
by Brad Elliott

24 **TIME IS ON MY SIDE**
The Rolling Stones Day-By-Day, 1962-1986
by Alan Stewart & Cathy Sanford

25 **HEAT WAVE**
The Motown Fact Book
by David Bianco

26 **BEATLEFAN**
The Authoritative Publication of Record For Fans of the Beatles, Volumes 3 & 4
Reprint Edition, With Additions

27 **RECONSIDER BABY**
The Definitive Elvis Sessionography, 1954-1977
by Ernst Jorgensen, Erik Rasmussen & Johnny Mikkelsen

28 **THE MONKEES: A MANUFACTURED IMAGE**
The Ultimate Reference Guide to Monkee Memories & Memorabilia
by Ed Reilly, Maggie McManus & Bill Chadwick

29 **RETURN TO SENDER**
The First Complete Discography Of Elvis Tribute & Novelty Records, 1956-1986
by Howard Banney

30 **THE CHILDREN OF NUGGETS**
The Definitive Guide To "Psychedelic Sixties" Punk Rock On Compilation Albums
by David Walters

31 **SHAKE, RATTLE & ROLL**
The Golden Age Of American Rock 'N' Roll, Volume 1: 1952-1955
by Lee Cotten

Available only through Popular Culture, Ink., P.O. Box 1839, Ann Arbor, Michigan 48106
Phone: 1-800-678-8828

32 **THE ILLUSTRATED DISCOGRAPHY OF HOT ROD MUSIC, 1961-1965**
by John Blair & Stephen McParland

33 **POSITIVELY BOB DYLAN**
A Thirty-Year Discography, Concert & Recording Session Guide, 1960-1991
by Michael Krogsgaard

34 **OFF THE RECORD**
Motown By Master Number, 1959-1989
Volume 1: Singles
by Reginald J. Bartlette

35 **LISTENING TO THE BEATLES**
An Audiophile's Guide to the Sound of the Fab Four, Volume 1: Singles
by David Schwartz

36 **ELVIS--THE SUN YEARS**
The Story Of Elvis Presley In The Fifties
by Howard A. DeWitt

37 **HEADBANGERS**
The Worldwide MegaBook Of Heavy Metal Bands
by Mark Hale

38 **THAT'S ALL**
Bobby Darin On Record, Stage & Screen
by Jeff Bleiel

✧ Remembrances Series ✧

1 **AS I WRITE THIS LETTER**
An American Generation Remembers The Beatles
Edited by Marc A. Catone

2 **THE LONGEST COCKTAIL PARTY**
An Insider's Diary of The Beatles, Their Million-Dollar Apple Empire and Its Wild Rise and Fall
Reprint Edition, With Additions
by Richard DiLello

3 **AS TIME GOES BY**
Living In The Sixties
Reprint Edition, With Additions
by Derek Taylor

4 **A CELLARFUL OF NOISE**
Reprint Edition, With Additions
by Brian Epstein

5 **THE BEATLES AT THE BEEB**
The Story Of Their Radio Career, 1962-1965
Reprint Edition, With Additions
by Kevin Howlett

6 **THE BEATLES READER**
A Selection Of Contemporary Views, News, & Reviews Of The Beatles In Their Heyday
Edited by Charles P. Neises

7 **THE BEATLES DOWN UNDER**
The 1964 Australia & New Zealand Tour
Reprint Edition, With Additions
by Glenn A. Baker

8 **LONG LONELY HIGHWAY**
A 1950's Elvis Scrapbook
Reprint Edition, With Additions
by Ger Rijff

9 **IKE'S BOYS**
The Story Of The Everly Brothers
by Phyllis Karpp

10 **ELVIS–FROM MEMPHIS TO HOLLYWOOD**
Memories From My Twelve Years With Elvis Presley
by Alan Fortas

11 **SAVE THE LAST DANCE FOR ME**
The Musical Legacy Of The Drifters, 1953-1993
by Tony Allan with Faye Treadwell

12 **TURN ME ON, DEAD MAN**
The Complete Story of the Paul McCartney Death Hoax
by Andru J. Reeve

✧ Trivia Series ✧

1 **NOTHING IS BEATLEPROOF**
Advanced Beatles Trivia For Fab Four Fanciers
by Mike Hockinson

"I thought he was a terrific rock'n'roll artist. He understood and appreciated Chuck Berry. He loved that music, but he also loved Cole Porter and Sinatra. He liked the glamour of Las Vegas, the Copacabana and all that. And he could do both quite handily."

·**AHMET ERTEGUN**, President, Atlantic Records

"He was one of the greats. He's kind of in the genre of Dion, but I think that because he headed in the direction of Sinatra, people don't relate to him as a rock figure. He was like a mentor to me. He convinced me that rock'n'roll was where it was at."

·**ROGER McGUINN**, singer, guitarist,
founder of The Byrds, Darin guitarist 1962-63

"In the record business in those days, nobody in their twenties used to produce. Young singers used to be an instrument of someone else. Darin did what nobody did in those days. He picked everything. It always had his thumbprint on it."

·**NIK VENET**, Capitol Records producer
(Darin, The Beach Boys, Lou Rawls, Linda Ronstadt)

"He did good work in so many different areas. He had a sense of ambition, desire and passion that is really part of the hallmark of rock'n'roll."

·**ROBERT HILBURN**, Pop Music Critic,
The *Los Angeles Times*

"He was one of the greatest performers I ever saw on the stage. I've worked with a hell of a lot of singers, and I don't think any of them had Bobby's essential performing ability."

·**BOBBY SCOTT**, jazz pianist, arranger, composer
("A Taste Of Honey," "He Ain't Heavy, He's My Brother"),
occasional Darin arranger and accompanist

"The thing I always respected about Bobby was that I totally believed every phase he was in. I believed his rock'n'roll phase, I believed his Vegas phase, and I believed his folk phase."

·**ALAN THICKE**, actor, television personality ("Growing Pains"), writer for "The Bobby Darin Show"

"I listened to him a lot as a kid. Darin was a white guy who was really in the groove. I identified with any white cat who could really sing in the groove, because there were a lot of white singers who did not."

·**TIM HAUSER**, vocalist, The Manhattan Transfer

"I've worked a lot with Frank Sinatra. Bobby was similar. When he came on in Vegas, he owned it. He was probably the best performer ever to play Vegas."

·**DICK BAKALYAN**, actor (appeared with Darin in "Pressure Point," "The Bobby Darin Show")

"Thinking back, he was probably one of the most talented, gifted entertainers I've worked with."

·**SAUL ILSON**, television producer ("The Smothers Brothers Comedy Hour," "Tony Orlando & Dawn"), co-producer of "The Bobby Darin Show"

"He was able to go in so many different directions. People, on the radio level in particular, like to be able to characterize an artist. He was going from Buddy Holly to Frank Sinatra. He liked it all."

·**TERRY MELCHER**, record producer (The Byrds, Paul Revere & The Raiders, The Beach Boys), Darin co-writer and associate

"He was very helpful in the studio. He cut right to the core of the matter and knew just what to do. He was an incredible professional and an incredibly great singer."

·**DON RUBIN**, co-producer of two Darin LPs

(Atlantic Records publicity photo)

That's All

Bobby Darin on Record, Stage & Screen

by

Jeff Bleiel

Popular Culture, Ink.
1993

Book design and layout by Tom Schultheiss.
Cover design by Diane Bareis.
Computer programming by Alex Przebienda.

ISBN 1-56075-031-6
LC 93-83934

Published by Popular Culture, Ink.
P.O. Box 1839, Ann Arbor, MI 48106 USA

PCI Collector Editions
are published especially for discerning collectors and libraries.
Each Collector Edition title is released in limited quantities identified by edition, printing number, and number of copies.
Unlike trade editions, they are not generally available in bookstores.

10 9 8 7 6 5 4 3 2 1
(First edition, first printing: 1500 copies)

Printed in the United States of America

"The best rock-and-roll books in the world!"

Contents

Part II: Appendices

Foreword

Through the years, I've been asked hundreds of times to reflect on my favorite artist of all time. Having dealt with thousands of performers, I've never been able to adequately answer. Quite frankly, I've always been afraid of offending the artists I didn't name. Having been asked to write a foreword to this book, I didn't feel as constrained. I've always admired Bobby Darin tremendously.

Bobby had a voracious appetite for variety. He wanted to do everything. As it turned out, he did it, and he did it well in a much-too-short lifetime. He is one of the most versatile performers I've ever met.

That's All: Bobby Darin On Record, Stage & Screen is a work that surveys the career of my friend Bobby Darin. Jeff Bleiel has purposely emphasized the professional side over the personal side of Bobby's life. But let me add a personal note. Bobby was one of the most complicated and interesting people I've known. You didn't always "get what you saw." He could be equally tough and gentle. He was autocratic and at the same time very democratic. He was generous to a fault.

There were things I always knew about him. If I were in trouble, no matter where he was, he would find me and come to my aid. Had I needed it, he would have given me money. I never asked for money but, like everybody else, I had my share of emotional setbacks. Bobby was always there to advise and console me. It was a reciprocal arrangement. I can illustrate the kind of friend he was with an example....If ever your home or your family are put in danger, the person who shows up to help put out the fire and take care of the kids is really a friend. I could always count on Bobby Darin. He knew he could count on me.

My appraisal of his extraordinary talent and contributions may be colored by my love for him. I hope that when you finish reading *That's All: Bobby Darin On Record, Stage & Screen*, you'll conclude that Bobby Darin was a true one-of-a-kind.

Dick Clark

Bobby Darin and his friend Dick Clark.
(Photo courtesy: Dick Clark.)

Acknowledgments

I wish to acknowledge and express my appreciation to the nineteen professional associates of Bobby Darin who were gracious in sharing their remembrances with me. Thanks to Dick Bakalyan, Ernest Chambers, Bob Crewe, Quitman Dennis, Steve Douglas, Geoff Edwards, Ahmet Ertegun, Saul Ilson, Charles Koppelman, Brent Maher, Billy May, Roger McGuinn, Terry Melcher, Tom Morgan, Walter Raim, Don Rubin, and Alan Thicke.

Special thanks to the two men who were most generous with their time, and without whose contributions this project would not have been nearly as revealing to the reader or rewarding to the author:

First, to the late Bobby Scott, whom I had the privilege of speaking with only eight months before his death in November 1990. I feel extremely fortunate to have had the opportunity to get his warm and vivid recollections about Bobby Darin on record.

And finally, to Nik Venet, whose initial kindness and openness was a tremendous boost to this effort. His continuing helpfulness was a great comfort and motivation throughout this entire project.

Thanks also to Bobby Darin's long-time friend and associate Harriet Wasser for sharing her insights and memories with me.

I would also like to thank Tim Hauser, Robert Hilburn and John Stewart for providing their comments.

Also thanks to the following for their assistance and/or encouragement: Stephen Allen, Jenny Berger, Renee Blumenthal, The Carnegie Library, Pat Durkin, Fred Dutton, The Federal Bureau of Investigation, Ron Furmanek, Erik Jacobsen, Georges LaForge, Gary Levine, The Library of Congress, particularly the staffs of the Motion Picture and Television and Performing Arts Reading Rooms, Richard Lorenzo of the ABC Direction Radio Network, Frank Mankiewicz, John May, Marlene Miller, The Museum of Broadcasting, Jack Newfield, Gordon Pogoda, Brad Rivers, Steve Ryan, Steven Shore, Ted Venetoulis, and Paul Walser.

I also wish to acknowledge and thank all the writers who have chronicled the Bobby Darin story in the past, most notably Alfred Aronowitz, Estelle Changas, and Al DiOrio.

Special thanks to Tom Schultheiss and the folks at Popular

Culture, Ink. for their belief in this project, and their efforts to bring it to fruition.

Thanks to Allen Wiener and Jeff Tamarkin for the special efforts they have made in offering suggestions and encouragement to me.

Finally, most special thanks to my wife Nicky for her assistance, patience, encouragement and love, both on this specific project and in my life in general.

Jeff Bleiel

CHAPTER 1

"In Memoriam"
Introduction

> "I used to be pissed off at Bobby Darin because he changed styles so much. Now I look at him and I think he was a fucking genius."
> —Neil Young, *Rolling Stone*, June 2, 1988

In his 1980 movie "One Trick Pony," Paul Simon includes a scene in which he and his band members kill time on a bus ride by playing a game of "Rock'n'Roll Deaths," rattling off the names of dead rock stars.

After a few obvious choices—Elvis, Buddy Holly, Otis Redding, Sam Cooke, etc.—Simon mentions Bobby Darin.

"He's not technically rock'n'roll you know," replies drummer Steve Gadd.

Simon insists that Darin qualifies, citing "Splish Splash" and "Queen Of The Hop." "That was early stuff," says Gadd. "Later he was strictly Vegas."

Simon differs, noting Darin's later hit recording of Tim Hardin's "If I Were A Carpenter."

"I still don't think he technically qualifies," says Gadd, "but let's not quibble."

Let's quibble.

Bobby Darin is in the Rock'n'Roll Hall of Fame. Yet there isn't a single sentence about him in *The Rolling Stone Illustrated History Of Rock'n'Roll.* Perhaps it is because three months after Buddy Holly's death, Darin was opening for George Burns in Lake Tahoe. Or because during the rock revolution of the 1960s, Darin was one of the highest paid performers on the Las Vegas strip.

Rock'n'Roll Hall Of Famers aren't supposed to record "Hello Dolly" or albums of Broadway show tunes or dozens of songs by the likes of Rodgers & Hart, Cole Porter, Irving Berlin and Johnny Mercer.

Yet, by the same token, crooners making $40,000 a week in Vegas aren't supposed to give it up to sing protest songs at the Troubadour with a four-piece rock band. Or be inducted into a Rock'n'Roll Hall Of Fame alongside The Who and The Kinks.

There has been little consideration given to Bobby Darin as a significant musical artist of his time. At best, popular critical consensus regards him as a hitmaker who used a couple of authentically good fifties rock'n'roll hits as a springboard to traditional show-business stardom.

It is an understandable opinion to hold. Someone interested in finding out why Darin is in the Rock Hall Of Fame might start with **The Bobby Darin Story**, a greatest hits album. And after hearing Side 2 of the album—with tracks like "Bill Bailey," "Clementine" and "Artificial Flowers"—a logical conclusion might be that Darin ceased to have any relevance to the "rock generation" after about 1960.

There has really been nothing to flag his artistry, his songwriting ability, his experimentation and risk-taking, the genre-busting and expectation-confounding nature which made his career one of the most unique and fascinating of the last thirty-five years. There were no rock heroes citing him as an influence, no journalists or disc jockeys rhapsodizing about his overlooked brilliance.

That is why this book was written.

No other artist of Bobby Darin's stature in the entertainment business made so many unexpected, surprising moves. Neil Young, who in the late eighties became the first major, critically acclaimed rock figure to wax enthusiastic about Darin to the press, called Darin an "extremist."

In a 1989 *Los Angeles Times* interview, Young surprised writer Robert Hilburn by naming Darin as the early rocker he most identified with.

"That guy went through more changes than anybody," Young told Hilburn. "Think of the swing from 'Queen Of The Hop' to 'Mack The Knife.' That was off the wall completely, but he managed to make two classics."

The differing styles displayed in Darin's hit singles is obvious, but his legacy as a songwriter is perhaps even more indicative of his unique ability to successfully cut across varying styles of popular music.

Buddy Holly, Rick Nelson, LaVern Baker, Dion, and The Coasters (all fellow Rock'n'Roll Hall Of Famers) recorded Darin-written songs. On the other end of the musical spectrum, so did Barbra Streisand and Wayne Newton. Darin has also been covered by cult folk artist Tim Hardin, country great Johnny Cash, and British Invasion bands The Searchers and Gerry & The Pacemakers. Darin also cut across generations: he wrote songs with both Johnny Mercer and Randy Newman. Had he never recorded a hit of his own, this alone should suffice to count him as one of the most interesting musical figures of his time.

So, professionally, the Bobby Darin story consists of much more than the forty-one hit songs he recorded (of which twenty-one made the Top 40 and ten of those reached the Top 10). Aside from his rock and middle-of-the-road (hereafter, MOR) success, there was a latent respect for Darin in the jazz community. And had he recorded only his six folk-oriented albums and then disappeared, he would no doubt be regarded as a cult favorite in folk circles today.

Darin's reach also extended into other areas. Most noteworthy, he appeared in thirteen films, playing prominent roles in eleven of them, and earned enough respect as an actor to receive an Academy Award nomination.

Indeed, one of the most rewarding things about researching Darin's career is the continual surprises one encounters: the shock of seeing a "teen idol" chillingly portray a bigoted Nazi in "Pressure Point"; the jar in the musical juxtaposition of albums such as **Hello Dolly** and **Commitment**, where a blindfolded, unknowing listener would never guess that they were the product of the same artist; the respect evident in the remembrances of figures as diverse as folk-rock pioneer Roger McGuinn of The Byrds and television actor Alan Thicke, both of whom referred to Darin as a "mentor"; the discovery of his largely-unpublicized activity in the social and political causes of his time.

Then there is the story of the personality behind this unique life and career. Darin earned, even cultivated, a reputation for being a brash, cocky (some go so far to say obnoxious) individualist. But nobody who worked closely with Darin remembers him that way. His good friend Dick Clark told *Rolling Stone*, "I used to laugh when people told me how Bobby was an arrogant little son of a bitch. But if you knew him, he was the kindest, gentlest person."

Likewise, each of the nineteen Darin associates interviewed for this book remembered him with respect and affection. Their recollections and anecdotes provide fascinating insights into the motivations that fueled Bobby Darin's fire.

However, the emphasis of this book is placed on Bobby Darin's professional career, rather than his personal life. This is not intended to be the definitive biography of Darin's life, but rather a detailed, comprehensive account of his work, complete with background, anecdotes, analysis, and the remembrances of numerous professional associates.

Some comments on Darin's character and personality are included, as are details on some "personal" events in his life. But a reader looking for gossipy tidbits about his marriage and divorce of Sandra Dee, or other items about his romantic or family relationships is advised that those matters will not be covered in these pages.

As Darin has long been underappreciated or miscategorized, it is hoped that this overview will give his career proper historical due. Ultimately, Steve Gadd was right when he said "Let's not quibble." The debate about whether Darin was a "rock artist" is irrelevant, if the accent is on "rock" not "artist."

He had the ability to make a rock fan appreciate "Mame" and a Sinatra fan appreciate "Roll Over Beethoven." He brought Bob Dylan songs to Las Vegas, and Rodgers & Hart songs to rock'n'roll caravan tours. No other artist of the past thirty-five years followed a similar career path. Because he was one of a kind, he was the last of a kind.

CHAPTER 2
"Long Ago And Far Away"
The Early Years

The two constants of Bobby Darin's youth were sickness and poverty.

He was born Walden Robert Cassotto on May 14, 1936. Bobby Cassotto was a frail, sickly child. At age three, he fell from a chair and broke his leg. When he was eight, he had his first attack of rheumatic fever. Before he was twelve, he would have three more attacks. Each night, members of his family would take turns checking in on the sleeping young boy to make sure he was still breathing.

Doctors told his mother that he probably would not live to be sixteen. Years after he outlived that prediction, he would talk of how, when he was a baby, neighbors would stop his mother on the street and say "Why do you want to wheel that thing around for? It's gonna die."

"My earliest recollections were of being in bed, stiff, hurting," the adult Bobby Darin would recall. "I used to read or do coloring books. I couldn't do what everybody else was doing."

He grew up without a father in a series of East Harlem and Bronx tenements. His mother, and a sister, born nineteen years earlier, raised him. "We were poor, on relief-type Bronx people," Darin would explain. "It was a poverty very hard for me to describe."

Bobby's parents were Saverio "Sam" Cassotto and Vivian "Polly" Walden Cassotto. Sam was the son of an Italian immigrant tailor. A cabinetmaker by trade, Sam Cassotto was reported to be close friends, and even partners in a bar, with Frank Costello, reputed head of the New York Mafia.

Convicted for participating in a pickpocket scheme, Sam was sent to Sing Sing prison in 1934. While there, he died of pneumonia.

While completely distancing himself from his father's shady connections, the adult Bobby Darin was not at all shy about relating the story of Sam Cassotto to the press. It made good copy, and in many ways, served the image Darin wished to create.

Vivian Polly Walden had show business in her blood. As a teenager, she ran away from home to join a road show. Using the stage name of Paula Walden, she later landed a featured role in a vaudeville revue. On a trip to Chicago, Sam had seen her on stage and sent her flowers. Soon she was off the vaudeville circuit and heading to Harlem as Sam's wife.

Nineteen years before Bobby came along, Sam and Polly had a daughter, Vanina (Nina) Cassotto. In 1936, it was the unmarried, teenage Nina who gave birth to Walden Robert Cassotto.

Not until he was about thirty years old did Bobby Darin learn the truth about the circumstances surrounding his birth—that Nina, whom he thought was his sister, was his natural mother, and that Polly, whom he called his mother, was his natural grandmother. Nina took the identity of Darin's biological father to her grave.

Because throughout his life, in every known interview or biographical profile, Bobby Darin referred to Sam and Polly as his parents and Nina as his sister, that is how they will be designated throughout this book. The true story was not made public until long after Darin's death.

A few years after Bobby's birth, Nina married Charlie Maffia, who moved in and helped support the family—and pay Bobby's medical bills. Years later, Maffia would work as a valet, chauffeur and road manager for Bobby Darin.

Bobby was always encouraged by his mother. "You don't belong in a tenement," she would tell him. "You're not like other boys. You're different." Indeed, an IQ of 137 enabled him to excel in school. He was an A student at Clark Junior High in the Bronx, and he did well enough to get into the respected Bronx High School of Science.

"I enjoyed doing homework," he would recall. "That made

me a freak to the kids on the block. My neighborhood was not geared to things scientific and scholastic. I was going to a fine school, then going back to a neighborhood where an education didn't mean a damn."

Despite his scholastic potential, Bobby was more interested in performing and entertaining. He loved the attention. At one point, he thought comedy was his calling, but he also picked up on music. He learned to play rudimentary piano by ear.

Toward the end of his junior year at Bronx High School, some musically-inclined friends of Bobby's decided to form a band. The group had a guitarist, Walter Raim, a pianist, Eddie Ocasio, a trumpet player, Richard (Dick) Behrke, and a vocalist, Steve Karmen. They needed a drummer, so that's what Bobby Cassotto became. He had never played before, but in three weeks he became proficient enough for this band.

"We were all learning our instruments, really," recalled Walter Raim. "Bobby was a talented, musical kid. He decided that he would be the drummer, then he learned to play afterwards. He was untutored. He just learned the drums himself."

Drumming was an unusual, potentially dangerous physical activity for Bobby. Even in high school, he was excused from calisthenics and had a special pass to use the school elevator. But he decided that playing music was worth the risk to his health. He also knew that he'd have to test his strength to follow another dream, becoming an actor.

"When we met him, he was hell-bent on being an actor," said Raim. "At the time we got involved with the band, he was trying to learn French, because he was trying to get a part in a play with a French-speaking company. He wanted to be an actor. Music was just another creative activity he thought would be fun."

The band played gigs like high school dances, private parties and lonely hearts clubs. Then in the summer of 1951, they got a job playing at a hotel in the Catskills called Sunny Land. For the princely sum of thirty-five dollars a week, they got to be the house band by night, bus boys by day.

"We were a real old-fashioned dance band," Raim recalled. "We played stock arrangements that you could send away for—three or four-part band arrangements of standards from the thirties and forties. It was the pop music of the time, which was the Frank Sinatra-Perry Como era."

The band repeated the engagement the following summer, another season of "Fools Rush In," mambos and waltzes. But with high school over, so was the band. However, this modest little group produced an impressive musical legacy. Bobby Cassotto became Bobby Darin. Both Walter Raim and Dick Behrke would go on to successful careers as musicians, often working with Darin. Steve Karmen would later write successful commercial jingles, including "I Love New York." Such potential, of course, wasn't so readily apparent at the time.

"At the time, I thought we were a fine band," said Walter Raim. "If I heard a recording now, I don't know what I'd think."

Following high school, Bobby enrolled at New York's Hunter College, intending to major in theatre arts. He appeared in productions of "Hedda Gabler," "The Valiant," and "The Curious Savage," but only lasted one semester. Later, he would explain that he was not interested in learning the technical side of the theatre, which was to have been the focus of his second semester.

He then spent some time on the road with a touring children's theatre company, performing in "Kit Carson." Back in New York, he and Dick Behrke shared an apartment at West 71st Street, and Bobby gave some free performances at an off-Broadway bar called Club 78.

At age eighteen, Bobby had one additional professional—and personal—experience which, in early interviews, he would cite as having a profound influence on his life. A thirty-one-year-old dancer invited Bobby to join her on the road and play bongos for her act.

The relationship turned out to be more romantic than musical, and it ended with the dancer using, then dismissing the naive Bobby. He had fallen hard, and he was crushed. "Before I met her, I was just a kid in the Bronx," Darin later told *Life* magazine. "Afterward, I was the most disillusioned human being in the world. But I was no kid."

The bitterness of the experience stayed with him for a long time, but he found a way to make it work for his career. "I know what I'm singing about," he would say.

Chapter 3

"I Have Dreamed"

On The Way

In 1956, Bobby Cassotto became Bobby Darin. With his sights set on breaking into the music business, he decided that a stage name would be beneficial.

Two stories exist about how the name "Darin" was chosen. One is that Bobby picked it out of the phone book. Another is that it came to him when he was passing a Chinese restaurant called the Mandarin, the neon letters "Man" burned out of the flashing sign.

Early that year, Darin had started writing songs with another former Bronx High School student, Don Kirshner. The duo copyrighted their first song, "Bubble Gum Pop," on January 17, 1956. Their earliest efforts included commercial jingles such as "The Rogers Cha Cha" for a local furniture store.

The co-composers were also making the rounds to music publishers, plugging their beginners pop songs. The demos featured Darin's voice. One day, they took a song called "My First Real Love" to George Scheck, the manager of Connie Francis. Though her first hit, like Darin's, would be almost two years away, Francis had a contract with MGM Records.

Scheck was impressed by both the song and the demo. With Scheck's name (as George M. Shaw) added to the songwriters' credit, "My First Real Love" became Francis' fourth single. The backing group credited on the record, The Jaybirds, was in fact, Bobby Darin.

It was also the beginning of a romance for Darin and Francis. In her biography, *Who's Sorry Now*, Francis describes Darin as her "first real love and a man I would love 'till the day he died and beyond." She reports that Darin proposed to her in the days before either of them became famous. However, their romance was opposed by Francis' domineering stage father, who, to prevent the young couple from seeing each other, reportedly once went after Darin with a gun on the set of the "Ed Sullivan Show."

Meanwhile, George Scheck helped Darin get a contract with Decca Records. His first single was the Leadbelly folk/blues classic "Rock Island Line." It was an ill-advised, unnatural choice for Darin. Opening with a spoken-word introduction, the record featured only a strumming acoustic guitar and drumming as accompaniment. Darin's off-key impression of a train whistle drove a nail into the record's coffin. Not that it would have succeeded anyway, competing with a version by British skiffle star Lonnie Donnegan which eventually reached the national Top 10.

The single's flip side was a Darin-Kirshner (and Scheck) original, "Timber." It was another work-type song, and though not very good, it was telling that one of Darin's earliest songs would fall into that genre.

Four days after the "Rock Island Line" recording session, Scheck and Decca arranged for Darin to make his first television appearance, a performance of the single on the "Dorsey Brothers' Stage Show" program.

Darin was so nervous that he tried to write the song's lyric on his hands, only to see the words perspire away. "I went out cold, scared to death and sang 'Rock Island Line,'" he told *TV Guide* later. "It bombed."

So did all of Darin's Decca recordings. For his second single, Darin dove into the rock'n'roll market with a novelty-style original called "Silly Willy." It was not quite hit material, but the song's bridge, which featured an energetic big beat and rock saxophone, showed potential.

Unfortunately, Darin's next, and final, two Decca singles veered away from rock'n'roll. On these tracks, Darin's vocals sound unlike his singing on any other record of his career, almost as if he were trying to impersonate another singer. Only "Dealer In Dreams," a Darin-Kirshner beat ballad with big band horns, rose above the mediocre level.

Darin went on the road for the first time, performing dates in small nightclubs with Kirshner backing him on guitar and acting as his manager. The two also continued to write songs, and managed to place a few with other singers. A seasonal novelty, "I Want To Spend Christmas With Elvis," was recorded by Little Lambsie Penn in 1956.

A more impressive list of singers would record Darin-Kirshner songs in 1957. Rockabilly great Gene Vincent took "Wear My Ring," R&B legend LaVern Baker recorded "Love Me Right" and jazz singer Bobby Short cut "Delia." But Darin was still trying for a hit of his own. When Decca dropped him, the outlook grew dimmer.

While on the road in Nashville in May 1957, Darin paid for a recording session himself. He recorded two songs he and Kirshner had written—"Wear My Ring" and "Talk To Me Something"—and two others, "Just In Case You Change Your Mind" and "I Found A Million Dollar Baby (In A Five And Ten Cent Store)", the latter an old Billy Rose standard. Influenced and inspired by Elvis Presley's success, Darin produced all in the rock'n'roll idiom.

Back in New York, Darin and Kirshner took the masters to Atlantic Records, and the tracks impressed Herb Abramson, who had helped Ahmet and Nesuhi Ertegun found the r&b-oriented label a decade earlier. Abramson oversaw the company's Atco label and he purchased the four masters from Darin.

Atco released "I Found A Million Dollar Baby" as its first Darin single. It was a quite respectable rock'n'roll effort with a good electric guitar sound and big-beat drumming. But backed with Darin and Kirshner's affected rock'n'roll ballad "Talk To Me Something," the record flopped.

Darin still wasn't entirely comfortable or confident as a rock'n'roll singer or songwriter. This was evident on his second Atco single, recorded on August 21, 1957. It was another pair of Darin-Kirshner originals, "Don't Call My Name" and "Pretty Betty." Both were certainly rock'n'roll in style, but the former was a rip-off of Fats Domino's "Ain't That A Shame" while the latter echoed Little Richard's "Ready Teddy."

Though the hit still hadn't arrived, Atlantic stood behind Darin, and their backing helped him achieve significant exposure. In July, he joined Chuck Berry, Frankie Lymon and Andy Williams on Alan Freed's TV show, "The Big Beat." He also got a spot in a Freed rock'n'roll revue playing at New

York's legendary Apollo Theatre.

In a twelve-minute segment, Darin sang a few of his Atco songs, Larry Williams' "Short Fat Fannie," and medleys of songs by Fats Domino and Ray Charles. Trying to please the Apollo audience was a tough assignment for any white performer, let alone an inexperienced one like Darin. "He patterns himself after Fats Domino," said a *Variety* review, "and the contrast is quite glaring. White singer is not in that class."

In December, Darin made his first appearance on "American Bandstand," performing "Don't Call My Name." His finger-snapping style was already in place and, chatting with Dick Clark, Darin proved to be a polished, natural TV interview. "I want to congratulate you on a really great thing," the smooth Darin told Clark. "Every city I've visited throughout the land, you know they said the best show on television in the afternoon is Dick Clark's 'American Bandstand'."

Darin and Clark struck up a close friendship which would last throughout Darin's life. Clark has called Bobby Darin "my all-time favorite performer" and "probably my closest friend in the business."

Atco tried another track from the Nashville session, "Just In Case You Change Your Mind" as a single in early 1958. It was another forced attempt at copping the "Elvis sound," even to the point of employing a Jordanaires-style backing group. Darin still sounded unnatural in the role.

It was three misses and no hits for Bobby Darin at Atco, and for Herb Abramson's money, that was enough. Then, Ahmet Ertegun stepped in.

"When Herb said he was going to release Darin from his contract, I said 'No. If you don't want him, I'll take him over,'" Ertegun recalled.

Darin and Ertegun had developed a friendly relationship in the Atlantic office. Ertegun's office was right next to the waiting room, where Darin would sometimes pass time before his appointments with Abramson. There was a piano in that waiting room, and Darin would catch Ertegun's ear with his piano noodling.

"On that piano, he would play music totally different from the masters Herb had purchased," Ertegun said. "I heard some terrific things."

Chapter 4

"Splishin' And Splashin'"

1958 Rock 'N' Roll Hits

The sound of bubbling water introduced Bobby Darin to the young American record buying public in the summer of 1958. The bubbling sound effect opened "Splish Splash," the record which would make Bobby Darin a rock'n'roll star.

Since signing with Atlantic, Darin had become friends with legendary New York City disc jockey Murray Kaufman, better known as "Murray The K." Kaufman's Portrait Music subsequently published several of Darin's compositions. One day, while visiting Kaufman's home, Darin met the disc jockey's mother, who suggested that "Splish, Splash, Take A Bath" would make a great title for a song.

Twelve minutes later, Darin had finished writing "Splish Splash." Because she had suggested the title, and because having half a songwriting royalty go to the mother of a famous disc jockey could only help airplay, Jean Murray received co-writing credit for the song.

On April 10, Atlantic Records had scheduled a recording session for jazz singer Morganna King. Ahmet Ertegun told Darin to show up with some of his new songs. Ertegun quickly produced two sides for King, which were soon forgotten. Before the session was over, three Bobby Darin tracks were recorded, including "Splish Splash" and "Queen of the Hop."

"They were cut in less than two hours with a pick-up band," Ertegun recalled. "We did the arrangements on the spot. That's the way I used to produce records in those days."

"Splish Splash" is one of the most fondly-remembered rock'n'roll hits of the fifties. Vocally, Darin showed that he was listening to Jerry Lee Lewis (the exclamatory "hey-yea!") and

An early publicity photo.

Fats Domino (the way "door" became "doe" and "floor" became "flo"). The lyrics were also full of rock'n'roll "in" references—Peggy Sue, Lollipop, Good Golly Miss Molly.

Though "Splish Splash" is often considered something of a novelty hit, it is in the same ballpark with many fifties rock classics, such as "Bird Dog," "Good Golly Miss Molly," "Bony Maronie," and even Elvis Presley's "Hound Dog," which also verged on novelty. The song's nonsense lyrical theme should not take away from its place as an authentic rock'n'roll effort: Note the pounding piano, big beat, wailing sax, and the rough edge on Darin's voice.

In fact, Darin's performance was so convincing that some listeners assumed he was a black r&b artist. The fact that Atco was an r&b label contributed to the misconception.

"Thank God we didn't have video then," Atlantic executive Jerry Wexler told author Joe Smith in *Off The Record*. "Nobody knew he was white."

It all added up to something which struck a chord with the rock-crazed teenagers of America. "Splish Splash" hit #3 in August 1958.

However, after the "Splish Splash" session, Darin wasn't entirely confident that the record would click. After all, he was 0-for-7. With only two weeks left before his Atco contract expired, Darin felt he needed some professional insurance.

In case Atco dropped him, Darin wanted to have a record to sell to another label. He went into the studio and produced his own recording of "Early In The Morning," a new song he'd written with Woody Harris.

Murray Kaufman sold the master to Brunswick Records. But when "Splish Splash" caught on, Atco renewed Darin's contract. A month after "Splish Splash" charted, Brunswick released "Early In The Morning" under the name The Ding Dongs. Atco was not fooled. Darin was now hot property, and they would not allow another label to release a Bobby Darin record.

Atco got the master back and, not wanting to compete with the still-climbing "Splash," released the record under the name The Rinky Dinks. Decca countered by rush-releasing Buddy Holly's cover of "Early In The Morning" one week after the Rinky Dinks disc charted. In the chart battle that ensued, the

Darin version (#24) edged out Holly's cover (#32).

Ertegun was upset, but understanding of Darin's action, given the conflicting status reports the singer was getting from Atco. "Herb (Abramson) probably told Darin we were going to drop him. I told him we weren't."

Likewise, Darin was very conciliatory when the press picked up on the fact that he was The Rinky Dinks.

"I thought there was a chance Atco wouldn't pick up my option," he told *Billboard*. "We were accused of all kinds of underhanded tricks, but no kidding, we didn't mean to hurt anybody. We were just trying to protect our own interests so we would have somewhere to turn."

The public also caught on when Darin appeared on Dick Clark's Saturday night show on July 19. After presenting Darin with a gold record for "Splish Splash," Clark announced that Darin would perform his follow-up hit, "Early In The Morning." Atco then started labeling the single as "Bobby Darin with The Rinky Dinks."

Lost in the shuffle was a fine flip side, "Now We're One." Featuring a prominently-strummed, loud-for-its-time electric guitar, the song was also covered by Buddy Holly (as the B-side of his "Early In The Morning").

Also in July, Atco issued Darin's first album, **Bobby Darin**. In addition to "Splash" and its flip, "Judy, Don't Be Moody," the album included the six flop sides which preceded the hit, and the Nashville session leftover "Wear My Ring."

Two tracks recorded in New York in January 1958 stood out. Another Darin-Woody Harris collaboration, "Brand New House," found Darin sounding much more comfortable in the r&b mode. And "Actions Speak Louder Than Words" was a fine r&b ballad co-written by future Motown founder Berry Gordy, Jr.

Darin also helped Atlantic out with his songwriting ability. In September, "This Little Girl's Gone Rockin'," which Darin wrote with Mann Curtis (who would later pen the lyric for "Let It Be Me"), became a pop and r&b hit for the label's Ruth Brown. It is one of only two Top 40 pop hits the legendary r&b singer would ever score.

In October, "Queen Of The Hop" was released and quickly shot into the Top 10. It was another Darin rock'n'roll classic.

Through the years, writing credit for "Queen Of The Hop" has gone to Woody Harris. But in 1987, when Warner Special Products released **The Ultimate Bobby Darin** CD, songwriting credit for the track was given to "Darin-Harris."

A search of copyright records at the Library of Congress showed that "Queen Of The Hop" was copyrighted three times. Twice, in August and September 1958, the song's copyright credits Darin and Harris. A November 1958 copyright cites only Harris.

Given the above information, and the nature of the song, it is highly likely that Darin co-wrote the hit version of "Queen Of The Hop," despite the fact that Harris' name continues to show up alone in most places. As with "Splish Splash," the song's lyric is replete with clever rock'n'roll catch phrases ("Bandstand" and "Sweet Little Sixteen" were added to Peggy Sue and Miss Molly), distinct elements of Darin's early writing style.

Darin also cut some other fine rock'n'roll records in 1958, including two more Woody Harris songs, "I Want You With Me" and "Pity Miss Kitty," and Pomus & Shuman's "I Ain't Sharin' Sharon." Most impressive was Neil Sedaka and Howard Greenfield's "Keep A Walkin'," a track which rocked far harder than the duo's songs recorded by Sedaka himself. If it had been released as a single, "Keep A Walkin'" almost certainly would have been a hit. However, Atco did not release these rock'n'roll tracks for almost two years.

This suited Darin just fine, because after three rock'n'roll hits, he was already getting antsy. Before the end of the year, he went into the studio to cut decidedly non-rock material with a big band, tracks that Atco would hold for about four months.

In press interviews at the time, Darin stressed that he did not want to be confined to the rock'n'roll genre, and wanted to reach an adult audience.

"I sing rock'n'roll because it sells records," he told *Billboard* in September 1958. "The young kids like it and want it and I can do it. But I try to be versatile. It's the only way to build a future in this business. In the night clubs, I lean to other things, ballads done fairly straight, special bits, etc. I even do 'Mack The Knife' from 'Threepenny Opera'."

In fact, Darin seemed downright perturbed that he was derisively labeled a rock'n'roller on the basis of "Splish Splash":

"I have a rock'n'roll hit," he said. "That makes me one of a thousand other guys. Now I've got to prove I can sing."

Ahmet Ertegun was not surprised that his label's first successful white rock'n'roll artist intended to move toward a more adult style. In fact, Ertegun believed Darin could successfully make the transition.

"I thought he was a terrific rock'n'roll artist, but he had aspirations to do bigger and better things," Ertegun said. "He understood and appreciated all the Chuck Berry and so on. He loved that music, but he also loved Cole Porter and Sinatra. He liked the glamour of Las Vegas, The Copacabana, and all of that. He wanted to do it all."

* * * * * * * *

Over the years, many music industry observers have contended that Bobby Darin didn't really like rock'n'roll music, and that he simply "used" the music as a springboard to traditional show business stardom. Such contentions were justified by the often-contradictory statements Darin made about rock'n'roll during the first years of his career.

On the pro-rock side, Darin never failed to praise Ray Charles. "I put Ray Charles on a pedestal," he said. "Ray Charles is the greatest thing since Beethoven." While Charles always made his list, the 1958 Darin would wax enthusiastic about other rock'n'roll stars, while the 1960 Darin would lean toward pop standard bearers.

In a 1958 *Billboard* interview, Darin listed his favorites as Fats Domino ("a great artist, with the sound of the Delta,"), Little Richard ("a wonderful church-type blues artist"), and Elvis Presley ("I'm crazy about Presley's understanding of what he does").

Speaking with *Down Beat* magazine in 1960, Darin changed his tune: "Rock'n'roll? I love some of it," he said. "There are only three singers who move me emotionally: Peggy Lee, Frank Sinatra and Ray Charles. These three people are my Rock of Gibraltar." He also discussed his admiration of Bing Crosby and Sammy Davis, Jr.

Darin's comment on Pat Boone in the *Down Beat* article was telling: "Boone was using rock'n'roll as a device—which is all well and good; it's exactly what I did."

In examining the question of whether Darin liked rock'n'roll, two things should be remembered. Darin seemed to change his mind as often as he changed his style, which was quite often. And Darin had a habit of telling interviewers what they wanted to hear, especially when it came to how he wanted to present himself to a particular audience.

His best rock'n'roll records speak for themselves; suffice to say that he made some great rock'n'roll records and performed credible live rock'n'roll intermittently throughout his career. His public leaning toward the Vegas style may have been more the result of a commercial career decision than a reflection of his personal taste.

"Nobody likes the good authentic early rhythm and blues any better than I do, but it's not right for me," Darin told the British music publication *Melody Maker* in early 1960.

In fact, Darin's personal taste in music was, as might be expected of anyone who stylistically experimented as much as he did, quite eclectic. But an appreciation of rock'n'roll was always there.

"He liked rock'n'roll music," asserted record producer Nik Venet, who would work extensively with Darin in the 1960s. "I traveled cross-country in a train with him, and we sure didn't play Sinatra. We played r&b stuff like The Five Keys, what they used to call race records. He could sing anything that the Keys did. He knew more about rock'n'roll than most people in rock'n'roll."

* * * * * * * *

Despite his imminent move away from rock, Darin hit the rock'n'roll caravan tour circuit in late 1958. In October, he joined a tour that included Buddy Holly & The Crickets, Frankie Avalon, The Coasters, and Clyde McPhatter.

He fit in well with the rock'n'roll artists he toured with. One tour included Duane Eddy & The Rebels, the hit instrumental group. During the tour, the band would occasionally back Darin on stage.

"He was a dynamite guy," said Rebels saxophonist Steve Douglas, who would later work extensively with Darin in the sixties. "All those things they say about him being cocky were certainly true."

On a tour with Dion & The Belmonts, Jimmy Clanton and Joanne Campbell, Darin became close friends with Dion DiMucci, the legendary rock'n'roller. "Even then, you could tell he had more on his wish list than just being a teen idol," DiMucci wrote about Darin in his autobiography, *The Wanderer*. "He was a great person to be around—positive, fun and extremely ambitious."

Entertainment critics who usually scorned or ignored rock'n'roll hitmakers began to take notice of Darin's versatility. A *Variety* review of Darin's December 1958 performance at Brooklyn's Town & Country called him "a promising performer" and a "singer of considerable savvy."

"Darin is a subscriber to no particular school," the review continued. "Although he works in an idiom closely resembling rock'n'roll, he can steer his catalog into a ballad or he can do a rhythm number in a manner that seems to be a lot of fun."

One of the few people not impressed with Darin in 1958 was Uncle Sam. Amidst all the excitement of Bobby Darin's career taking off, Walden Robert Cassotto forgot to report for his induction for military service with the Selective Service Board in New York.

It took an investigation by the FBI to finally track down the missing Walden Robert Cassotto. He told them he had not intentionally sought to avoid military service and that he failed to show up for induction because he had never received his induction notice.

The United States Attorney decided not to prosecute Darin if he would agree to immediate induction. Darin agreed, knowing he would never pass the physical. Indeed, Darin was rejected for induction due to his rheumatic heart condition.

Chapter 5
"The Big Time"
1959

Darin's first single of 1959, "Plain Jane," a rather ordinary rock'n'roll number, stalled at #38 on the *Billboard* charts. But the lapse in quality and commerciality was only temporary. In March, Darin went into a New York studio and cut two of the best records of his career.

Of all the songs Darin ever wrote, "Dream Lover" is the one that has stood the test of time and become a true pop standard. It has been recorded by Rick Nelson, Glen Campbell, Dion, Tony Orlando, Johnny Nash, Don McLean, and the Paris Sisters, among others.

"Dream Lover," which reached #2 in July 1959, was an important transitional record for Darin. It still had something of a rock'n'roll feel, and it was still the teenage audience which made it a hit. But it also gave Darin the opportunity to croon, to show off the more traditional singing style he was using in his nightclub act.

More and more, adults started to take notice of Bobby Darin. When he performed "Dream Lover" on the "Ed Sullivan Show" in May 1959, the audience saw a suave entertainer snapping his fingers, twirling, and shrugging his shoulders with the beat of the song. He came across with the confidence and polish of a showman twice his age.

Darin explained the songwriting process behind his most often-covered and commercial songwriting effort: "I had just discovered the C-Am-F-G7 progression on the piano," he said. "I stretched them out and I liked the space I felt in there, and the words just flowed."

The arrangement of "Dream Lover" differed from Darin's

Darin receives show-biz advice from George Burns.
(Las Vegas News Bureau)

earlier rock productions in that strings and background vocalists were used rather than a saxophone section. Another contributor to its success was Neil Sedaka, who played piano on the record, as well as its flip side, "Bullmoose," another Darin original.

Although it did not become a hit, "Bullmoose" is perhaps the greatest rock'n'roll record Darin ever made. It features a loud, Holly-like electric guitar and absolutely wild piano playing that is very uncharacteristic of Sedaka. Exuberant vocals from Darin and the background singers are the icing on the rocking cake. "Bullmoose" could actually qualify as a great lost fifties rock'n'roll gem, and those who doubt Darin's credentials as a rock'n'roller should give this side a listen.

But Darin still had his sights on nightclubs and traditional show business stardom. His biggest break came in May 1959, when George Burns invited Darin to be his opening act at Harrah's in Lake Tahoe.

Darin sang "Splish Splash" and two songs from his newly-issued Atco album of standard pop material, **That's All**: "Mack The Knife" and "Some of These Days." Together, he and Burns would do a vaudeville-style soft-shoe routine on the song "I Ain't Got Nobody."

Sharing the stage with Burns gave Darin the chance to exchange shtick with an old show business professional. "The old-timers in show business have given me some good tips," Darin would say to Burns on stage. "Elvis helped me out a lot."

Personally, Darin grew very close to Burns. "I love the man," Darin told an interviewer. "My father died before I was born. If I had to pick a father, it would be George Burns. I'd work with him anytime he wants me."

When Burns' show moved to Las Vegas, Darin went along. "George Burns taught me more in six weeks in Las Vegas than twenty others could have done in ten years," Darin said. In addition to dispensing show business advice, Burns also looked out for Darin in other ways.

One night, after Darin lost $1,600 gambling, Burns was so angry that he refused to shake Darin's hand on stage. After Darin begged for the customary handshake, Burns told the audience the story and made Darin promise from the stage that he'd never gamble again.

Darin at The Sands.
(Las Vegas News Bureau)

Jazz pianist and arranger Bobby Scott, who was about to start working with Darin, saw the Burns-Darin show in Vegas, and was knocked out by Darin's opening set.

"By the time Burns came on stage, that audience was so warm and so delighted with what Bobby had done that they were in George's hands," Scott recalled. "Bobby knew he was the opening act, and he prepared the audience for George. He took them to the limit; they were really primed. That's no mean accomplishment."

Darin impressed the show business establishment on his first foray into the big-time showrooms. Many celebrities, including Burns, were on hand for Darin's opening as headliner at The Cloister in Hollywood in August. "His presentations have a surety that belies the performer's youth," wrote *Variety*.

Even the jazz publication *Down Beat* was laudatory: "Self-assured, almost cocky in manner, young Bobby Darin cradled a sophisticated house in the palm of his hand...and made his bid as leading contender to the title, Young Sinatra. Clearly, Bobby Darin has emerged from the juvenile rock and roll league and is now preparing to carve himself a hefty slice of adult big time."

In October, Darin became the youngest performer to ever headline at the Sands in Las Vegas. *Variety* called him "one of the most versatile, polished young performers around today."

Darin brought a trusted friend on the road with him. His old high school bandmate and West 71st Street roommate Dick Behrke acted as his pianist and conductor, a role Behrke would retain in Darin's stage shows for years.

Darin was now performing almost all of the **That's All** album in his act, and his acceptance on stage was enhanced by the fact that the album was starting to take off on radio and in record stores. With brilliant, exciting arrangements by Richard Wess, the album featured full string and horn sections and a clever selection of songs. Among the members of the big band assembled for the sessions was future "Tonight Show" bandleader, trumpeter Doc Severinsen.

Darin's snappy, frantic-tempo reading of the title song, recorded by many other vocalists (including Nat King Cole) as a ballad, was a classic. On this, as well as other superb tracks such as "I'll Remember April" and "Softly As In Morning Sunrise," Darin showed an absolute mastery of the "swingin'" style associated with Frank Sinatra.

Another highlight was Darin's lone songwriting contribution to the album, "That's The Way Love Is," which proved that he could effectively write a new song which sounded like a standard. Darin put a clever lyric over a melody which echoed Sinatra's "Love Is The Tender Trap," and the fact that the effort sounded so natural on an album of established standards was an impressive testament to Darin's writing credentials.

Throughout **That's All**, with a big band swinging behind him, Darin was given the opportunity to project his youthful personality onto older popular standards. Brash, loud, hip, alive—all could be used to describe **That's All**. Darin was giving pre-rock music a shot in the arm. Sure, he had made great rock'n'roll records. But **That's All** was a great *Bobby Darin* record—there was no separating the success of the songs from the style of the delivery.

The acceptance was so encompassing that in the summer of 1959, only six months after "Queen Of The Hop," Darin was invited to sing at the Hollywood Jazz Festival. But even as Darin was wowing them there and in Vegas, Atco had yet to release a single from **That's All**.

The hesitation was understandable, as the next single would follow-up "Dream Lover" and **That's All** had no track with such obvious youth appeal. But the choice was made by radio, which did not sit back and wait for a single, but jumped on the album's lead track, "Mack The Knife."

"Moritat" or "Mack The Knife" was written by Kurt Weill and Bertolt Brecht for "Threepenny Opera," then enjoying a successful off-Broadway revival. The English lyric was written by Marc Blitzstein. The song had already been a hit for numerous others, as five different instrumental versions (including records by Lawrence Welk and Les Paul and Mary Ford) charted in 1956. But the version which most influenced Darin was a '56 vocal hit by Louis Armstrong.

Atco released Darin's "Mack The Knife" as a single in August. Although it was quite a departure from the rock'n'roll style which had garnered Darin five Top 40 hits (three in the Top 10) over the previous year, Ahmet Ertegun knew there was something special about the track.

"I knew it could not miss," Ertegun said. "Once in a while you hear something and say 'That's it! The magic is there!' Bobby worked out the arrangement with Dick Wess and it was fabulous. We put together a great band. It was just one of those forever records."

The single entered the *Billboard* charts on August 24, 1959. Six weeks later, it was the number one single in the country. It stayed number one for nine weeks, making it the third biggest hit to that point in the rock era, which began in 1955. Only Presley's double-sided "Hound Dog"/"Don't Be Cruel" and Guy Mitchell's "Singing The Blues" stayed at number one for more weeks. Even after thirty-two years of rock, the span of 1955-1987, "Mack" was the sixth biggest hit of the era, according to Joel Whitburn's *Top 1000 Singles*.

"Mack The Knife" became Bobby Darin's signature song. Instantly, he was accepted by adults. But the record also received heavy airplay on the same youth-oriented stations that played "Dream Lover" and "Splish Splash." The kids knew it wasn't rock'n'roll, but they could sense—and relate to—the hip attitude inherent in Darin's performance. "Mack" was almost the very definition of an "across the board" smash. The single sold two million copies.

Darin's performance on "Mack The Knife" is one of the most famous vocals of all time—instantly recognizable, eternally dramatic, simply immortal. Outswinging all competition, Darin used every measure of Richard Wess' arrangement to his advantage. His "eek!," "Ho! Ho!," and other stylistic improvisations with the song are now as imbedded in the popular culture as the lyrics themselves.

In fact, the vocal was such a *tour de force* and so overshadowed everything else that few of the millions who bought the record ever stopped to think that they had no idea what Darin was singing about. In Darin's hands, the song's lyrics were strictly a vehicle, something he could stylize.

The lyric Darin sang, which was similar to the one in Louis Armstrong's version, was much lighter than a literal translation of the original German lyric in "The Threepenny Opera." Of course, MacHeath, "Mack The Knife," is a murderer, not the swingin' character depicted by Darin. In fact, many "Threepenny Opera" and Brecht-Weill purists ridicule Darin's "Mack The

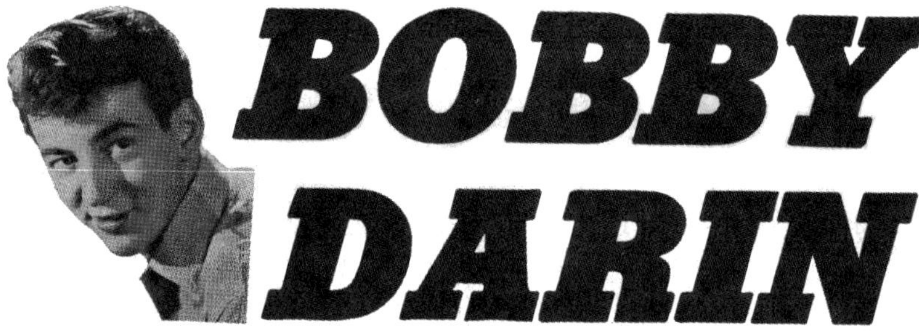

AMERICA'S HOTTEST SHOW-BUSINESS PERSONALITY

"THAT'S ALL"
(Atco LP 33-104)

the hottest album in the country contains

"MACK THE KNIFE"
(Atco 6147)

the hottest single in the country together with 11 other swingin' standards

Available Stero and Monaural

ATCO 157 W. 57th Street
New York 19, N. Y.

"Mack the Knife" is also available in Atco EP 4504, along with "That's All", "Beyond The Sea", and "That's The Way Love Goes."

Knife" because it is a complete bastardization of the song's original *mise en scene*.

So, in essence, Darin created a new "Mack," one that would be forever his. In a nice touch, one of the names Darin drops in the lyric is Lotte Lenya, Kurt Weill's widow, who was then starring as Jenny in the revival of "Threepenny." Unbeknownst to Darin, Lenya had suggested to Ahmet Ertegun that some Atlantic artists should record her late husband's songs.

"I told her we were not a general record label, that we just did rhythm & blues and rock'n'roll," Ertegun said. "But I said I'd think about it. I didn't have the opportunity to mention it to Bobby. So when he came up with 'Mack The Knife,' I said 'I can't believe it—three days ago I had lunch with Lotte Lenya and I was going to suggest it to you.'"

As "Mack" made him a true star, Darin was candid about his jumping off the rock'n'roll bandwagon. "I had to go beyond rock'n'roll," he said. "'Mack' introduced me into the adult world."

"My record, which is completely away from rock'n'roll, came at a time when tastes were shifting," he told *Melody Maker* in 1960. "It was perfectly timed and turned out to be the luckiest thing I ever did. It's the sort of thing I intend to concentrate on because adults like it as well as the kids."

The same week "Mack The Knife" hit number one, **That's All** finally cracked *Billboard*'s album chart. It would eventually climb to #7 and remain on the best-seller charts for fifty-two weeks.

Big-time television also came calling. In September, Darin showed up on the special "An Evening With Jimmy Durante," performing "Mack" and "That's All," as well as two ducts with Durante. Two months later, he reprised his nightclub shtick with George Burns in "George Burns in the Big Time." Big time, indeed: Burns' other guests were legends Jack Benny, Eddie Cantor and George Jessel.

Darin even had a chance to return to the dramatic acting he had given up years earlier. In October, he appeared on the CBS series "Hennesey," portraying a young entertainer unhappily serving a stint in the navy.

But the highpoint would come on November 29. The music industry's second annual Grammy Awards ceremony was held at the Beverly Hills Hotel. Darin and "Mack The Knife" were up for four awards.

Richard Wess' arrangement of "Mack" was nominated for Best Arrangement, an award which went to Billy May for Frank Sinatra's "Come Dance With Me." The same two records also paired off in the Best Vocal Performance, Male category, with Sinatra taking the award.

For the first time, a Best New Artist award was given. Darin's competition was Edd Byrnes, Mark Murphy, Johnny Restivo and Mavis Rivers. In (speaking in retrospect) one of the few times the Academy would get this award right, Darin was the winner.

The nominations for Record Of The Year were "Mack The Knife," Sinatra's "High Hopes," Elvis Presley's "A Fool Such As I," Andre Previn's "Like Young" and The Browns' "The Three Bells." The winner was "Mack The Knife."

Darin had not only performed "Mack" on the show (telecast by NBC), but received two Grammys—heady "establishment" recognition for a singer who was derisively labeled a "rock'n'roller" nine months earlier.

It was the ultimate night of triumph for Bobby Darin. But the next day, the press would be awash with news not of what Darin did, but what he said.

Chapter 6

"Two Of A Kind?"

Darin Vs. Sinatra

"I hope to surpass Frank in everything he's done."

Frank, of course, was Sinatra. And the above quote, reportedly uttered by Bobby Darin on Grammy night, would follow —and help define—Darin until his death.

The Darin-Sinatra comparison was an easy item for the press to pick up on in the wake of Darin's singing (and swinging) style on **That's All**. And the fact that they and their records shared Grammy nominations made comparisons almost inevitable after Darin took two awards.

So after UPI's Vernon Scott asked Darin about challenging Sinatra, Darin's "hope to surpass" quote was picked up off the wire by hundreds of newspapers in the following days. It caused a stir and painted Darin as a brash, cocky kid whose accomplishments had yet to match his mouth.

Such a portrayal wasn't entirely inaccurate, but Darin spent the next year denying and clarifying the remark, especially in an effort to offer an olive branch to Sinatra, who reportedly did not appreciate the upstart's boldness.

Darin claimed he was misquoted. He told the *New York Post* that he actually said "There's no question of beating Sinatra. Please don't use the comparison. I want to do everything that anybody's ever done, but better."

Vernon Scott stuck by his story: "I don't blame him for denying it," Scott told the Post. "It wasn't the brightest thing in the world to say. But he didn't say it spitefully. He just said it exuberantly, flush from the victory of his awards."

There *was* good reason to compare Darin and Sinatra, and the comparisons would have come up even if Darin had kept his

Holiday

THANKS

Who Made It

BOBBY

"Best Pop Record Of 1959"

"MACK THE KNIFE"

by

Bobby Darin

(Voted No. 1 in the Annual Cash Box Music Operators Poll)

Personal Management

STEVE BLAUNER

8744 Arlene Terrace • Los Angeles 46, Calif.

Exclusively On

ATCO RECORDS

mouth shut on Grammy night. But to counter the perceived brashness of his comment, Darin would spend almost every interview of the next two years talking respectfully about Sinatra.

"It's an insult to Frank to compare him with a twenty-four-year-old punk like me," he told the *New York Post*. "I don't want to be a second Frank Sinatra. I want to be a first Bobby Darin."

Even as late as 1962, Darin still occasionally found himself having to fend off charges of riding Sinatra's coattails. "I'll admit Frank's vocal style influenced me—but so did Bing Crosby, Louis Armstrong, Eddie Fisher and a lot more," he told *Melody Maker*. "In the future, somebody might be as great as Frank Sinatra. But never greater than him."

Of course, these treatises on Sinatra only helped Darin. As *New York Post* writers Alfred G. Aronowitz and Jack D. Fox put it, "The aura of controversy which has followed Sinatra throughout his career now hovers over Darin like a halo." Even Darin acknowledged that, publicity-wise, the quote "did an awful lot of good."

But Darin did eventually tire of the matter. In a 1962 interview with *Newsweek*, he said, "The biggest single fallacy that has been built up (about me) is that I think the sun rises and sets on Frank Sinatra."

Indeed, the mini-furor over Darin's statement overshadowed the important issue: The ways in which Darin the entertainer was influenced by the master.

"It is Sinatra as a person more than Sinatra as a singer that has influenced me," Darin told *Down Beat*. "His outlook on the business and his attitude to performance are the important things."

"My approach to singing is not the same," he continued. "Sinatra has a clipped speech. I'm a slurrer. But let's face it, he's the boss. Frank Sinatra is the greatest living lyric interpreter."

But some critics were starting to suggest what Darin himself would have gotten slammed for saying—that comparisons to Sinatra were absolutely valid.

"Darin today is unquestionably the only young pop singer who handles standards with something approaching the polished intensity of Sinatra," wrote *Down Beat*'s Gene Lees in

May 1960. "To those who would offer the rejoinder that Darin does not have Sinatra's vocal finesse and musicianship, it should be adequate to point out that Sinatra is 42 while Darin in 23."

The *New York Post*'s Aronowitz and Fox wrote "Like Sinatra, Darin generates an in-personality which lights up a night club floor beyond the wattage of other show business dynamos. Like Sinatra, Darin makes every performance a command performance and it is Darin who is always in command."

Sammy Davis, Jr., who authored a laudatory telegram about Darin which was reprinted on the back cover of **That's All**, commented on Darin-Sinatra similarities in a 1960 interview.

"I think what people really compare is their attitudes on stage," Davis said. "Certainly Bobby's style is more physical than Frank's ever was."

An interesting perspective on the comparison of the two singers came from musician and arranger Bobby Scott, who worked with many of the giants of jazz, as well as more contemporary vocalists such as Darin, Aretha Franklin and Marvin Gaye.

"Bobby belonged, as a performer, in the age that produced a Sophie Tucker, an Al Jolson," Scott observed. "He was in the great performing tradition, and I kind of think of him as the last hurrah of the preceding Golden Age of Performing.

"I don't put Sinatra in that category," Scott continued. "Sinatra is a product of the record industry. Had Sinatra been born earlier and tried to perform during the vaudeville era, we'd have never heard of him. I don't think Bobby was a product of the record industry. If Bobby had never made a record, but had secured some kind of employment where he could perform, he would have become a star in any case.

"I think Sinatra needed a band. I don't think Bobby ever needed a band. I think Sinatra had to learn things that were inherent in a guy like Bob."

Despite Darin's almost reverential comments about Sinatra subsequent to the Grammy night quote, Sinatra never publicly complimented Darin. This led to lingering speculation that there was an official (and lifelong) "feud" between the two singers. Credence was given to this theory by a report that Sinatra and Dean Martin were seen tossing darts at a picture of Darin after the Grammy comment.

In reality, however, it appears unlikely that there was ever serious animosity for Darin on Sinatra's part. Though Darin and Sinatra were never seen publicly together, Darin was openly accepted in the Sinatra "circle" in a way that would have been impossible if Sinatra harbored any true resentment.

Throughout his life, Darin was close to Sinatra's daughter, Nancy. He was also close friends with other members of the so-called "Rat Pack"—including Dean Martin and Sammy Davis, Jr.

Record producer Nik Venet, who worked extensively with Darin in the sixties, was also friends with Nancy Sinatra and worked with her first husband, singer Tommy Sands. Venet dismissed any notion of a Sinatra-Darin feud.

"That was all bullshit made up in the papers," Venet said. "Sinatra never snubbed Darin. I think he respected him. I think the 'fued' was something made up in the trades. Those two names rang a bell, they got a response, and the press just ran with it."

Still, it would be 1984, eleven years after Darin's death, before Sinatra made what appeared to be his first complimentary gesture toward Darin—a recording of "Mack The Knife" in which he respectfully alludes to Darin's earlier version.

Some reports to the contrary, Darin was not crushed by any thought of a Sinatra "rejection" of him. In fact, he went so far as to express admiration for one particular Sinatra swipe at him.

When, shortly after the controversy began, Sinatra was asked "What do you think of Bobby Darin?," he replied "I sing in saloons. Bobby Darin does my prom dates."

Calling that "one of the greatest single lines of all time," Darin told *Down Beat* "All I can say is that I'm only too happy to play his prom dates...until graduation."

CHAPTER 7

"Actions Speak Louder Than Words"

The Personality

"It is impossible not to like the guy"
—Gene Lees, *Down Beat*, 1960

"In person, Bobby Darin is fully as offensive as he is in public"
—Richard Gehman, *TV Guide*, 1961

The Frank Sinatra comment was not the first time Bobby Darin's personality and attitude attracted as much attention as his skills as a singer and entertainer. Even the liner notes to **That's All**, released before Darin had broken into "big time" show business circles, referred to his reputation as an "Angry Young Man."

By the time Darin reached star status with "Mack The Knife," the press was only too ready to shine the white hot spotlight on Darin's personality. It made great copy.

In the wake of "Mack," Darin's Grammy success, and his appearances on major TV variety shows, Darin was profiled with major articles in *TV Guide*, *Life*, and *Down Beat* magazines. When he played the Copacabana in September 1960, Darin was the talk of New York: both the *New York Post* and the *New York Journal-American* ran multi-part, in-depth hometown-boy-made-good profiles.

Articles would inevitably turn to Darin's brashness, cockiness or ill manners. And that appeared to be precisely the way Darin wanted it. He knew what it took to make a good story—to separate himself from the hundreds of other entertainers who were written about constantly—and he played the role to the hilt.

"I like people who don't know me to dislike me," Darin told the *Journal-American*'s Anita Ehrman, who described Darin's life as "a series of temper tantrums punctuated by laughter."

"It gives me a great pleasure to get bum-rapped," Darin said. "I thrive on it."

"When you write about me, make it tough," he told the *Post*. "Ruin me."

But most writers, while relating every detail on how Darin rubbed people the wrong way, couldn't help but admire their quotable, candid subject. "The white heat of his temper has become part of the glow of his charm," wrote *Post* series writers Alfred Aronowitz and Jack D. Fox.

The Darin life story read like a legend in the hands of the New York press. The poverty and sickliness of Darin's youth were submitted as sympathetic counterbalances to the excesses of his star personality.

But the Darin persona was built far more on ambition than arrogance. The defining statement of Darin's career, one that would literally follow him to death (it was part of most obituaries) came from Shana Alexander's *Life* profile of January 11, 1960.

There, Darin bluntly expressed his goal—"To establish myself as a legend by the time I'm 25." An instant headline.

"I want to make it faster than anyone has ever made it before," he said. "I'd like to be the biggest thing in show business by the time I'm 25 years old."

Rather than being taken at face value, as the honest ambition of a talented young performer who was newly-rich, in great demand, and being acknowledged as a potential giant by his peers, the comment was perceived as a prediction. Darin might as well have said "I *will* be a legend by the time I'm 25."

So the statement was viewed as another example of Darin's gall. It fit in nicely with other stories making the rounds, such as Darin ordering noisy nightclub patrons to behave during his act. Or refusing to go on stage until a certain record industry executive who had snubbed him in his pre-fame days was removed from the club.

Not all of the negative appraisal of Darin's personality could be chalked up to misconception, or a carefully-orchestrated publicity front on Darin's part. He did often court trouble.

Before Darin left Hollywood to go to New York and open at the Copa, Nancy Sinatra and Tommy Sands planned an elaborate send-off and good luck party for him. Angered over a minor oversight (a friend of his was left off the guest list), Darin skipped the party.

Darin's reputation got around the show-business community. "I've never seen someone so disliked," Paul Anka told the *Post* in 1960.

In a brutal January 1961 *TV Guide* profile ("The Astoundingly Brash Character of Darin"), Richard Gehman made his intense personal dislike of Darin explicit—"He does not merely talk rudeness, he lives it." Yet, even Gehman could not pronounce Darin completely unappealing.

"There is more than a suspicion in my mind that the extreme cockiness is merely a device for attracting attention," Gehman wrote. "All I can report is that for all his faults and offenses...Bobby Darin still is somehow an appealing, interesting fellow...There is a single-minded honesty about him and a candor that is all too rare in the strange show-biz world he inhabits."

Darin did not often publicly discuss his concern about his health—surely the most justifiable explanation of his impatience and lack of regard for the usual show-business niceties. But occasionally he would drop a telling tidbit to the press.

"I have the feeling I'm going to die young," he told the *Los Angeles Times* in 1959. "So I've got to do what I'm going to do now."

"The whole key to Bobby's personality was his illness," said Darin's friend Harriet Wasser, who first met him in 1957 and did some publicity work for him early in his career. "If it wasn't for his illness, he probably never would have done what he did. He could be really obnoxious. He did things that I felt were just unnecessary. But by the same token, he had this attitude which was, 'If the only way I can get to be a star is to be Mr. Nice Guy, I don't want it.' He loved Sinatra for that reason.

"We talked about his illness," she continued. "He wasn't sickly, in the sense that he was home a lot, in the hospital, etc. But he couldn't take the train, because he couldn't walk up all the stairs [at the station]. There were certain things that he couldn't do, but he didn't let everybody see those things."

Wasser was with Darin in September 1959 when he became very ill after a rehearsal for his appearance on "The Ed Sullivan Show." "He grabbed my arm and I thought he was going to collapse backstage," she recalled. "I mean the guy was ready to die."

Pianist/arranger Bobby Scott, who began working with Darin in 1960, recalled Darin telling him "I'm not going to be around here very long." Scott also believed that the specter of death was Darin's principal motivation.

"It colored his existence and his personal life," Scott said. "To those who didn't know about his ailment, there was no chance they'd understand what motivated him. He made a bargain with himself: The world was going to know he'd been here."

Bobby Scott met Darin in 1959 and began working closely with him in the studio—as the arranger and pianist for three albums worth of material—in 1960. Scott's musical credentials were impressive. He'd worked with jazz greats such as Gene Krupa, Lester Young and Stan Getz, and even scored a pop hit of his own, "Chain Gang," in 1956. (Scott would later compose two pop standards, "A Taste Of Honey" and "He Ain't Heavy, He's My Brother.")

In addition to their close professional ties—Scott would also play piano for many of Darin's live dates in New York City and would later work for Darin's publishing company—these two products of the Bronx struck up a close personal relationship. But Scott remembered that his initial meetings with Darin were tense.

"We had a little bit of difficulty at first," Scott recalled. "On the first couple of arrangements I wrote for him, he wanted to change this, and change that. I told him 'Why don't you learn to write your own goddamn arrangements?'

"He did not suspect that I would be proprietorial about what I wrote," Scott said. "He thought that since he paid for it, he owned it. I said 'Oh no you don't. You don't fuck up my music because my name goes on it too.'"

Legendary arranger Billy May also found his initial contacts with Darin to be difficult. May, who played with Glenn

Miller's orchestra and arranged classic fifties recordings by Frank Sinatra and Nat King Cole, among others, did not appreciate the young Darin's manner of challenging the orders of older music industry veterans.

"He really was a smart-ass little kid in those days," said May. "He came in and started telling us how to do it. I figured if the record company hired me, they knew that I knew what to do, and I didn't need him to help me.

"I'll tell you what got me off on the wrong foot with Bobby Darin,." said May, recalling their first session together. "The first number involved a bright tempo and there was about eight bars of band, and then a drum break. So we started running it down. The drummer played the break, and Darin stopped the band and went over and started to tell the drummer how to play the break. I thought, 'Who the hell is this?'"

May, whose work with Darin included arranging two albums and music for a TV special, eventually grew somewhat more tolerant of Darin as their work together became less strenuous.

"Everything was amicable, you know," he said. "I took his suggestions. A couple of times, we had cross words, but we never really got into any beefs or anything. It's just that he was more difficult to work with than other people. But as he grew older, he became a little more knowledgeable. He turned out to be a pretty good guy. He was friendly and we got along very well."

It didn't take Bobby Scott long to soften his initial impression of Darin. He became a Darin confidante. "I got to know him on a level that other people did not, in that he was never evasive with me," Scott said. "He leveled. He liked my calling a spade a spade, and I enjoyed the way he kicked the usual music business procedures in the butt.

"If I served him at all, I believe it was through being as honest as I could be with him," Scott said. "I may be patting myself on the back, but I think it was refreshing to him, considering all the 'yeses' he was hearing."

For that reason, Scott's remembrances of dealing with Darin professionally and personally offer insights into Darin's character that are often missing from the "public" record promulgated by the press (and, in some cases, Darin's own publicists).

"I know he had the reputation of being an arrogant bastard, but I don't think so," Scott said. "I think he was like a whole lot of other people: He was a bright enough guy that he did not suffer fools easily.

"I'm a Bronx kid," Scott continued, "and there's a certain kind of belligerency in people that come from the Bronx. Bobby had a hell of a lot of that. Bobby was not the kind of guy that somebody mugged, because you might mug him, but you're going to get a broken jaw, too. He was enough of a street kid for that."

But Scott also saw another side of Darin, a friendly nature apparent to friends and associates, but rarely relayed in the press.

"I'm not putting a halo on his head, he deserves no halos," Scott said. "But if you run across somebody that really paints him out black, you can best believe they didn't know him.

"He was put down by almost everyone I'd met in the business," Scott said. "But I never met anyone who had a decent idea about who and what he was. The reason I found this contempt odd was that Darin was a remarkably convivial fellow."

Darin was also a loyal friend. When Bobby Scott's wife was in the hospital delivering their first child, Scott was broke. When it came time to bring his wife and newborn daughter home, the hospital wouldn't accept his check, essentially holding his family until he could come up with some cash.

"Bobby Darin came to the rescue," Scott recalled. "He offered to give me money with no strings attached. He gave me enough work—arranging and accompanying—over the next couple of weeks to tidy everything up for us financially.

"The first gift my daughter got—delivered to the house by messenger when the baby got home—was from Bobby," Scott said. "He beat the relatives."

Darin's loyalty was also evident to other friends, such as actor Richard (Dick) Bakalyan, who appeared with Darin in the 1962 film "Pressure Point" and later, on Darin's television series.

"Bobby was one of the guys, one of the boys," Bakalyan said. "He'd go to the wall for you if there was trouble.

"I'd heard that he was a cocky guy and this and that,"

Bakalyan recalled. "He was far from that. He was a gentleman and he treated everyone with great respect and they responded in same."

Not that Darin's friends never saw his infamous impatience, especially when it came to his work. "He insisted on holding all the aspects of his performing life in his own hands, and in making all the decisions," Scott said. "He was correct in assuming that if you wanted things done right, do them yourself.

"But he was not a malicious person," Scott continued. "Not at all. A lot of people thought he was a smart aleck; he wasn't. I think he threw up a lot of defenses and gave the wrong ideas to people. I think he was, at core, really a very, very good person.

"If I told Bobby 'I need something,' he got it for me," Scott said. If I said 'Six strings ain't gonna work, I want twenty,' twenty would have been there. He was as good as his word in all those departments."

Darin's intense ambition carried over from his career to his personal life. Never forgetting the poverty of his youth, the adult Darin relished the discovery of "finer things" such as great literature, art, and classical music. He delighted in the opportunity his fame provided him to associate with "important" people.

"He used to come to my house for dinner," recalled Ahmet Ertegun, whose father had been the Turkish ambassador to the U.S. "I'll never forget the first time he came, he saw photographs that were given to my father by Roosevelt, Truman, the president of Turkey, and so on. He said 'My God.' He came from a very poor background, and he loved the big life."

So despite the intense dislike some members of the press felt for Darin—and described to the public—there would be the occasional writer, such as *Down Beat*'s Gene Lees, who would portray Darin as a disarming fellow.

Of course, it is not unusual for press descriptions to fail to completely capture all aspects of a celebrity's personality, especially those qualities most apparent to "insiders" such as friends or close professional associates.

In looking back at what was written about Darin in the early sixties, hindsight also comes into play. The combination of Darin's youth and brashness understandably rubbed some members of the mainstream entertainment press the wrong way. Ten years later, after the "rock" explosion and some of the personalities it spawned, Darin's early behavior would seem almost gentlemanly.

There was also the recognition that it was the temperament of an artist. As the years went by, and Darin dispelled any "flash in the pan" notions, it became obvious that his talent transcended that of a mere rock'n'roll hitmaker or Vegas crooner. What was initially perceived as cockiness became confidence, a badge of artistic honor.

Los Angeles Times writer Estelle Changas summed it up best in a 1972 portrayal of Darin:

"Early in his career, Darin was branded brash, cocky and arrogant, labels which clung tenaciously for years," she wrote. "Though intended as insults, they really served to confirm the disquieting candor Darin refused to relinquish, an individuality which became increasingly visible."

CHAPTER 8

"Beyond The Sea"

1960

"I want to be in the upper echelon of show business to such an extent it's ridiculous," Darin told *Life* magazine in 1960.

As the year dawned, it appeared as if that upper echelon was only a short step away for Darin. Professional acceptance poured forth from his peers and the press.

"Do you realize you're alone in your generation?," Jerry Lewis told Darin. "Sammy, Dean and I are all ten years ahead of you. Unless you destroy yourself, no one else can touch you. You're alone."

Influential music critic Gene Lees of *Down Beat* called Darin "probably the most fascinating singer to watch on this side of the Atlantic...With his combination of excellent movement and intense, driving singing, Darin is one of the most stimulating and vital acts in show business today."

As Lees alluded to, as much focus was placed on Darin's performing style—his on-stage movements—as on his voice. Darin told *Life*'s Shana Alexander that he strove to be regarded as "a singer who moves like a dancer. That is my billing, and I intend to sell the hell out of it."

"I'm not just a singer," Darin told *Newsweek*. "I really try to sell my personality. For me, it's got to be a salesmanship job, not just a good voice. Singing isn't enough. Spontaneity and personality are the things."

Darin discussed the selling of another commodity with Gene Lees: "The sex element is the most important in this business," he said. "The fact remains, you must sell sex. It must not be conscious, however. You're either sexy or you're not. I don't know whether I am. I will know, fifteen years from now."

From the stage, accompanist Bobby Scott analyzed Darin's performing genius. "Bobby, I always used to feel, danced through his numbers," Scott said. "An arrangement was very important to him if he could use it—for his feet, a turnaround here, a turn there.

"He viewed arrangements for their extramusical value," Scott said. "No singer I knew made more performing use out of brass syncopations and licks than did Bobby Darin. He'd drop the mike and catch it to coincide with a brass burst, or turn himself around when the musical materials did so. He would even stop a song if the band tempo wasn't in accord with his idea of what it ought to be.

"He knew how to read an audience. He knew how to use his hands. He knew how to use his clothes, even to loosen his tie," Scott observed. "He knew things it took other singers twenty or thirty years to gather.

"I've worked with a hell of a lot of singers, and I don't think any of them had Bobby's essential performing ability," Scott concluded. "I mean, he could come on hoarse and carry off the show. He'd have been dynamite in vaudeville. He was one of the greatest performers I ever saw on the stage."

Darin continued to be a ubiquitous presence in the media. In December 1959, he was the subject of TV's "This Is Your Life." Murray The K, George Burns and Sammy Davis, Jr. joined Charlie and Nina Maffia, Don Kirshner, Dick Behrke and other old friends for the tribute. In January 1960, Darin was reunited with old flame Connie Francis on the "Ed Sullivan Show"; the pair sang a charming duet version of Cole Porter's "You're The Top."

Like most rock'n'roll hitmakers, Darin couldn't avoid having his name brought up in the payola scandal. On December 4, Darin, along with Les Paul and Mary Ford, was questioned by the New York district attorney about payola and his radio appearances on Alan Freed's show. He denied paying Freed. (Apparently, Darin's relationship with Murray Kaufman never came under question.)

Darin saw the payola scandal for the political charade it was. "What is it going to do?," he said in an interview at the time, "win a few new Senatorial seats?"

With an artistically and financially successful year behind

him—his 1959 gross income was reported to have been $250,000 —Darin began the new decade on the right foot.

His first single of 1960, his follow-up to "Mack The Knife," was "Beyond The Sea," another **That's All** track. Darin's vocal moved him even closer to Sinatra territory (this one was a little harder for the rock'n'roll crowd to get into) and Richard Wess' arrangement brilliantly alternated between the gentle and the blaring.

"Beyond The Sea" proved that "Mack The Knife" was no accident: Darin was a *bona fide* stylist. As with "Mack," the song wasn't new and it wasn't his. But Darin turned it into his second straight standard, another definitive reading. The record clicked, reaching #6 in February.

In May 1959, while **That's All** was still climbing the charts, Darin and Wess had gone into the studio to record a follow-up in the same style. The result, **This Is Darin**, was released in February 1960, and while the album lacked any bursts of glory as bright as "Mack" or "Beyond The Sea," it was a successful effort.

In many ways, the album opened more eyes to Darin than its predecessor, which cynics had been inclined to regard as a fluke. Now that Darin was starting to be mentioned in the same breath as Sinatra, it seemed as if a gauntlet had been thrown down, challenging Darin to keep up the quality. **This Is Darin** satisfied the doubters.

Down Beat exclaimed, "Darin can sing and he can swing. He may even be the heir apparent to Sinatra's mantle...If Darin can become the big thing among our teenagers, perhaps all is not lost."

New York Times reviewer John S. Wilson was even more effusive in praising the album. Calling **This Is Darin** "the most striking instance of the renaissance of showmanship" on pop records, Wilson wrote, "Any doubts that Mr. Darin can stand up on his own are dissipated...[his] musical personality comes across in electrifying fashion...This is a disk that belongs with the best work of such masters of the genre as Bing Crosby and Frank Sinatra."

This Is Darin peaked a notch higher than **That's All**, reaching #6. The album's single, Darin and Woody Harris' reworking of the chestnut "Clementine," hit #21. The track

Bobby Darin's *Eagerly Awaited* NEW LP!

"This is DARIN"

ATCO 33-115

Available stereo & monaural

Arranger-Conductor RICHARD WESS

A new triumph for Bobby Darin!

From Bobby Darin's last album came "Mack The Knife," the No. 1 hit of 1959—and "Beyond the Sea," his current hit single. Much can be expected of a follow-up to such an LP, and Bobby has brilliantly fulfilled this promise in his new album, THIS IS DARIN.

THIS IS DARIN is an impressive collection of great swingy ballads from which, we feel certain, several singles of the magnitude of "Mack The Knife" will emerge. This LP shows the full range of Bobby's phenomenal talent and his flair for showmanship.

THIS IS DARIN is an album to dazzle the eyes, as well as the ears. Its silver foil sleeve makes it a million dollar keepsake.

You don't gamble with a "sure thing." Swing with Darin!

THIS IS DARIN is the smash hit LP of 1960!

Songs in the Album

Clementine — Caravan
I Can't Give You Anything But Love
Black Coffee — My Gal Sal
Have You Got Any Castles, Baby
Guys and Dolls — Pete Kelly's Blues
Don't Dream Of Anybody But Me
Down With Love — All Nite Long
The Gal That Got Away

THE OTHER DARIN LPs

- **33-102 BOBBY DARIN**
- **33-104 THAT'S ALL** (contains "Mack The Knife" and "Beyond The Sea".)

was again designed to subjugate the song in order to showcase Darin's show-stopping style. While it succeeded at that, it was a little too forced to match the appeal of "Mack" or "Beyond The Sea." Instead, Darin's relatively straight handling of standards such as "Caravan," "The Gal That Got Away" and "I Can't Give You Anything But Love" highlighted the album.

A strange Darin single appeared shortly thereafter. "Moment Of Love" and "She's Tanfastic" were two Darin-penned rock'n'roll style numbers recorded in February 1960. It appeared to be an effort to reach out to the young audience left behind by the past two LPs, but to avoid confusion with an "official" single release, Atco labeled it as a "special premium record" with the cryptic production credit "Produced by Ferron, Inc."

In March, Darin headed off to Britain to headline a concert tour with rockers Clyde McPhatter and Duane Eddy. During his opening night show in Lewisham, Darin was surprised to be greeted with boos when he began "My Funny Valentine." A small, but vocal percentage of the audience had come expecting 100% rock'n'roll, and though Darin brushed off his hecklers with "I thought you people lived on the other side of town," the boos dogged Darin throughout the tour.

It became a major controversy in Britain when *Melody Maker* bannered "Darin Slams Back At British Rock Fans" on the front page of an issue during the tour. Darin told the publication "I'll never tour Britain again in a rock'n'roll package show."

Back home, Darin's next single was another re-working of an old public domain workhorse, "Bill Bailey." On February 2, Darin had recorded an entire album with a small jazz combo and arrangements by Bobby Scott. The session was over when Darin and Scott started messing with "Bill Bailey."

"We got rid of a few musicians and we ended up with just a rhythm section: bass, drums and piano," Scott recalled. "It was an afterthought."

The restrained jazz arrangement contrasted nicely with the big band swing of Darin's previous three hits. "Bill Bailey" reached #19. It's flip side, Darin's ballad "I'll Be There" (recorded in July 1959) also became a minor hit. In time, the song would come to be regarded as one of Darin's top pop songwriting efforts: Britain's Gerry & The Pacemakers scored a Top 15 hit with it in 1965.

For a performer of Bobby Darin's ambitions, the mecca was not Carnegie Hall, but the Copacabana. The major showrooms of Vegas, and clubs like the Cloister in Hollywood were prestigious bookings, but the Copa was the crowning achievement. It unquestionably placed a performer in the upper strata of nightclub stars.

For Darin, a Bronx kid, headlining at the Copa was an even sweeter triumph. He could, for a few days, rule his hometown. And Darin did rule, as the New York press hyped his return to the hilt, building up anticipation for his debut in June. Previews pegged Darin as "the potentially greatest talent in the business."

The Copa timed Darin's debut for June in order to bring in a younger crowd during the prom season. But Copa boss Jules Podell found out he didn't need to hedge his bets with Darin. The place was standing-room-only every night.

As *Variety* pointed out, "The premiere audience was composed almost entirely of adults, and it's these clients that seem to swing along more robustly than the youngsters."

In addition to clicking at the box office, Darin's show received rave reviews. "Darin's finger-snapping, jazzy and extremely hep delivery has its moments of humor, ease and at all times, a singular brand of charm that make it big at this particular scene," commented *Variety*. Rave reviews also appeared in the New York newspapers: the *Journal-American*, *Mirror*, *Post*, and *World Telegram & Sun*.

Darin's repertoire consisted of a few hit singles—"Mack," "Clementine" and "Bill Bailey"—a handful of numbers from the two hit Atco albums, and some standards not yet recorded by Darin: a couple of Cole Porter songs, Rodgers & Hammerstein's "I Have Dreamed" and "traditional" material such as a medley of "Swing Low Sweet Chariot" and "Lonesome Road." Darin also took turns on the vibraphones, drums and piano.

There were a few nods to his early rock'n'roll roots. Darin played piano on a credible version of Ray Charles' "I Got A Woman." "Splish Splash" and "Dream Lover" were also included in the nineteen-song repertoire, though it was fairly obvious that Darin was giving them a little less attention than the remainder of his set.

"He didn't like to do those hits," explained Bobby Scott, who often played piano for Darin's Copa shows. "At the time, he had moved on to a new area and they kind of stuck out like a sore thumb, and he knew it. He did them because there were people out there who had bought the records. But he did them a little bit tongue in cheek."

To compound the excitement of the Copa dates, the June 15 and 16 shows were recorded for a live album. **Darin At The Copa** became his third straight Top 10 album, climbing to #9 in the fall. The entire Copa show was documented, with the exception of three songs which were edited from the release: "Birth Of The Blues," "My Funny Valentine" and "Splish Splash."

The album gave listeners a taste of Darin's show-business *savoir-faire*, which was knocking out nightclub audiences. But in retrospect, Bobby Scott felt Darin's subsequent Copa performances were superior and he wished the live album had not been rushed out so soon.

"The recording was so bad in there," Scott observed. "They just did not get the band. The sound was horrible. I don't think they should have done it. I think it was a little early in his career for a live album."

Reminiscing about Darin's now-legendary early sixties appearances at the Copa, Scott most remembered the sense of excitement that surrounded Darin in those days.

"I remember in between shows, in the apartment in the Hotel 14 above the Copa," Scott recalled. "Jesus Christ, it was like a show business pantheon. Everybody came out. I remember Judy Garland bringing Liza Minnelli in. I remember Lee Remick complimenting Bobby on his show.

"There were so many people who wanted to see the show," Scott said. "The crowds were so large that they filled the stage area and Bobby sang about three feet from me, pressed up against the grand piano. Bobby was at the height of his performing abilities. They were really great times."

One of Darin's biggest boosters at the time was Walter Winchell, the influential and nationally syndicated *New York Mirror* columnist. A regular attendee at Darin's shows at the Copa, the Cloister, and Washington, D.C.'s Casino Royale, Winchell dropped Darin's name into his column quite often.

AMERICA'S MOST VERSATILE YOUNG SHOWMAN

BOBBY DARIN

In A Fabulous Piano Hit!

BEACHCOMBER

AND

Autumn Blues

Atco 6173

With Orchestra Conducted by Shorty Rogers

ATCO RECORDS

"The Winchell thing happened quite unexpectedly," Darin explained to the *New York Post*. "He saw me working, he liked me, and he came down to tell me. The next night, he and I had an argument about a certain individual in politics...The net result of that argument was a very close friendship."

While Darin was playing in D.C. in May, Winchell telephoned the office of his friend, FBI Director J. Edgar Hoover, to request an FBI tour for himself and Darin. Although Hoover did not accompany them, Darin and Winchell did receive a special tour of FBI facilities.

All the while, Atco continued to pump out the product. Strangely, an instrumental single, "Beachcomber," was released in the fall and barely dented the chart at #100. A quick follow-up, "Artificial Flowers," paired with "Somebody To Love" (the latter a Darin composition) fared better, with both sides charting. "Somebody To Love," the lesser hit, was recorded in 1959 at the same session as "I'll Be There" and was decidedly more youth-oriented than any Darin hit since "Dream Lover."

Along those lines, Atco released an album in September called **For Teenagers Only**, a title indicative of the label's marketing strategy for Darin. The album package included a photo spread and pull-out poster. With the exception of "Somebody To Love" and "You Know How" (another track from the July 1959 session), the entire album consisted of leftover material from 1958. For the most part, teenagers stayed away; the album did not chart.

Atco's bad habit of keeping Darin material in the can increased in 1960; two entire albums were shelved, held from release until 1963 and 1964, after Darin had left the label.

Atco did have some understandable concern about the glut of Darin product, and the commerciality of the material in question. The label released four Darin albums in both 1960 and 1961, so finding a hole in the schedule would have been difficult.

But by burying the albums until '63 and '64, when Darin was on another label and his record sales in a down-cycle, Atco virtually insured that two of the greatest albums of Darin's career would go virtually unheard. The label didn't know what to make of the albums, and it was easier to throw together a greatest hits album, a collection of unreleased rock'n'roll for teenagers, or a **Live At The Copa** than to take a chance with the material Darin recorded in January and February of 1960.

"We just thought at the time we would go with things that were more commercial," acknowledged Ahmet Ertegun about the shelved LPs.

The first of the rejected albums was **It's You Or No One**. The concept was Darin's, right down to the album's artwork, which featured a bright color picture of a smiling Darin on the front, a black and white shot of a forlorn Darin on the back. The photographs symbolized the style of the album: upbeat songs, arranged by Torrie Zito, on Side 1; melancholy songs, arranged by Bobby Scott, on Side 2.

Featuring jazz-style arrangements, the album was heavily orchestrated, with Darin's reading of Sammy Cahn and Jule Styne's title track standing out. Acclaimed jazz guitarist (and future Phil Spector session stalwart) Barney Kessell played guitar on Side 1.

Bobby Scott's arrangements for Side 2 were unique in that the accompaniment consisted solely of a string quartet, a flute, a clarinet, French horns, and bass. Neither guitar nor drums were utilized. Slow versions of Duke Ellington and Bob Russell's "Don't Get Around Much Anymore" and Irving Berlin's "How About Me" were highlights.

"I think Bobby did a wonderful job bringing them off," Scott said of the material. "But Atlantic didn't like it at all. They thought it was so esoteric."

An even better album resulted from sessions held a week later, on February 1 and 2 (the session that produced the "Bill Bailey" single). Ten of the fourteen other tracks were finally released on the 1964 Atco LP **Winners**.

Winners was a true jazz vocal album, as Darin shone in a "swingin'" style, but with more relaxed instrumentation than found on **That's All** or **This Is Darin**. Scott assembled a true—and great—small jazz combo: he played piano, with Howard Roberts on guitar, Joe Mondregon on bass, Ronnie Zito on drums, Larry Bunker on vibraphone and Jack Costanzo and Carlo Vidal alternating on congas. The six-piece band's restrained arrangements provided a new, effective showcase for Darin's singing. Here, Bobby Darin was a jazz singer, although arranger Bobby Scott was not fond of that term.

"I don't believe that there is such a thing as a jazz singer," Scott said, "but I would call Bobby a jazz singer as much as I call Ray Charles kind of a jazz singer. Bobby easily went over that line, and had that relaxed thing, and could improvise, certainly much better than Sinatra, or Vic Damone or the 'straight up' singers. He was much better at improvising and moving things around. Bobby was ingenious. He could come up with some interesting phrasing."

A few of the session's tracks rank among the best of Darin's career, particularly "When Day Is Done," "What A Difference A Day Made" and "Easy Living." The latter stood out in Bobby Scott's mind.

"'Easy Living' is a classic record," Scott said. "Bobby sang beautifully on it. That record holds up today. A lot of people who are good singers today would have been proud to make that record."

Regarding Darin's rendition of Dinah Washington's classic "What A Difference A Day Made," writer Ken Emerson, who penned the liner notes to the 1991 CD compilation **Mack The Knife: The Best Of Bobby Darin, Volume Two**, raved "[Darin] murmurs with tender initimacy, an almost feminine delicacy you'd never expect from a performer with Darin's range...Darin was multi-faceted, but here is yet another side of him that he seldom revealed."

George Burns dropped by the sessions for the only "guest vocal" on a Bobby Darin album, providing the "Ho-Ho's" on George and Ira Gershwin's "They All Laughed."

In August 1960, Darin, again with arrangements by Scott, began work on an album which would be released that fall—a Christmas album called **The 25th Day Of December**. The seasonal theme not withstanding, Darin viewed the project as a gospel album.

Thus, most of the songs sported a gospel feel and Darin was able to display his r&b roots more decidedly than in most of his recent pop success. There was some shouting, and a definite edge in Darin's voice. The album contained no "secular" seasonal fare; in fact, only two selections—"Silent Night" and "Oh Come All Ye Faithful"—could be called "traditional" Christmas material.

In a strange marketing move, Darin's 1960 Christmas single,

Sandra Dee.

"Christmas Auld Lang Syne," was not included on the album. This track, using the "Auld Lang Syne" melody with new Christmas lyrics, charted at #51 that December.

On October 3, 1960, Darin joined Patti Page and Joan Crawford as guests on Bob Hope's TV special. Darin performed "Artificial Flowers" and "Lazy River" (slated to be his next single), as well as duets with Page and Hope.

He also took another crack at TV drama, appearing on "Dan Raven" that fall. The series revolved around a detective whose beat was the supper clubs and jazz spots on the "Strip." In the series' very first episode, Darin played himself.

But Darin also had his sights on the big screen. In the *Down Beat* profile in May, Darin reported that he had already received "20 or 25 scripts," but turned them down: "I want the right roles," he said. "I don't want to do an exploitation picture. I want to do drama, light comedy, the whole range. And someday, I want an Academy Award."

Darin's first motion picture appearance was in "Pepe," released in December 1960. In the three-hour, fifteen-minute bomb, Darin cameoed in a nightclub scene, singing "That's How It Went All Right." The track was released by Colpix Records as a single, but received even less attention than the movie.

But in the summer of 1960, Darin was cast in his first major big-screen role. "Come September," starring Rock Hudson and Gina Lollobrigida, began shooting in Rome in the late summer.

Darin's received fourth billing in the role of an American student who, while vacationing in Italy, falls in love with another young American tourist. The love interest was played by Sandra Dee.

The eighteen-year-old Dee was already an established film star, having starred in two smash 1959 movies, "Gidget" and "A Summer Place." She had been a child model, moved into television, and landed her first film role before she was fifteen. Known for playing innocent young girls in the throes of teenage romance, Dee was very popular among teenage movie audiences. Her other previous credits included "The Reluctant Debutante," "The Restless Years," and "Portrait In Black."

Darin and Dee were inseparable on the set. The pair fell deeply in love and after a whirlwind, brief courtship, Bobby Darin and Sandra Dee were married on December 1, 1960, only a few weeks after their return from Italy.

The ceremony, planned on the spur of the moment, was held at 3:00 a.m. in the living room of Don Kirshner's apartment in Elizabeth, New Jersey. Darin borrowed a ring from Kirshner's father-in-law, and Richard Behrke stood as the best man.

America had a new teen idol dream couple.

Chapter 9
"Multiplication"
1961

As Bobby Darin looked into the NBC cameras in January 1961 and sang the opening lines of the Gershwins' "I Got Rhythm," one could not help but think he was describing the state of his own life. Who could ask for anything more?

A finger-snapping medley of "I Got Rhythm" and "I Got Plenty Of Nothing" opened another milestone in Darin's career—his own television special. Produced by Bud Yorkin & Norman Lear, "Bobby Darin & Friends" aired on January 31, 1961.

Anyone who had heard Darin's albums, or seen his nightclub act should not have been surprised that his showmanship could successfully carry an hour of television variety. Still, the savvy that the twenty-four-year-old displayed during this big-time show-business showcase was impressive.

The opening medley segued into a dance number and Darin nicely hoofed his way through some rudimentary choreography. His comic acting skills were evident in a cute musical skit with guest Joanie Sommers, in which the couple played shy high-schoolers (with Darin as the prototypical nerd).

Darin also had the chance to perform a vaudeville routine with a master of the form, Bob Hope. Though Darin over-did the mugging slightly, it was obvious that the pair was having a great time with the loosely-scripted bit, and their comic rapport appeared quite genuine.

In addition to his finger-snapping, swingin' style on numbers such as "Some People," Darin (accompanied by Billy May's orchestra) also played the ultra-smooth balladeer on "I Have Dreamed," which flowed into a ballet number performed by

BOBBY DARIN's

LAZY RIVER

Richard Behrke, arranger-conducter

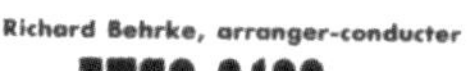

Bobby's Biggest since "MACK THE KNIFE"!

b/w

"OO-EE TRAIN"

Ernie Freeman, arranger-conducter

Tony Charmoli's dancers. Other musical highlights included a long duet number with Sommers, and a Darin-Hope-Sommers soft-shoe through "Bill Bailey."

"Darin works with the aplomb of a stage-scarred veteran," said *Variety*'s review of the special. "The whole performance [was] super-charged with his self-assured air. He used his talent to the hilt and gave this variety hour the benefit of his sharp personality edge."

Executive producer of the special was Steve Blauner, who became Darin's manager (the fifth in five years) in 1960. The headstrong Blauner immediately produced results, such as the TV special, regular Copa bookings, and a new Las Vegas contract—three years at the Flamingo at $20,000 per week.

"It's a great pairing," Darin told the *New York Post* of his teaming with Blauner. "Let me put it this way. I know where I want to go. Steve knows how to get me there."

Darin's single version of "Lazy River" made the charts in February, eventually reaching #14, his biggest hit in a year.

"Lazy River" completed the trilogy, begun with "Mack The Knife" and "Beyond The Sea," of older popular songs which came to be regarded as "Bobby Darin standards." Darin made the song uniquely his own with another show-stopping vocal. This time, the wonderful arrangement, which built from simple bass and acoustic guitar to a full-scale swing attack, was courtesy of Dick Behrke.

Darin's first album of 1961 was **Two Of A Kind**, a collection of duets with the legendary Johnny Mercer, one of the finest popular song lyricists of the century. Unfortunately, the project was misguided in several respects. Though billed as a "Bobby Darin & Johnny Mercer" album (probably for commercial reasons), Mercer opens, and dominates nearly every track.

Mercer's considerable catalog of classics was largely bypassed in favor of, as the liner notes mention, "some of the long neglected corners of Tin Pan Alley." But if the album was designed as some rediscovery-of-lost-gems musical project, the amount of humorous banter Darin and Mercer exchange calls attention to their rapport—not the songs—as the album's centerpiece.

The pairing did produce one masterpiece in the title track, a Darin-Mercer writing collaboration. Darin's true "standard" melody and Mercer's typically clever lyric combine for a wonderful song which singing duos should be performing for ages.

Darin was very proud of the project, which was another example of his acceptance in the community of pre-rock musical greats. During Darin's Copa engagement that year, he coaxed a reluctant Mercer on stage with him for a song.

"Bobby forced Johnny to come on stage and sing a tune," recalled Bobby Scott. "Johnny hated being thrown into the lights. He and Bobby carried it off, as consummate pros will, but John was still blushing when they finished."

Two Of A Kind did not chart, the third consecutive Darin LP which failed to do so. There was a glut of Darin LPs on the market and each of the previous three had been a "special project"—the duet album, the Christmas album, and the collection of unreleased rock'n'roll for the teenagers. Thus, Darin's momentum as a record-seller slowed, making it easy to second-guess about what might have happened if Atco had seen fit to release the stronger **It's You** or **Winners** collections.

The next Atco LP was a can't-miss. **The Bobby Darin Story** collected Darin's twelve most popular sides, evenly split between rock'n'roll and standards. It marked the first album appearance for many hit singles such as "Queen Of The Hop," "Dream Lover" and the concurrent hit "Lazy River." The album sold quite respectably, reaching #18 and staying on the charts for nearly a year.

Darin was back in the swingin' mode for his next album, the tasteful **Love Swings**. The album concentrated on often-recorded standards to an even greater degree than **That's All** or **This Is Darin**, with songwriting credits full of luminaries such as Rodgers & Hart, Ira Gershwin, Jerome Kern, Hoagy Carmichael and yes, Johnny Mercer.

With arrangements by Torrie Zito, Darin turned in very stylish readings of "It Had To Be You," "Skylark" and "I Didn't Know What Time It Was." He updated "How About You" with contemporary references to JFK, Sandra Dee, and rock'n'roll.

The album did not include his latest single, a remake of the Nat King Cole standard "Nature Boy." Though not rock'n'roll, the track's production aimed for the younger Top 40 crowd far more than "Lazy River." For whatever reason, Darin was gravitating back to rock'n'roll.

"You Must Have Been A Beautiful Baby," his next single, was indeed a standard (with lyrics by Mercer), but Darin gave it a pounding rock'n'roll arrangement (later picked up by The Dave Clark Five) and put the edge back in his voice. Commercially, it clicked big, taking Darin back into the Top 5.

On August 9, nearly a year after filming began, "Come September" opened in Minneapolis. While Hudson and Lollobrigida were still major box-office attractions, Darin and Dee's standing as Young America's Sweethearts helped attendance.

"I can't go wrong," Darin told Bobby Scott when the film opened. "The box office people will come out to see the stars, they'll see me, and maybe I can build something out of it."

Darin's reviews were relatively promising for a newcomer. "Darin does a workmanlike job, and gives evidence he'll have more to show when the parts provide him with wider opportunity," wrote *Variety*.

Darin composed two songs for the movie, including the instrumental title theme, released as a single under the name "The Bobby Darin Orchestra." Though it only reached #113 in the U.S., it did better in Britain, hitting #50. Bobby Scott remembered the occasion when Darin first played the song for him on the piano. Scott thought the melody's pseudo-classical aspirations were a bit much.

"'It's pretentious, Bobby,' I told him," Scott recalled. "He laughed and told me to play it; his piano playing left a little to be desired. So I played it, cleaning up the harmonic design. He leaned over the keyboard and said, 'There, now it's so pretentious, it works.'"

The second Darin-penned number, which he performed in the film, was "Multiplication," a clever pop song in the loose novelty style of "Splish Splash." Although it was released as a B-side, it still became a fair-sized hit, reaching #30. (It was a #5 hit in Great Britain.)

The A-side of that December 1961 single was "Irresistible You," a horn-driven rock'n'roll number whose appeal lived up to its title. Darin's "Let's twist awhile" exclamation at mid-song drove home that the record's intended audience was teenagers on the dance floor. "Irresistible You" reached #15.

Darin's not-so-subtle move back into the rock'n'roll arena

was intentional, said Ahmet Ertegun. "No pop singer was having a series of hits then, including Tony Bennett, Sinatra and so forth. Their records weren't big pop records. Darin was trying to get back, to find something that would go both ways. It was the right thing to do, because those records became hits."

Both sides of the hit single and "You Must Have Been A Beautiful Baby" were included on **Twist With Bobby Darin**, the first Darin rock'n'roll album which sold well. The remainder of the album was filled out with old tracks such as "Bullmoose," "Queen Of The Hop," the Rinky Dinks singles, and a few tracks recycled from the **For Teenagers Only** album.

Though it can't be considered a true album project because it was a mish-mash of so many old tracks, **Twist With** is one of Darin's most enjoyable albums. It's a great party record and could almost serve as a time capsule capturing the joys of fifties rock'n'roll.

1961 was capped off with another personal milestone for Bobby Darin. On December 16, his son, Dodd Mitchell Darin, was born at Cedars of Lebanon Hospital in Hollywood.

Chapter 10

"Look At Me"

The 1962 Movies

"Bobby Darin is not yet the biggest thing in pictures, but he is just about the busiest." So proclaimed a *Newsweek* story on Darin in April 1962.

If any newcomer to the silver screen ever ran the risk of wearing out his welcome, surely it was Darin in 1962. Coming off "Come September," Darin corralled prominent roles in five movies that year.

"The pictures are my first love," Darin now announced to *Newsweek*. "I've attacked the movies with the same ferocity I did other things."

For critics who were used to pop or rock stars taking on bubbly roles in inconsequential fluff, Darin was a welcome change of pace. "He is good," *Newsweek* exclaimed with apparent surprise. "Singer Darin belts out his material with elaborate gusto, but actor Darin's style is as natural and understated as that of Bing Crosby or Frank Sinatra."

Darin's first film of the year was "Too Late Blues," for which he shared top billing with Stella Stevens. The film was directed by John Cassavetes, making his first Hollywood picture after receiving acclaim for the low-budget, independently-produced "Shadows." "Too Late Blues" premiered in Paris in November 1961 before a January 1962 U.S. opening.

Darin portrayed John "Ghost" Wakefield, a pianist in a small-time jazz combo. His acting was low-keyed and sophisticated, entirely appropriate for his character. "Darin is effective," said a *Variety* review. "His flaccid, unformed face and his fumbling idealism fuse well." The *New York Times* concurred: "An arrogant punk of a hero [is] played to perfection by Mr.

Darin (center) in "Too Late Blues," his first starring role.
(Paramount Pictures Corp. publicity photo)

Darin."

Unfortunately, the film's reviews were deservedly negative. Without a directional plot, the narrative intended to be a character study, but development was nil and motivation was unfounded. As the *Times* review began, "All that 'Too Late Blues' needs to make it one of the best movies ever about jazz musicians is substance."

Darin's next film was his first and only true musical, "State Fair." The 1962 version, which also starred Pat Boone, Ann-Margret and Pamela Tiffin, was the second remake of the venerable Rodgers & Hammerstein favorite.

Darin portrayed Jerry Dundee, a fast-talking, worldly television announcer involved in a mating ritual with Tiffin's small town girl. Darin sang "This Isn't Heaven," a new song written for the film by Richard Rodgers, and participated in an ensemble number, "It's A Grand Night For Singing." The film's soundtrack album was a sizeable hit, reaching #12 in the summer of 1962.

However, Darin found himself in another film panned by critics, and this time, their barbs didn't stop at the story. "Pat Boone and Bobby Darin emerge rather bland and unappealing," wrote *Variety*, while the *New York Times* called Darin "rather awkward as an actor." Though critics almost universally agreed that the whole idea of the remake was miscalculated, the film was a commercial success, finishing twenty-third on *Variety*'s list of "Big Rental Pictures of 1962."

Critics were kinder to Darin's next film, "Hell Is For Heroes." Although Darin received second billing, his role in actuality was merely supporting. When first introduced in the movie, Darin's character (Private Corby) shoulders the role of comic relief, although later Bob Newhart steps in and Darin becomes just another soldier.

Except for Steve McQueen, none of the actors were given much character to work with. Again, Darin did quite well with what he was given, as *Variety* noted—"Bobby Darin has a colorful role of a battlefield boarder which he portrays with relish."

The movie was ultimately confusing and often sluggish, with battle strategy and battle scenes all portrayed at length on screen. Admirers of the film were intrigued by McQueen's

Darin (second from left) in "Hell Is For Heroes."
(Paramount Pictures Corp. publicity photo)

character, although from the post-Vietnam perspective, the qualities which were then regarded by some as heroic appear more questionable. "Hell Is For Heroes" was a solid, if unspectacular, box office hit, finishing at #59 on *Variety*'s tally of the top films of 1962.

Darin's next role would not only elicit his greatest on-screen performance, but also result in the finest, most thought-provoking film of his career, "Pressure Point." Sharing top billing with Sidney Poitier, Darin portrays an unnamed character simply referred to as "The Patient," a prison inmate under the psychiatric care of Poitier's "The Doctor."

A black and white film set in 1942, "Pressure Point" finds Darin as a racist, anti-Semitic Nazi sympathizer arrested for subversive activities in the German American Bund. Considering Darin's image, it was a fascinating role for him to take on.

He convincingly put across the character's hatred, insulting FDR and donning a Nazi uniform. But he also superbly handled scenes in which the roots of his character's sickness are explored. One of the best is the scene in which Darin's character attends his first Bund meeting. As the audience sings "The Star Spangled Banner," and Darin eventually, reluctantly joins in, the confusion and doubt on his face is telling.

Though the film did not attract audiences, Darin's performance gained wide recognition. "Bobby Darin gives a strong performance, delivering a believable, natural characterization," said *Variety*. "He plays with a frighteningly realistic attitude of distrust and psychopathic fear." Even the usually reserved *New York Times* was complimentary: "As was intended, Mr. Darin's portrayal should make anyone recoil."

Effusive in praise, the *New York Herald Tribune* wrote of Darin: "That this usually light, romantic young man undertook such a vicious portrayal is evidence of his seriousness. That he brings it off with such ghastly sureness of touch underlines his talent with unexpected incisiveness."

Darin and Poitier, who was also superb, were given a relatively strong script to work with. There are a few weaknesses, such as Darin's character needing more motivation for his anti-Semitism than being rejected by a Jewish girl. But for the most part, the writing hit home.

The movie's pivotal scene comes when the patient chal-

From "Pressure Point."
(Paramount Pictures Corp. publicity photo)

lenges his black doctor's love of America: "Can you walk on a bus or a streetcar or a train and sit down with a little dignity like a free human being, like a free man?" he goads. With voice-over narration, Poitier then chillingly observes "I knew then what I was so afraid of."

Another scene showcasing The Patient's anti-social nature depicted a Darin-led gang terrorizing a bar. Eventually the members go so far as to play tic-tac-toe on the body of the owner's wife (played by actress Mary Munday). For this scene, Darin was joined by actor Richard (Dick) Bakalyan. During the shoot, Darin and Bakalyan played chess every day, and the two struck up a lasting friendship.

Darin and Poitier also became close. (Ironically, given the film's anti-bigotry message, "Pressure Point" was the only film of 1962 to feature a black actor in a lead role.) Just as Darin admired Poitier's consummate professionalism as an actor, Poitier admired Darin's musical integrity. Once, Poitier stopped by one of Darin's recording sessions.

"Poitier had come fully assuming he was going to hear a guy singing 'My Funny Valentine,'" recalled future Darin producer Nik Venet, who attended the session. "Darin, myself, an engineer and one of the violin players were the only four white people at the session. Poitier was stunned. He couldn't believe that he was coming to a session that was so funky."

After proving his mettle as a serious dramatic actor, Darin returned to the expected for his fifth film of 1962, "If A Man Answers." It was the first vehicle concocted especially for the Darin-Dee team. *Time* pretty well summed up critical consensus with "Actor Darin and Actress Dee, who are Mr. and Mrs. in real life, just sort of stand there like Tweedle Dumb and Twiddle Dee [*sic*]. And the production is in the cheapest kind of expensive bad taste."

But the box office appeal of Dee was still strong, and the film was a moderate hit. More than any of his previous, more respected efforts, "If A Man Answers" placed Darin, albeit briefly, in the exclusive category of "movie star."

Darin was riding high. The film opened shortly after he signed his lucrative new contract with Capitol Records. His first single for the label was the movie's title song, the first record he made with Capitol producer Nik Venet.

Darin starred with Sandra Dee in "If A Man Answers."
(Universal International publicity photo)

A few nights before the film's opening, Darin, Dee and Venet were taking a late night cab ride down Broadway, driving past the theatre where the movie would premiere. The theatre had just erected 30-foot high cutouts of Darin and Dee to hang above the marquee. To savor the moment, Darin asked the cab driver to pull over just across the street. Darin and Venet got out.

"In the privacy of the night, we stood there in total awe," Venet recalled. "He said to me 'Can you believe this?' For two guys who came from parents who didn't have much, it was amazing."

The cab driver, who did not recognize any of his passengers, finally concluded that there was a celebrity in the back seat of his car. The driver turned to Darin and said "Your friend looks like somebody."

"He sure is somebody," Darin replied.

"I knew it," the driver replied, turning to Venet. "Mr. Mineo, can I have your autograph?"

"Sal will do anything for you," replied Darin. Venet obligingly signed Sal Mineo's name on a piece of paper. When time came to pay the fare, Darin told Venet, "Sal, the guy recognized you, give him a big tip." Venet reached for a ten dollar bill, but Darin yanked a fifty out of Venet's wallet.

"Darin and I laughed our asses off," said Venet. "That's the kind of sense of humor he had. He didn't say 'But I'm Bobby Darin' to the driver, he went along with the gag."

Darin on stage at The Famingo, August 1962.
(Las Vegas News Bureau)

Chapter 11

"Things"

1962 Music

Despite Darin's full slate of film projects in 1962, he devoted just as much time to his music as ever. Before jumping labels in July, Darin capped off his Atco stint in grand style.

One of the most intriguing albums of his career was **Bobby Darin Sings Ray Charles**, recorded in November 1961 and released in the spring of 1962. Darin tackled eleven songs written by or associated with Charles in very impressive fashion. Driving versions of "The Right Time," "Hallelujah I Love Her So" and "Leave My Woman Alone" showed that Darin hadn't lost any touch with his r&b roots.

Some impressive help was on hand. Jimmy Haskell arranged the album. Saxophone was supplied by future Phil Spector session ace (and soon-to-be "Deep Purple" hitmaker) Nino Tempo. Background vocals were provided by The Blossoms, whose Darlene Love stepped up to the microphone for some wicked solo vocal parts on "The Right Time."

Darin's four-minute version of "What'd I Say" was split in half and released on both sides of a single. Part 1 reached #24, while the album reached #96. Ahmet Ertegun, who produced the sessions, considered the album too ahead of its time to succeed commercially. Darin himself was ambivalent about the results.

"It wasn't the greatest LP I've ever made," he told *Melody Maker* later that year, "but I had to get it off my chest. It seems to be the fashion now to admire Charles. I'm proud to have been admiring him for a long time."

Darin's version of "What'd I Say" received a Grammy nomination for Best Rhythm & Blues Recording. In entirely appropriate irony, Ray Charles won that year's award for his rendition of the country classic "I Can't Stop Loving You."

* * * * * * * *

Rumors about Darin working with legendary producer Phil Spector have popped up in many published accounts of Spector's career, and they are usually placed at about this time period—1962. The assertion that Spector produced some tracks for Darin is presented as fact in many "rock history" tomes, with no specification or documentation. This despite the fact that no Darin single or album bears a Spector production credit and no track has an obvious "Spector sound."

Atlantic chief Ahmet Ertegun, who served as supervisor (sometimes solely, often in tandem with brother Nesuhi and/or Jerry Wexler) for all of Darin's Atco sessions—a role which over the years ranged from actually producing to acting as "executive producer"—said that Spector had no involvement in Darin's records.

However, Ertegun reported that he did intend to have Spector work with Darin, and arranged for the two to meet.

"By that time, Bobby had married Sandra Dee and was living in Beverly Hills," Ertegun said. "So Phil and I went to this big mansion, with a butler serving drinks around the pool and everything. We walked in, and I introduced Bobby to Phil."

"See, Bobby was a very prolific writer, and he would write fifteen or twenty songs and play them all for me. And out of the fifteen or twenty, there would be three or four really good ones. So he started playing me songs like 'Jailer Bring Me Water' and I said 'Well, that's great.' He played another and I said 'That's great.' The songs weren't good, but I knew the good ones would come up.

"Phil turns to me and says 'Just a second man, are you crazy or am I? Those songs are horrible.' So Darin says 'Who the hell is this son of a bitch?' He was ready to throw Spector out, so we left.

"A year later, when Spector was hot, Darin says to me 'Do you think you could get this kid to work with me?' I told him it was the same guy he threw out. He didn't remember."

Despite the inauspicious meeting described by Ertegun, Darin and Spector did become acquaintances. In the 1989 Spector biography *He's A Rebel* by Mark Ribowsky, Spector cowriter Terry Phillips related a story about he and Spector pitching songs to Darin and getting a favorable response.

Los Angeles Times pop music critic Robert Hilburn, while on a road trip with Spector in the early seventies, received first-hand evidence that Darin and Spector had a cordial relationship.

"In Vegas, Spector and I went to see Elvis at the International, then to the Desert Inn to see Darin," Hilburn recalled. "After the show, Spector and Darin sat around for four, five, six hours, reminiscing about the old days in New York."

* * * * * * * *

Darin's final Atco single was "Things," a finely-crafted country-pop effort which became his biggest pop hit since "Mack The Knife," reaching #3. Darin described "Things" as "sorta polite country and western. It was a gamble that paid off."

The lyric displayed Darin's ability to drop a relatively unusual phrase such as "Heartaches are the friends I'm talking to" into a simple pop song. Though "Things" was not a country hit at the time, it has since made the country charts in three cover versions, including one by Anne Murray which also became a minor pop hit.

Atco hastily assembled a corresponding **Things And Other Things** album, which was filled out with various single A and B sides from '58-'61 which had not appeared on Darin LPs before.

In July, Darin signed a new, lucrative contract with Capitol Records, ending his five-plus year association with Atco.

"That was a big shock to me," Ahmet Ertegun recalled. "Darin was the only really big pop artist we had at the time. He was being influenced by his managers. He was always told 'You're a big pop star, you shouldn't be on this funky little r&b label.'" Indeed, it was that exact pitch by Capitol which won Darin over.

"At that time, Capitol, RCA and Columbia were very prestigious labels," said Nik Venet, the first Capitol producer to work with Darin. "If you played nightclubs and wanted to do TV and film, Atlantic and those companies—which were really doing well—didn't have the prestige, or production offices in California. It was quite a thing to get on Capitol. The deal was so prestigious for Bobby."

Venet produced Darin's first Capitol single, the piano-driven, rock'n'roll-style theme from "If A Man Answers." It reached #32, but was hardly the smash the label was hoping for. In fact, they were hoping for a replacement for Frank Sinatra, who had left Capitol two years earlier to form his own Reprise label.

Darin tried to oblige with his first album, **Oh! Look At Me Now**, a collection of standards arranged big-band style by Billy May, who had worked extensively with Sinatra. (May had also handled arrangements for Darin's TV special and the **Two Of A Kind** LP.) Capitol staff producer Tom Morgan produced the album.

"Bobby wanted to do a Capitol type of album—with Billy May and the big studio orchestra," said Morgan. "I spent some time with Billy May and Bobby over at Bobby's house, where we picked the tunes and talked over what the charts were going to be. Bobby sang great, the music was great, and it was a very good album."

May, who had no appreciation for rock'n'roll, came to respect Darin's vocal ability. "I think Darin was a better singer than people in my generation classify him," May said. "I think he sang well in-tune. He phrased OK and all. He had the ability to develop a staying quality."

The Darin-May pairing sounded perfectly natural. Darin was not overwhelmed by the arrangements and didn't try to overexert himself. The albums's few ballads, hampered by Ray Conniff-like background singers, tended to drag, but an upbeat romp such as "A Nightingale Sang In Berkeley Square" was an absolutely classic Darin vocal (and the great brass arrangement was classic May).

Three Irving Berlin songs—"All By Myself," "Always" and "Blue Skies"—stood out as highlights. Darin's swingin' style also shone on "There's A Rainbow 'Round My Shoulder" and a jazzy reading of Duke Ellington's "I'm Beginning To See The Light."

Though the faux-Sinatra approach resulted in some excellent tracks, **Oh! Look At Me Now** stiffed. But Darin was interested in pursuing his usual array of differing styles at Capitol.

"He didn't want to abandon the teenage audience," Nik Venet said. "He wanted to be able to do whatever he wanted, but he didn't want to offend anybody. He didn't want to offend teenagers by playing Vegas, and he didn't want to offend Vegas by making records that would appeal to young people. He didn't want to pander to anybody. He wanted to be a multiple talent. In those days, that was a problem. You were either a teenage singer or Frank Sinatra."

Of course, Darin had been both for Atco. His *modus operandi* was to consider all options—and occasionally the label's input—when it came time to choose which songs, and in which style, he would record.

"Bobby would let everybody at the table speak," Venet recalled. "If you had an idea, and you argued with him, he'd go with you. You had to prove your conviction to him. You became his friend with your integrity. He made you put your money where your mouth was."

Darin and Nik Venet became close friends. Still in his twenties, Venet was by far the youngest producer at Capitol. In addition to Darin, he worked with The Beach Boys, The Lettermen, Ray Anthony, Jack Scott and Tommy Sands. (He would later produce Linda Ronstadt and John Stewart.)

Venet produced three Darin albums and six singles. In the course of their work together, Venet also estimated that he would spend ten to fifteen weeks a year on the road with Darin. Those times gave Venet a unique perspective on, and understanding of, the Darin personality.

"Darin was a remarkable human being," Venet said. "I've worked with some heavy duty people, from Stan Kenton to Linda Ronstadt. But Darin was probably the most impressive person I've ever met in my life. Had he not been a musician, he would have been a senator or congressman."

Venet's close relationship with Darin gave him an insight on Darin's generosity toward his friends. For example, Venet received an XKE from Darin. Darin gifts would often be surprises.

"I once saw a wristwatch he was wearing and said 'That's beautiful,'" Venet said. "The next day, there was a knock on my door. It was a messenger, with a $5,000 wristwatch. There was a little note attached to it—'Thank God you didn't admire my wife.'"

"The guy would give you the shirt off his back, and he did," Venet said. "He was the most generous man in the world."

Venet also learned how important loyalty was: Darin would never let one friend say something negative about another friend. Once Venet started to complain to Darin about Don Kirshner. The beef was nothing terribly nasty; Venet was just upset that some Kirshner-published songs he thought he had secured for the Lettermen were given to another act.

"Darin told me 'Stop. Continue this conversation and I'm going to move to another table,'" Venet said. "I couldn't even begin a conversation about someone he knew—someone that was part of his 'family'—with one negative word. He wouldn't even entertain the thought of discussing it."

There were also many moments of humor. Sometimes, Darin and Venet would astoundedly discuss their good fortune.

"I remember once, we were three sheets to the wind, laughing," Venet said. "He was married to Sandra Dee and I was dating Tuesday Weld. We were saying 'Jesus Christ, this is amazing, that this could happen to jerks like us from New York and Baltimore.' Talking like kids."

Darin could also be a practical joker. Once, after a long work session in which Darin and Venet had gone three nights without sleep, they stopped at a barbershop. When Venet fell asleep in the barber's chair, Darin paid off the barber to give him a crewcut.

"Touring with some other acts was a chore," Venet said. "Darin was great, because we were identical in our political beliefs, we had great conversations, and we met great people."

"Darin introduced me to Allen Ginsberg," said Venet. "He was a great fan of *On The Road* by Jack Kerouac—that was one of his favorite books. Darin was counter-culture before counter-culture had a title."

Chapter 12
"Earthy"
The First Folk Phase

Though the Kingston Trio had been popular since 1958 (their breakthrough came only months after Darin's), folk music did not really become a stronghold in popular music until 1962. The upper echelons of the album charts, still the domain of soundtracks to movie musicals and Mitch Miller, were suddenly invaded by Peter, Paul & Mary, The Limeliters and Joan Baez.

Like many others, Bobby Darin liked what he heard. Previously, he had dabbled with a Vegasy arrangement of the spiritual "Swing Low Sweet Chariot," and even taken a crack at writing a gospel-folk number in "Jailer Bring Me Water." But in early 1962, Darin decided to more deeply pursue folk music and to do some performing in that style, on stage and on record.

While it was easy to accuse Darin of jumping on a bandwagon (as some critics have done), his interest in and respect for folk music was genuine. Darin was not only into the newly-popular folk of Peter, Paul & Mary and the Kingston Trio, but also some other, quite respected artists old and new—in the folk tradition.

"I remember packing tapes for when we would travel," recalled Nik Venet. "We used to play a lot of folk music: a lot of music from the Dust Bowl days, the thirties, the WPA albums. It was a favorite period of ours for digging up music."

"Cisco Houston (a compatriot and sometimes singing-partner of Woody Guthrie) was a big favorite of ours," said Venet. "Darin was also a big Tom Paxton fan. He had all of Paxton's records."

Live, Darin's first forays in the folk area were a gentle

reading of "Danny Boy" and the chain-gang-style blues "Work Song." He was working towards a "folk" segment of his concert act, during which the big band would rest, and Darin would take off his jacket and tie and sing with minimal instrumental accompaniment.

While Darin was mulling this over, he and Steve Blauner went to see Lenny Bruce perform at the Crescendo in Los Angeles. The opening act was another of the folk groups which had achieved a fair level of popularity, The Chad Mitchell Trio. During the show, Darin was quite impressed by the Trio's back-up guitarist, who not only had great instrumental chops, but also would delight the audience with his clowning.

With his own folk segment in mind, Darin decided that the guitarist would be the perfect addition to his band. After the Mitchell Trio's set, Darin went backstage and offered the nineteen-year-old musician a job at double the weekly salary he was being paid by the Mitchell Trio.

The guitarist was Jim McGuinn, who after one-and-a-half years in Darin's band, would go on to found The Byrds, the seminal and hugely-influential folk-rock band of "Mr. Tambourine Man" and "Turn Turn Turn" fame. (While with the Byrds, McGuinn changed his first name to Roger.)

McGuinn, who had also previously backed The Limeliters, was making $150 a week. When Darin offered him a job, McGuinn hedged; he was bored with the Mitchell Trio, but was also considering an offer to join the New Christy Minstrels. Darin convinced McGuinn that he would get lost in the shuffle in that multi-member folk troupe.

McGuinn was leading something of a musical double life at the time. He was into the protest and topical forms of folk music, and hanging out in Greenwich Village with a hip crowd that included Bob Dylan. Those friends tended to look down on more "commercial" acts such as The Limeliters and The Chad Mitchell Trio (and it's hard to imagine that their view of Darin would have been any more charitable).

In some interviews over the years, McGuinn has been quoted as saying he was somewhat ashamed of his early "commercial" associations. However, in an interview about his work with Darin, he insisted that he is nothing but proud of that particular pre-Byrds association. McGuinn was adamant in his defense of Darin's musical integrity when questioned about whether Darin was sincere about folk music.

"Absolutely," he said. "There's no question in my mind. Bobby was more sincere than the other groups I had worked with."

"When he did something, he had an integrity about it that I didn't feel with The Chad Mitchell Trio," McGuinn said. "I felt they were more fluff than anything. Bobby was very interested in folk music and felt he wanted to be part of it."

McGuinn was brought into the fold to play twelve-string guitar and sing harmony during the folk segment of Darin's show. Rather than rehashing the Kingston Trio/Peter, Paul & Mary folk at the top of the charts, Darin concentrated on more "traditional" material during the segment, which was part of his shows throughout 1962 and 1963. Songs included Leadbelly's "Cottonfields" (for which Darin accompanied himself on guitar), "Long Time Man," "I'm On My Way" (also known as "Canaan's Land"), "Boil That Cabbage Down" and, in one nod to pop-folk, The Rooftop Singers' hit "Walk Right In."

The segment went over well with both audience and critics. "He sings his folk section with power and precision," said a *Variety* review, which noted that Darin seemed to put more effort into the folk segment than the rest of the show: "He has a tendency to casually throw away the numbers the audience is waiting and clamoring for, yet conversely, to work with great respect and discipline on less familiar material."

The interest in folk carried over into the recording studio, and Darin would take advantage of his Capitol contract to release two theme albums of folk material. To help out, Darin called on an old friend from his high school band days, Walter Raim.

Raim had drifted into the folk scene, hooking up with the Harry Belafonte organization, occasionally playing with Belafonte on stage, and doing other musical work for the organization. Darin saw Raim's name on the back of a Belafonte album and phoned his old friend to ask for help with an album of folk songs.

"He saw in folk music a sophistication of some kind, a higher calling," recalled Raim. "He had in his mind that he was doing something more important than singing Las Vegas standards. He was attracted to the realness, the down-to-earth thing."

Although Capitol would hold its release for almost a year, Darin's first "folk" album, **Earthy**, was recorded shortly after the **Oh! Look At Me Now** sessions. Tom Morgan, who was not crazy about the project, oversaw the production. Raim helped Darin choose the songs, and wrote out the arrangements.

Earthy's theme was folk music from different cultures, which further differentiated Darin's project from the popular folk music of the day. The album was a varied collection of spirituals, blues, Latin American folk dance songs, and ballads.

Darin's vocal approach to the songs was markedly different from the way he sang rock'n'roll or popular standards. He substituted his voice's usual polish and strength with a restrained, softer, occasionally world-weary style. It seemed as if he was intentionally holding back, because that's how he felt the songs should be interpreted.

"I think he was trying to achieve another dimension as a singer," commented Raim, "just as a character actor would try to be someone else. Unlike someone like Sinatra, who always sounds like himself, I think Bobby was trying to be a different character when he sang those songs."

The project moved Darin to some of his all-time greatest performances. "Fay-O," a Haitian lament adapted and arranged by Raim, is one of Darin's most beautiful recordings; his absolutely moving vocal is framed in a lovely minimalistic arrangement of acoustic guitar, bass, bongos and flute.

Likewise, Darin cut a top-notch version of Tom Paxton's mournful protest "Strange Rain," almost whispering his vocal over an acoustic guitar. Recorded less than a year after Dodd's birth, the song's line "What will become of my son?" may have made it particularly meaningful to Darin.

Earthy was not the swinging, cocky, in-control Bobby Darin the public had come to expect, but it showcased Darin as one of the great interpreters of his generation. While somewhat outside the thematic framework of the album, "Work Song," written by Oscar Brown, Jr. and Nat Adderly, was another Darin *tour de force*, arranged in the bass-driven, dramatic jazz-blues manner of Peggy Lee's "Fever."

While "Fay-O" was sung partially in Haitian, two other

cuts, "La Bamba" and "Guantanamera" were sung entirely in their Latin American languages. Harry Belafonte received credit for the adaptation of "La Bamba" (radically different from the Ritchie Valens' rock'n'roll hit). Darin was also strong on the gospel songs "I'm On My Way," "When Their Mama Is Gone," and "The Sermon Of Samson" (which Peter, Paul & Mary recorded as "If I Had My Way").

Throughout the album, the vocal and instrumental arrangements were solidly in the folk tradition.

"I don't think we thought much about being authentic; just about being true to the spirit of the song," said Raim. "We were not trying to be ethnic or pure. To do a folk song with anything but a guitar was considered commercial. We were trying to make a commercial album that would sell."

Though **Earthy** failed to chart, Darin did not give up on folk, recording a second album in that style called **Golden Folk Hits**. Darin's folk sessions featured an impressive guest line-up. Glen Campbell played on both records. Legendary guitarist James Burton can be heard on **Golden Folk Hits**.

From the folk community, Bud Dashiel (of the duo Bud & Travis) played on "La Bamba" and "Guantanamara." The folk group The Tarriers, who hit with "The Banana Boat Song" in 1957, were also employed. (The group included Marshall Brickman, who would later perform with John & Michelle Phillips in their pre-Mamas & Papas folk outfit, The New Journeymen). In 1962, the Tarriers also accompanied Darin on a tour and backed him during the folk segment.

Roger McGuinn played on some sessions, but believes his playing was pretty much lost in the mix: "I was just sort of along with the other guitarists in there. I don't know how much of my input got onto the record," he said.

Nik Venet also recalls that one of the giants of the sixties folk scene, the late Phil Ochs, was a frequent guest at the sessions.

"If someone tries to tell you that Darin didn't know his folk music," said Venet, "or that he was making folk music because it was hot, why would Phil Ochs come down to the session? Why would he hang out with us, if Darin was ripping that segment of music off?"

Venet produced **Golden Folk Hits**, released in November

1963. With accompaniment consisting of guitar, banjo, bass and background vocals, and very tasteful, faithful acoustic arrangements of the more familiar folk of the early sixties, the album was more contemporary, but less ambitious than **Earthy**. If less thought went into this album on Darin's part, even less care was displayed by Capitol, which didn't even bother to put a picture of Darin on the front cover.

Still, it was interesting to hear Darin throw his hat into the ring of the top-of-the-charts folk familiarized by Peter, Paul & Mary ("Where Have All The Flowers Gone," "If I Had A Hammer"), The Kingston Trio ("Greenback Dollar," in which Darin chickens out of the "damn" that got the Trio censored), and the New Christy Minstrels ("Green, Green").

But the most noteworthy facet of the album was Darin's recording of two Bob Dylan songs. The first time McGuinn told Darin about a kid in Greenwich Village named Bob Dylan, Darin laughed and thought the kid was ripping off his name. But Darin was one of the first, if not the first, of the so-called "legitimate" singers to recognize Dylan and to incorporate Dylan songs into his recorded and live repertoire.

"Darin was impressed with the songs," recalled Venet. "He thought Dylan was important. We thought Dylan wasn't getting the shake he deserved. Some people weren't getting the message because of Dylan's singing style."

"I remember Darin in Vegas, sitting at the piano, playing Dylan's 'Don't Think Twice' with a big band," said Venet. "He was tearing up the house. The audiences at the ten o'clock and two o'clock shows were people in their twenties and thirties—it was the youth of Vegas. He was starting to get the message across."

The album's version of "Don't Think Twice" is marred by the inappropriate Jordanaires-style "Bop-bop-bop" of the background vocalists. (Darin would later record a superior version of the song for Motown.) However, Darin's reading of "Blowin' In The Wind," in his subdued voice, is a standout, and holds up very well against the myriad other recorded versions of the classic.

Darin's work in the folk idiom is largely overlooked, and often merely considered a side-track in his career. Even Walter Raim would comment, "Although he wanted to do this very much, it was not who he was." Still, precisely because it was so left-field a move at the time, Darin's 1962-63 foray into folk is fascinating. He would call upon his love of stripped-down, acoustic music to varying degrees throughout his career.

And there is a legacy left from this era, considering how effusive Roger McGuinn is in his praise of Darin, and how important a band The Byrds became.

Although the legend is that The Byrds were folkies who decided to plug in and play with a beat when they heard the Beatles, McGuinn suggested that at least some of the impetus toward rock came from his days with Darin.

"Bobby had a lot of influence on me," McGuinn said. "He convinced me that rock'n'roll was where it was at. He oriented me in that direction.

"It was a good training ground," McGuinn said of his days in Darin's band. "It gave me a lot of seasoning in the business. I knew things that the guys in The Byrds didn't know.

"It was almost like coming up in vaudeville or something. Bobby was like an old trouper. It was like he was from another era. He was a more professional performer than most people I know in the business today. He was punctual and he was precise and he hit the mark all the time. He was a brilliant guy, real bright, and he could do anything he wanted to do very well."

During this time, Darin got his first notions of how a performer might be able to do more than entertain an audience. Perhaps, through music, he could express his concerns about society, perhaps act as a catalyst for thought. Though it would be years before Darin would fully embrace this notion, the seed was planted. He also saw the potential volatility in the mix of the supper club circuit and liberal artistic vision.

"I remember him doing a show in the Catskills," recalled Nik Venet, "and I remember people saying, 'What happened to Bobby Darin? Did you hear those songs he was singing? He sounds like a communist.' Somebody else said, 'I came here to hear Frank Sinatra, not this rock'n'roll shit.'

"Some people were very disappointed in the show, because Darin was mixing it up. He used to say 'Just let 'em think about it.' He was so far ahead of his audience sometimes."

Chapter 13

"Commitment"

Political And Civil Rights Activism

Though it has not been extensively publicized previously, Bobby Darin was very interested and active in the political and social causes of his time. Although much of the FBI's ninety-six-page file on Darin (of which the agency released forty-three pages to this author) concerns White House-requested name checks on entertainers or details on Darin's delinquency regarding induction into the military in 1958, the agency did not overlook his participation in marches and demonstrations.

In the early and mid-sixties, Darin's attention was captured by the cause of civil rights. He often spent long hours discussing his feelings with Nik Venet, who shared Darin's liberal views and accompanied him on the March on Washington.

"Darin thought the civil rights movement was the great revolution of the twentieth century," Venet said. "The man was civil rights conscious long before it became radical chic. It was a passion of his."

Darin knew the Reverend Dr. Martin Luther King, Jr. and introduced the great civil rights leader to Venet. On another occasion, Darin introduced King to a less receptive audience, attendees of one of Darin's shows at the Copacabana.

That night, King came to the Copa during Darin's second show, entering through the back entrance. Darin stopped the show to introduce King. The reaction from the older, white, decked-out Copa crowd was less than enthusiastic.

"It was silent," recalled Venet. "Then two guys in the back, and I think they were waiters, started applauding, and then slowly the applause rode from the back to the front.

"They finally applauded," Venet said, "but Darin felt that if he had introduced Sammy Davis, Jr., it would have been easier."

Indeed, Darin did not like the racial discrimination in the Las Vegas entertainment industry, which accepted Davis and Nat King Cole on stage, but seemed less receptive to blacks anywhere else.

"He'd say 'I can't believe it—you guys don't even have blacks as waiters here,'" said Venet. "They used to get mad at Darin. He'd threaten to bring in an all-black orchestra. He'd say 'Next time I play here, you're not going to see a white face up here except mine.'"

While on marches, however, Darin would try to keep a low profile. Whenever a member of the press would recognize him, he would decline to make a comment, saying "I'm here as a concerned citizen, not an entertainer."

The trips to Washington weren't without their lighter moments. Darin had just completed a run at the Copa and neither he nor Venet had bothered to make travel arrangements. Hours before they had intended to head to the nation's capital, they found that all flights out of New York, and all hotels in D.C., were booked solid.

Their only option was to become true "limousine liberals"—they made the trip from New York to Washington in a limousine, hardly the mode of transportation favored by too many of the other civil rights demonstrators they would join the next day. "We felt terrible about having to take a limousine," Venet recalled.

For accommodations, they stayed at the home of Venet's brother, Ted Venetoulis, who was then working on the staff of Texas congressman Jim Wright. Venetoulis admired entertainers such as Darin and Sammy Davis, Jr. who participated in the civil rights marches without seeking publicity for it.

Darin was wearing a toupee by this time in his life, a piece for the front of his head to disguise his receding hair line. Just before turning in for the evening at Venetoulis', he took off the toupee and hung it on a doorknob. During the night, it fell to the floor. Thinking it was a dead mouse, the maid who came early the next morning flushed it down the toilet.

Though Darin would later laugh heartily about the incident, when he awoke to find no toupee that morning, he was livid. The first order of business would be finding him a hat.

"He was always conscious of the hair, but in a good-natured way," said Venet. "He just didn't think the world was ready to see him without the front of his hair."

Naturally, with the city abuzz with tension and excitement, and the streets full of people, Darin was content to buy the first hat he could find. Unfortunately, it turned out to be a little straw hat, with a beer can on it, and the message "In case of accident, get me a beer." Thus, so properly attired, did Bobby Darin attend the March on Washington.

Darin made sure he personally practiced what he preached. "He wouldn't treat a porter secondarily, and then go march in a civil rights campaign," said Venet.

Once, while driving through a Chicago ghetto in a limousine, Darin spotted a group of kids playing stickball with broomsticks and balls of rolled-up tape. Against even the advice of the limousine driver, who was black, Darin decided to get out and play with the kids, eventually sending off the driver to a hardware store to purchase better equipment.

"There we were in an all-black neighborhood, and Darin played stickball with a bunch of kids for an hour-and-a-half," recalled Venet. "Those kids still have no idea that the guy they played with was Bobby Darin."

Darin was a big supporter and admirer of John F. Kennedy, and was devastated by Kennedy's assassination on November 22, 1963. "That was the beginning of a lot of changes in his feelings," recalled Venet.

Just days after the assassination, Darin began taping for a guest appearance on "The Judy Garland Show." The atmosphere on the set, and within the studio audience, was naturally somber, but Garland, Darin and Bob Newhart, the other guest, put on their best "the show must go on" faces. (The show would air December 29, 1963.)

Darin was every bit the assured show business professional, joining Garland for a long medley of songs with the loose theme of railroad travel, such as "Sentimental Journey," "Chattanooga Choo-Choo" and "The Atchison, Topeka and Santa Fe."

For his own solo segment, however, Darin came out without his suit and tie. In a darkly-lit setting, he sang two of the spiritual-style songs from his "folk" albums—"Michael Row

The Boat Ashore" and "I'm On My Way." It was an intense, superb performance, almost as if Darin was using this serious, religious music as a catharsis for his sorrow, for the nation's shock, in those troubled days.

Darin's commitment to issues such as civil rights would continue through his life. For instance, he joined the march from Selma to Montgomery, Alabama, to protest voting discrimination on March 24, 1965. While FBI records note plans for "singing and entertainment" by Darin, Dick Gregory, Harry Belafonte and Peter, Paul & Mary at the conclusion of the march, it is not believed that Darin actually performed.

Darin's actions in the social arena may seem unremarkable, viewed from the context of twenty-five years later, especially when it is now commonplace for pop stars to lend a hand to numerous causes. But while some folk singers had gained activist reputations in the early 1960s, few in the pop field, especially among the younger generation of stars, had yet to become active in such causes.

"You didn't have your younger entertainers at that time going on campaigns about civil rights," said Nik Venet. "The mainstream entertainment industry was hands-off that subject. Talking about it now seems mild, but at the time, Darin put his whole career, and the possibility of getting blacklisted, on the line."

CHAPTER 14
"Settle Down"
1963

1963 was another busy year musically for Bobby Darin. Four new albums were released (five, if the Atco from-the-vaults release of **It's You Or No One** is counted), and Darin scored back-to-back Top 10 hits for the first time in three years.

In addition to the two folk albums discussed earlier, two new Capitol LPs produced by Nik Venet were built around the hit singles. The first was **You're The Reason I'm Living**.

The Darin-penned title-track single, which reached #3 in March, was a return to the country-pop style which clicked on "Things." In a 1969 overview of Darin's career, *Los Angeles Times* pop music critic Robert Hilburn called "You're The Reason" "one of the best country-pop records ever made."

The song again found Darin emulating Ray Charles, whose **Modern Sounds In Country & Western Music** album was a huge hit a year earlier.

In fact, "You're The Reason" seems patterned after Charles' "I Can't Stop Loving You" in its piano-based, relaxed tempo and use of a female backing chorus to sing the title line. However, while Nik Venet admitted that "You're The Reason" was borrowed, he said it was not from Ray Charles.

"It's influenced by two songs," Venet explained. "Bobby and I were talking about how Sam Cooke built 'You Send Me' from 'Blue Moon' and how Sharon Sheeley wrote 'Poor Little Fool' from a Diamonds record slowed down. The joke was to work on 'Happy Birthday.'

"The other song that's used is 'Red Sails In The Sunset,'" Venet said. "If you sing the chorus 'You're the reason I'm living / I'd be lost without you,' it's really 'Red sails in the sunset /

Happy birthday to you.' That's an inside joke."

Full of songs which overwhelmingly came from country backgrounds, the corresponding **You're The Reason** LP is often considered Darin's "country" album. However, a listen to the arrangements, which often veer into big band territory, shows that Darin wasn't interested in making the run-of-the-mill country album.

"I always get pros and cons about whether Darin was chasing a trend," Nik Venet said. "He wasn't. He was always gathering contributions to music. He felt country music had contributions that could cross over to pop and jazz, and vice versa."

Thus, songs written by Harlan Howard, Don Gibson, Gene Autry, and Glen Campbell were turned into swing numbers with heavy brass, courtesy of Shorty Rogers' arrangements. Highlights were renditions of Hank Williams' "(I Heard That) Lonesome Whistle" and Buck Owens' "Under Your Spell Again."

"The horn players were all from Stan Kenton's band," Venet said of the **You're The Reason** sessions. "We were using dedicated jazz musicians, who played with Kenton and Miles Davis. We brought them on this session and they had the time of their lives. We worked charts there; they contributed a lot of the riffs.

"On every session with Darin, the musicians would all leave knowing they did something they felt good about," said Venet.

You're The Reason I'm Living also included Darin's first—and only—official recorded duet, with Mary Clayton on "Who Can I Count On." (After changing the spelling of her first name to "Merry," Clayton went on to enjoy some success in the seventies, and in 1987 her song "Yes" from the "Dirty Dancing" soundtrack became a hit.)

Darin's West Coast sessions featured some of the top-name studio musicians who later contributed to Spector's famous Wall of Sound. But according to Nik Venet, Darin wasn't terribly picky about personnel, with one exception. He insisted that the drummer always be Earl Palmer, whose inventive beat had propelled the early rock'n'roll hits of Little Richard and Fats Domino.

"Bobby would tell me, 'Nik, if you don't get Earl, don't bother building the band,'" Venet said. "Once, I called for Earl, and the contractor said he had him. We got to the studio and we had forty or fifty musicians, but there was another drummer.

"It's the only time I ever saw Darin mad enough to punch somebody in the mouth," said Venet, recalling that Darin confronted the contractor. "Darin got into it with him. He cocked his fist. We had to grab Darin and pull him away."

In the studio, Darin was also very involved in working out arrangements. In fact, Venet goes so far as to say that Darin was co-arranger on nearly all of his Capitol tracks. Capitol producer Tom Morgan concurred that Darin was always there to chip in his two cents.

"Even with Billy May," Morgan remembered. "Bobby was trying to give Billy May total control, but he still had some influence." Morgan also recalled an instance in which Darin worked out an arrangement with Jimmy Haskell.

"We were in Studio A at Capitol, running down some tune," Morgan said. "We got to the ending and Jimmy Haskell, a brilliant guy without a big ego, asked Bobby 'What kind of ending do you want?'"

Bobby said 'If you're in the key of C, go to an A flat chord first,'" Morgan recalled. "I was impressed with that. I thought, goddamn, Bobby Darin doesn't have time in his life to fully study music. So as an arranger, he was not a thorough musician, but he would know, for instance, all the white notes on the keyboard."

Meanwhile, Darin was on a hot streak as a songwriter. "18 Yellow Roses," his follow-up to "You're The Reason," also shot into the Top 10. Another country-style track (this time the influence was Marty Robbins), its too-corny lyric was saved by a surprise concluding twist.

The single was arranged by Jack Nitzsche, Spector's longtime arranger. The production's double-tracked lead vocal (in which Darin sang harmony with himself), was a relatively unusual feature on his records. Venet recalled that Capitol Records was initially displeased with the results.

"They told me they weren't going to put it out," he said. "They didn't think it was a hit song. They thought they were getting Sinatra; they had no idea who Darin was."

The album **18 Yellow Roses And 11 Other Hits** was the

first Darin LP to include cover versions of then-current Top 40 hits. Bobby Scott provided some interesting arrangements for Pomus & Shuman's "Can't Get Used To Losing You" (an Andy Williams hit) and a rockin'-with-horns take on Dion's "Ruby Baby." Most interesting was "Rhythm Of The Rain," in which Darin's relatively straightforward version was suddenly interrupted by Scott's jazz instrumental break.

The album's best track was Darin's reading of Skeeter Davis' "The End Of The World." Darin treated the classic weeper with the same restrained manner he used on **Earthy**'s folk tracks like "Strange Rain," and the performance was superb. Unfortunately, he coasted through the album's two genuine folk-based numbers, "Walk Right In" and "Reverend Mr. Black."

The sessions for the "18 Yellow Roses" single and album were grueling, recalled saxophonist Steve Douglas, who acted as contractor for the dates.

"I remember we did one of the longest sessions in the history of the union at the time," Douglas said. "We started a session at two in the afternoon. At 4:00 a.m., I'm on the phone calling musicians, because guys are falling out. I think that session went until ten in the morning, non-stop. A few of us got rich in one night."

Naturally, Capitol was not pleased with Darin's expensive approach to studio time. Douglas, who later produced some Darin sides, recalled Darin's attitude about the label's rules.

"Bobby didn't give a damn," said Douglas. "He kind of ran roughshod over everybody. He ruffled a lot of feathers over there. Of course, Bobby was only a mild taste of what was to come with the rock bands."

For two additional 1963 singles, Darin abandoned country for the Brill Building teen-pop style associated with the his old friend Don Kirshner's publishing empire. The Drifters-ish "Treat My Baby Good" (with a snatch of its melody lifted from "Spanish Harlem") and "Be Mad Little Girl" (which echoed "Go Away Little Girl") almost sounded like genre exercises for Darin. While both were decent, neither stood out enough to make the Top 40.

In the midst of all his recording activity, Darin was still knocking out audiences at spots like L.A.'s Cocoanut Grove, Harrah's Lake Tahoe, the Copa, and the Flamingo in Las

Vegas. But in October 1963, he dropped a bomb. Darin announced that he was retiring from nightclub performances.

"Somehow [Flamingo chief] Morris Lansburgh got the idea that I wasn't going to work here anymore," Darin announced from the stage during his October 24 Flamingo opening. "Oh yes, I remember how he got the idea: I wrote him a letter and told him."

Variety wrote: "It will be a great loss to Las Vegas, because his act has hit a peak; he has definitely joined the few powerhouse performers who appear on the Strip."

Darin said his exit from the nightclub scene would allow him time to "widen his scope" in the entertainment business. No one could argue that he wasn't busy. But aside from the fact that he would have more time to devote to recording, films and television, there were three chief reasons for Darin's decision to give up the stage.

One was that he hoped it would save his marriage. In March 1963, Darin and Dee officially separated. Though they reconciled a few weeks later, Darin felt that giving up live performing was a sacrifice he could make to strengthen the marriage.

There was also a scare regarding Darin's health. He spent two days in the hospital after he collapsed following an outdoor concert at Freedomland in the Bronx in July 1963. Harriet Wasser recalled the scene backstage.

"He almost died," she said. "We thought it was going to be all over. They got the oxygen for him. The feeling was that he could not continue working the way he was working. That he would have to start thinking about other things."

The third reason was that Darin had found yet another area of the music industry to branch into. He had his own business to run.

Chapter 15
"Green Green"
The Music Publisher

Though Bobby Darin had always pronounced his respect and admiration for performers such as Ray Charles, Frank Sinatra and Donald O'Connor, there was another side of the entertainment business he was intrigued by. It was the side exemplified in many ways by his old friend Don Kirshner—the role of business mogul.

In the years since his initial work with Darin, Kirshner had built a pop empire of his publishing business. The company's stable of writers included Gerry Goffin and Carole King, Barry Mann and Cynthia Weil, and Jeff Barry and Ellie Greenwich. Without singing, playing or writing a note, Kirshner became a major force in the music industry.

Having seen the financial rewards it generated for Kirshner and others, and confident in his own ability to write and choose hit songs, Darin entered the publishing business with a bang in early 1963. He shelled out a half million dollars to purchase Trinity Music from his former managers Joe Csida and Ed Burton. As the Trinity umbrella included Adaris Music and Towne Music, Darin now gained publishing control over his own compositions.

Darin dubbed his new operation T.M. Music. In addition to its publishing activities, the firm would also act as a record production outlet for Darin. He would oversee a roster of songwriters, and new recording artists signed to the company.

While T.M. never built a staff to rival Kirshner's empire, Darin did assemble some formidable talent. T.M. writers Kenny Young and Artie Resnick teamed up to write the Drifters' classic "Under The Boardwalk," and its hit follow-up "I've Got

Sand In My Shoes." Another writer, Rudy Clark, delivered "The Shoop Shoop Song (It's In His Kiss)," a 1964 smash for Betty Everett. Clark and Resnick collaborated on "Good Lovin'," which The Young Rascals took to #1 in 1966.

Darin initially set up shop in New York's Brill Building. One of his first hiring decisions was to bring in his old friend and associate from the Atco days, Bobby Scott.

"I don't know what the hell you'd call me," Scott said of his approximately eighteen-month stint at T.M. "I was kind of director of personnel in the measure that Bobby had hired some young writers and was paying them a stipend every week and they were turning out material. And it was my job to kind of oversee what they were doing."

Scott felt Darin's branch into publishing was a wise move, based on Darin's own track record in the music industry: "He didn't pick losers very often. He knew how to write a hit song and he knew what good craftsmanship was. He was an excellent producer of records."

One artist brought into the T.M. fold by Scott was Jesse Colin Young, who would later go on to success with the Youngbloods (the band which recorded the sixties classic "Get Together") Young's first album was produced by Scott under the T.M. aegis.

Scott enjoyed his T.M. experience, but he was a bit taken aback by Darin's style when he put on the hat of publishing mogul.

"I saw that he naturally treated administrative people, of which I was one, better than he treated the talent he had gathered together," Scott said. "He played the businessman well. I was surprised."

While Scott held great respect for Darin's songwriting ability, he felt that Darin expected other writers to share the same writing philosophy. As Ahmet Ertegun alluded to, Darin's method was "crank 'em out"—some will be great, some will be average, and some will be dogs—and you lived with that. Scott said Darin did not believe in the philosophy of a writer pouring himself into a pop composition at great length.

"The idea of 'great pains' totally escaped him," Scott said. "His understanding of the differing processes in differing talents was non-existent." Because of such philosophical differences, Scott eventually left T.M. on amicable terms.

Another past Darin associate, Jim McGuinn, also hitched up with T.M. McGuinn worked as a staff writer for the firm—at thirty-five dollars a week—for about a year. "The stuff I wrote wasn't commercially successful, but it was a good experience," he said.

McGuinn's most fondly-remembered T.M. composition was "Beach Ball," co-written with fellow staffer Frank Gari. After finishing the song, the duo played it for Darin, who liked it and immediately booked studio time. The demo for "Beach Ball" was recorded by a quartet consisting of Darin (on drums), McGuinn, Gari, and Kenny Young, with all four providing vocals.

After the session, Darin decided that the recording was too good to be a mere demo. He released it as a single under the name "The City Surfers," with the production credit "Produced by T.M. Music." Though not a hit, "Beach Ball" became a collectible among surf music fans and was so well-regarded that it was included in the compilation album **Summer Means Fun**, a volume of the "Pebbles" series of overlooked sixties gems.

"Somebody had fun making this one!," the album's liner notes say about "Beach Ball." "The track itself is a remarkable transmutation of Spector's 'Da Do Run Run' into the beach idiom." A cover version of "Beach Ball" became a major Australian hit in 1964.

Darin also opened up a T.M. office in the Capitol Tower in Los Angeles, and continued to show he had a keen eye for talented personnel. For a while, the office was headed by Steve Douglas, the ace session saxophonist who played on Darin's records, Phil Spector's productions, the records of The Beach Boys, and many others.

Another T.M. staff writer and producer in California was Terry Melcher. The son of Doris Day, Melcher had achieved some success as the youngest staff producer at Columbia Records. Along with his partner, future Beach Boy Bruce Johnston, Melcher had hits as lead singer of the Rip Chords ("Hey Little Cobra") and Bruce & Terry ("Summer Means Fun"). He would later go on to produce The Byrds and Paul Revere & The Raiders.

Darin with Wayne Newton.
(Las Vegas News Bureau)

Shortly after opening the West Coast office, Darin called Melcher and lured him away from Columbia.

"There was a little celebrity enclave in Toluca Lake," Melcher recalled. "Bobby and Sandra were living in a house Sinatra used to have, by the Lakeside Golf Club, near Bob Hope's house. I used to go over on Sundays. Bobby was very personable. He was funny and he had a lot of magic and a tremendous amount of energy."

Darin and Melcher collaborated on a few songs, including "Hot Rod U.S.A.," an authentic, superb Beach Boys/Jan & Dean-style rocker Melcher recorded with the Rip Chords. It was proof that Darin could appreciate, and excel in, another genre of music. Another collaboration, "My Mom," was a minor hit for the Osmond Brothers. Also for T.M., Melcher and Bruce Johnston composed "Beach Girl," a minor 1964 hit for Pat Boone.

* * * * * * * * *

T.M.'s greatest success came with Wayne Newton, whom Darin signed personally. Because many of Newton's records bore only the "Produced by T.M. Music" production credit, the extent of Darin's involvement in Newton's career was not widely known until years after Darin's death.

At the suggestion of Paul Anka and Dick Clark, Darin went to see an act called the Newton Brothers at the Copacabana in 1963. He was impressed by Wayne Newton, and signed the act to T.M. with the intent of spotlighting the young vocalist. The first couple of single releases were credited to "Wayne Newton with The Newton Brothers"; after that, Wayne Newton received solo credit.

Darin intended Newton to be a pop artist and many of Newton's initial releases produced under Darin's auspices bear little resemblance to the Vegas-style material Newton would become famous for.

For Newton's first single, Darin dipped not into his own T.M. bag, but into Don Kirshner's Screen Gems-Columbia Music for Barry Mann and Cynthia Weil's "Heart." With production supervised by Steve Douglas, the track had a solid, commercial sound, and reached #82 on the charts.

Newton's second single for T.M. would become his signature song—"Danke Schöen." The story of how "Danke Schöen" became a Wayne Newton record is legendary—and somewhat convoluted. But one fact all parties agree on is that the song was supposed to have been recorded by Bobby Darin.

Nik Venet first heard "Danke Schöen" while visiting Europe and searching for songs for a Ray Anthony album he was producing. It was a German instrumental hit, composed and performed by orchestra leader Bert Kaempfert (who had a huge American instrumental hit with "Wonderland By Night" in 1960). When Venet expressed interest in recording the song with Ray Anthony, the song's publisher, Hal Fine, informed him that an English lyric was being written, and that it would be ideal for a Bobby Darin vocal.

On the condition that Darin would agree to record the song, Fine offered Venet a United States exclusive—no other American artist or producer would even hear the song until Darin's record came out. After playing the demo for Darin, who agreed that the song was a smash, Venet, Capitol and Darin were granted the exclusive first crack at "Danke Schöen."

"In those days, when you got an exclusive on a song, that was a guarantee the song was being recorded," Venet said. "You never went back on your word."

According to Venet, Darin recorded "Danke Schöen" and then went into the studio with Newton. At that point, Newton recorded a vocal, using the instrumental track co-produced by and intended for Darin.

The session was then turned over to Steve Douglas to complete production. Production credit for "Danke Schöen," like "Heart," reads "Produced by T.M. Music. Production Supervised by Steve Douglas."

The finished product sounded like a "Mack The Knife" sequel, and was one of the most vibrant non-rock records since "Mack." Jimmy Haskell's arrangement swung, and Newton's savvy vocal sold the song brilliantly. The record eventually reached #13 pop and #3 on the Easy Listening charts.

When the record was released, everyone was pleased except "Danke Schöen"'s publisher, Hal Fine, who wanted the song done by the proven hit-maker Darin, not the young upstart Newton.

"The publisher just shit," Steve Douglas recalled. "He was really furious, and I guess rightfully so. Bobby was very generous in giving that tune to Wayne. Bobby wanted Wayne to have a hit record."

Afraid that this "sure-fire" hit would be overlooked because Newton was still unknown, Fine called his initial contact, Nik Venet on the carpet.

"I had to guarantee him," Venet recalled, "that if Newton's record didn't go to number one, Darin would do a 'Danke Schöen' single and album with five of Hal's songs on it. I had to guarantee him on my life. And while I was on the phone with Hal, Darin was in the other room, laughing his ass off, knowing that I was putting my life on the line with this publisher."

"Danke Schöen" didn't reach the top, although Fine was apparently pleased enough with the record's performance. Still, some who know the inside story questioned Darin's decision to give the song away.

"I think if Darin would have done it, it would have sold five times as many records as Wayne Newton," Capitol's Tom Morgan said. "It's really Bobby Darin's record, a 'Mack The Knife' feeling."

After "Danke Schöen," Darin continued to serve as a kind of "executive producer" of Newton's tracks, with most sessions being handled by Steve Douglas. While Newton's albums tended to veer toward middle-of-the-road standards, his singles retained a relatively contemporary pop sensibility.

Darin and T.M. staffer Rudy Clark co-wrote "Shirl Girl" as a follow-up to "Danke," but it reached only #58. A Darin-Artie Resnick collaboration for Newton, "Dream Baby," was a blatant re-write of "Dream Lover." Newton also recorded early compositions by Bruce Johnston ("Someone's Ahead Of You") and Barry Gibb ("They'll Never Know").

One of the strangest—and best—Newton records of that era was "Comin' On Too Strong," released in early 1965. Produced by Terry Melcher and Bruce Johnston, the track was styled after The Beach Boys' "Don't Worry Baby." Given instructions to produce a hit, Melcher and Johnston handled the bulk of the vocals themselves, with Newton only chiming in a few lines at the beginning of the verses.

"That was funny for Wayne, and I know it was a little

awkward," Melcher recalled. "But my instructions were pretty much to go in and make it sound like a real 'West Coast' recording. We didn't think Wayne could handle the falsetto part."

The record charted at #65. In his autobiography *Once Before I Go*, Newton wrote that he asked Darin to "pull the record" after a couple of weeks because he did not want a hit he could not reproduce on stage, *sans* Bruce and Terry. According to Newton, Darin concurred, and promotion on the record stopped.

Darin's eye for recording and songwriting talent, combined with publishing royalties from his own compositions such as "You're The Reason I'm Living" and "18 Yellow Roses," made T.M. a success. The firm's gross business climbed from $321,000 in 1963 (Darin's first year) to $450,000 by the end of 1964. At that point, Darin predicted that the company would pay for itself by the end of 1966. Thirteen T.M. copyrights charted in 1964, and T.M. Music was ranked eighteenth in the Top 100 BMI affiliates for the year.

CHAPTER 16

"The Good Life"

1964

The most acclaimed film role of Darin's career came in "Captain Newman, M.D.," which opened in Los Angeles on Christmas Day, 1963.

Darin received "co-starring" credit amidst an impressive cast including Gregory Peck, Tony Curtis, Eddie Albert, Angie Dickinson and Robert Duvall.

Something of a precursor to "M*A*S*H," the film is set in the psychiatric ward of an army hospital in 1944. Darin, Albert, and Duvall play patients under the care of Peck's Captain Newman. The script calls for all three actors to give over-the-edge performances in confronting their characters' problems.

Darin's gained the most attention. His character, Corporal Tompkins, carries around a load of guilt for deserting a friend in a burning aircraft. To get Tomkins to confront the problem, the doctor administers sodium pentothal.

The next ten minutes of the film are Darin's. In a long, tough, serious scene full of physical twisting, yelling and crying, Colonel Tomkins relives the experience of watching his comrade die in the crash.

Darin gave an intense, full-tilt performance which walked a fine line between remarkable dramatic characterization and scenery chewing. While the *New York Herald Tribune* wrote "Bobby Darin is a gem of miscasting...his contortions under sodium pentothal are at best embarrassing," *Variety* called his "high-powered histrionics...the film's most moving passage." Even the *New York Times* viewed the performance positively: "Believe it or not, Bobby Darin plays the kid touchingly."

Darin did the scene in one take, astounding director David Miller and the rest of the cast and crew. Nik Venet met Darin as he came off the set.

"I've made reservations for us to have lunch," Darin told Venet. "I knew that if I didn't get this scene done in one take that we couldn't have lunch, and I wanted to put myself up against the wall."

Venet never did find out if Darin was serious: "I still don't know if he was pulling my leg."

Despite an ultimately pointless plot which continually drifts from one story to another only to kill time, "Captain Newman, M.D." was a solid box office hit, the twenty-first biggest picture of 1964, according to *Variety*.

The film's success was helped by notice of Darin's performance. *Variety* remarked, "In addition to serving as a box-office stimulant via word-of-mouth, [it] may earn Darin a supporting nomination in the Oscar derby."

The prediction was accurate. The Academy Award nominations were announced on February 24, and Darin received a nomination for Best Supporting Actor for his "Captain Newman" role.

The ceremony was held on April 13 in the Santa Monica Civic Auditorium. Though the Best Supporting Actor Oscar went to Melvyn Douglas for his performance in "Hud," Darin called his brush with Oscar "the most exciting event of my life. The fact that I didn't win was totally unimportant."

Darin's performance also gained notice overseas. He received the Foreign Press' Golden Globe nomination, and the French Film Critics' Award for best foreign actor. Feeling that his acting abilities were more appreciated abroad, Darin considered moving to Paris. In a 1972 interview with the *Los Angeles Times*' Estelle Changas, Darin expressed regret about not making that move.

"I didn't have the courage to do what I knew was right," he said. "I felt the French would have allowed me to have a career as both an actor and a performer. I didn't respond perhaps because it meant I would have to pull up stakes and forsake comforts. I'm not a man of regrets, but reflecting on this doesn't make me happy."

Darin was involved in one other 1964 picture, though not as

an actor. He wrote the music for the teen film "The Lively Set," starring James Darren and Pamela Tiffin. Five Darin pop songs appear, including two numbers sung by Joanie Sommers and a Darin-Terry Melcher collaboration, "Boss Barracuda," sung by the Surfaris (of "Wipe Out" fame).

The most interesting writing credit was on "Look At Me," sung by future game show host Wink Martindale. The song was written by Darin and Randy Newman, in their only collaboration.

Darin also appeared in two television dramas in 1964—an episode of the series "Wagon Train" and an hour long "Bob Hope Chrysler Theatre" drama called "Murder In The First."

On the music end, 1964 was a low point for Darin. It was the first year he couldn't manage a Top 40 hit since 1957. Of course, 1964 was the year of the rock revolution ushered in by The Beatles and The British Invasion. Despite the fact that he was one of the American singers displaced by the Liverpudlians, Darin admired The Beatles.

"He loved them," recalled Nik Venet. "He had no negative reaction whatsoever. He just hoped there was enough time on the air for other people to be played. He felt The Beatles were a phenomenon like Presley.

"Bobby always thought Presley was a cosmic happening," Venet said. "He used to say 'There have been two cosmic happenings in this century—Presley and Kennedy.' When The Beatles came, he said 'I think I'm into my third cosmic happening.'"

Darin was also open to The Beatles' less-polished rivals, The Rolling Stones.

"He loved the way the Stones recorded," Venet said. "He liked that haphazard feeling. He liked Mick Jagger. He used to say 'If that guy ever hits Vegas, we're going to have to pack it up.' Of course, at that time, we thought everybody would eventually play Vegas. Bobby admired Mick Jagger for his recklessness with a song."

There was no chance that Darin's first single of 1964 could compete with the new sounds on the airwaves. Darin had recorded "I Wonder Who's Kissing Her Now," a song which dated back to 1909, at his first Capitol session in July 1962. Dusted off for single release in February, it charted at #93.

Its flip side was a leftover from the **Oh! Look At Me Now** session with Tom Morgan and Billy May. The snappy "As Long As I'm Singing" was perhaps Darin's greatest songwriting effort in the "standard" style and far superior to any performance included on the earlier album. For a while, Darin used the number as his show opener.

Darin tried the country style again on his next effort, "The Things In This House," but this time the country affectations seemed too forced. In fact, the song can be looked at as a bit of a parody, with lyrics such as "our dog won't eat." Still, it was a fine vocal, with solid production by Jim Economides.

The flip side, "Wait By The Water" was a rocking adaptation of the standard "Wade In The Water." With a big beat and electric guitar, it was Darin's most "contemporary" sounding single side since joining Capitol.

Ironically, Darin's highest chart success of '64 came when Atco dug out his 1960 French language recording of "Milord" (which had earlier been a hit for Edith Piaf). The record picked up a fair amount of airplay, hitting #45 on the pop charts, and #11 on *Billboard*'s Easy Listening chart. Atco slapped "Milord" and its flip "Golden Earrings" on a "new" album called **Winners**, which otherwise consisted of the Bobby Scott-arranged jazz material recorded in 1960.

Some material Darin recorded for Capitol remains in the can. An unreleased live album was recorded in Vegas in 1963. Also, Nik Venet reports that a studio album of standards, recorded with radically different arrangements than usual, remains unissued.

One track from those sessions was a Darin-Peggy Lee duet on the song "Angry," which came about accidentally. While Tom Morgan was producing Lee in one Capitol studio, Venet was recording Darin in another. The two producers met in the men's room and decided to get the two superstar vocalists together for a track. It remains in the Capitol vaults.

Chapter 17
"Don't Rain On My Parade"
1965-66

For Darin's first single of 1965, he joined the seemingly endless parade of singers who recorded "Hello, Dolly!" Re-doing a Louis Armstrong hit had worked for him once before, with "Mack The Knife." To make the connection even clearer, arranger Richard Wess was brought back to the fold.

"Hello, Dolly!" opened with the "Mack" bass line, and its arrangement basically recreated the "Mack" swinging style. Fingers snapped in the background, and Darin even gave it a "Look out, old Dolly is back!" closing, but the song had already been beaten into the ground too much to duplicate the original's success. It reached only #79 on the *Billboard* pop chart, but became a respectable Easy Listening hit at #18.

The **From Hello Dolly To Goodbye Charlie** album found Darin explicitly back in the big band sound for the first time since **Oh! Look At Me Now**. Highlights were Darin's snappy, superb renditions of Henry Mancini and Johnny Mercer's "Charade" and Anthony Newley and Leslie Bricusse's "Once In A Lifetime." The album also featured Darin's own version of the song he and Randy Newman co-wrote for "The Lively Set," "Look At Me."

Darin's next single was an imported European ballad, "Venice Blue." For the single and corresponding album, Darin teamed up with Steve Douglas, then working as a staff producer at Capitol.

"By no means did I produce Bobby's records," Douglas explained. "I was the guy in the booth. He made his own records. You just kind of stood out of his way."

Douglas recalled Darin's enthusiasm about "Venice Blue": "I got a call from Bobby and he said 'I found this fantastic song. We've got to get in the studio right away.' He was very enthused, very excited. A few days later, he played me the song, and I must say I wasn't too excited about 'Venice Blue.' I thought it was a fairly ordinary tune. I never did understand what he was excited about. He wanted the record rushed right out."

Despite a lush orchestral production and a fine Darin reading, "Venice Blue" could only "bubble under" to #133. Even Easy Listening stations stayed away from it.

Douglas' assessment of the song was much closer to the bone than Darin's. The song's semi-appealing melody was sabotaged by its English lyric, which contained gems such as "To pigeons in the square I say my last goodbyes / Goodbye, oh vanished dreams, goodbye old bridge of sighs."

Despite the fact that MOR songs were having extreme difficulty cracking the pop chart, Darin inexplicably thought "Venice Blue" would click.

"I have a vivid memory of Bobby reading *Billboard* magazine," Douglas recalled. "I'm looking at him and he's real somber. He says 'This is the first time a record of mine didn't get a Pick of the Week.' He was really quite upset by that. He genuinely believed that was going to be a hit record."

The **Venice Blue** album, like **Hello Dolly**, was strictly an MOR collection. Another Newley-Bricusse song, "Who Can I Turn To," stood out, as did Darin's version of the "West Side Story" song "Somewhere." The only stylistic variations came in two Darin compositions. "In A World Without You" (written with Rudy Clark) was perhaps Darin's best country-oriented song, with a fine lyric. It would have been perfect for Connie Francis. "You Just Don't Know," loosely in the style of "You're The Reason I'm Living," was the most interesting pop-oriented song on the LP.

"I think the rest of the album was just done to get an album out," Douglas said. "It went by pretty quickly. I said 'Gee, Bobby, how 'bout some more Bobby Darin songs?' I wish I could have worked with him on his stuff—the rock'n'roll stuff."

If Darin's recent efforts had seemed anachronistic in the pop world of 1965, his next single, released in June, would be surprisingly contemporary. "When I Get Home," co-written by Darin and Russell Alquist, opened with the loud bang of a drum, and progressed into a very contemporary folk-rock production. The record had "1965" written all over it and was Darin's best non-MOR single since "Multiplication." Though it stands as one of

Darin's most appealing pop-rock singles, it was completely overlooked.

However, Liverpool's Searchers took notice and scored a British hit with the song later in 1965. It was the second time in '65 that a Liverpool beat group hit with a Darin song. Earlier, Gerry & The Pacemakers cover of Darin's 1960 ballad "I'll Be There" became a Top 20 hit in both the States and Britain. Perhaps Darin wasn't so anachronistic after all.

Darin's final Capitol single, released in August 1965, was the title song he composed for "That Funny Feeling," the third and final Darin-Dee movie. Its flip side, "Gyp The Cat" was another "Mack The Knife" rip-off, this one written by Darin and Don Wolf.

"That Funny Feeling" opened in Britain in June and in the U.S. in August. Though it was inoffensive fluff, it—combined with an eighteen-plus month absence from the screen—halted the momentum Darin's acting career gained with "Captain Newman, M.D."

"Darin handles an undemanding role well," wrote *Variety*, while noting the "tortuous contrivance" of the film's screenplay. On the plus side, Darin had a chance to work with one of his idols, Donald O'Connor, who received third billing immediately after the Darin-Dee team.

During Darin's three-year time span at Capitol, his status declined from one of pop's most dependable hit-makers to an artist who couldn't seem to buy a hit. Though he scored two Top 10 hits at the label ("You're The Reason" and "18 Yellow Roses"), neither are considered "essential" Darin and no Capitol recordings have survived as oldies radio staples the way a half-dozen of his Atco hits have.

When his Capitol contract expired in the summer of 1965, Darin decided it was time to move on. He moved to familiar waters—back to Ahmet Ertegun and Atlantic Records. Though Darin had left Atco more than three years earlier, the label hadn't given up: they continued to release old Darin records well into 1965, the last of which was a five-year-old recording of "Minnie The Moocher."

Darin's first single for the label found him squarely back into the contemporary rock scene. With a Searchers-like guitar, a big-beat, and an angry protest lyric, "We Didn't Ask To Be Brought Here" is literally the most "electric" record Darin ever made.

Atlantic Records Proudly Presents
America's outstanding recording artist

BOBBY DARIN

with his first Atlantic smash...

WE DIDN'T ASK TO BE BROUGHT HERE

b/w Funny What Love Can Do
Atlantic #2305

Great song!
Great message!
Great performance!
Great Darin!

1841 BROADWAY, NEW YORK, N. Y. 10023 (212) PL7-6306

Though not an explicit anti-Vietnam protest, Darin's lyric exhibited the same kind of undefined anti-establishment disenchantment that characterized Sonny & Cher's "I Got You Babe." Like the earlier "When I Get Home," it should have been a hit, and perhaps only Darin's name held it back. The record "bubbled under" the charts at #117 in October.

Never appearing on an LP, "We Didn't Ask To Be Brought Here" remains perhaps the greatest overlooked gem of Darin's career. It was another example of how easily—and how successfully—Darin could relate to another genre of music, one which no one of his show-business stature had embraced before.

Its flip side, "Funny What Love Can Do" opened with Darin's wailing blues harmonica. Credited to Darin, the song lifts its melody from Jimmy Reed's "Baby What Do You Want Me To Do" and features a very heavy electric guitar. It was another sharp break from the expected Bobby Darin style, but the surprise element made it that much more effective.

The single's style aside, Darin was still not about to throw his hat into the rock ring, and since The Beatles' arrival, no artist had successfully straddled the Vegas and rock sides of the music scene. The camps weren't warring, they merely had no relation to each other.

After "We Didn't Ask To Be Brought Here" bombed, Darin at least temporarily chose the familiarity of the Vegas world. The timing was right, anyway. Darin had grown restless during his "retirement" from the stage, and decided to return to live performances. He would open 1966 in the familiar confines of the Flamingo Hotel in Las Vegas.

It had been two-and-a-half years since Darin had performed on stage. Recording, writing, acting and his T.M. business certainly kept him busy, though not satisfied. "I'm a singer of songs and anything I do other than that is an offshoot," Darin explained at the time.

Vegas welcomed Darin back with open arms. "Bobby Darin is back with an exciting act which is even better than the one he had here when he established the showroom's all-time attendance record," *Variety* wrote of his Flamingo return. "Darin is one of the few nitery performers who click with all age groups."

Groucho Marx attended Darin's opening night. Darin introduced him and briefly turned over the microphone to the legendary

Darin at The Flamingo, 1966.
(Las Vegas News Bureau)

comedian. "When I first saw you, you were only a singer," Marx said to him. "Now you're a singer and an actor."

Darin's act now included a 10-minute impression routine, in which he would impersonate James Cagney, Cary Grant, Marlon Brando, Walter Brennan, Dean Martin and Jerry Lewis, Clark Gable, Burt Lancaster, Jimmy Stewart, Robert Mitchum and W.C. Fields. The routine was set in a Hollywood barroom and framed by the song "One For My Baby." Richard Wess conducted a twenty-nine-piece orchestra.

That spring, Darin also set his sights on television, as he starred opposite Eve Arden in "Who's Watching The Fleshpot," a pilot for a projected comedy-drama series to be called "It's A Sweet Life." The pilot aired as an episode of the popular drama "Run For Your Life," with Darin playing a friend of Ben Gazzara's who operated a tour service at a fashionable resort on the French Riviera. "It's A Sweet Life" did not make NBC's fall schedule.

Darin returned to the Copacabana in April for the first time in almost three years. He performed The Beatles' "Yesterday" and accompanied himself on guitar for "I Got Plenty of Nothing" from "Porgy & Bess."

His first Atlantic album also hit stores that month. Called **Bobby Darin Sings The Shadow Of Your Smile**, the collection's first side featured all five songs nominated for the 1965 Academy Award song of the year. The album's title was not decided until the awards were announced—and "Smile" took the Oscar. Prior to that, however, an extended play 45 called "Bobby Darin's Academy Award Song Kit," featuring all five songs, was sent to radio stations around the country and received a fair amount of airplay.

Darin's lovely renditions of the title track (from "The Sandpipers"), and "I Will Wait For You" (from "The Umbrellas of Cherbourg") were top-notch. Side 2 of the album was a hodge-podge of standards highlighted by fine versions of "Lover Come Back To Me" and "It's Only A Paper Moon."

On May 14, 1966, Bobby Darin reached a milestone it was once thought he would never achieve—his thirtieth birthday.

Some press members whom Darin had rubbed the wrong way noted the occasion. In a vicious article titled "Egotist Bobby Darin At 30 Hits Low Note As Legend," *New York Post* writer Bob Ellison concluded "This Saturday is his birthday...It is not a national holiday."

(L. to r.): Eddie Fisher, Andy Williams, Bobby Darin
on the "Andy Williams Show."
(NBC publicity photo)

For his next album, Darin shifted his sights from motion picture scores to the Broadway stage. The result was one of his most appealing albums and singles of the decade.

Darin was back in his prime swinging mode for "Mame," the title song of the Jerry Herman musical which had yet to open. The track crackled with the show-stopper pizzazz that had been absent from Darin's non-rock singles since the days of "Lazy River." While the single was too adult-oriented to crack the pop Top 40 (it peaked at #53), it climbed all the way to #3 on *Billboard*'s Easy Listening chart, becoming Darin's biggest all-time hit in the "good music" format. (The chart did not exist at the time of "Mack The Knife.")

The corresponding **In A Broadway Bag** was classic Darin, arguably the best album of standard material he ever recorded. Darin's vocal performance was strong and stylistic on the uptempo songs, and tender and interpretive on the ballads.

Darin shone on yet another Newley-Bricusse composition, "Feeling Good" (from "The Roar Of The Greasepaint—The Smell Of The Crowd"), a rare show tune which incorporated some r&b overtones.

Two songs Sinatra got to first—"I Believe In You" and "Once Upon A Time"—also stood out, and Darin certainly gave Old Blue Eyes a run for his money with these two performances. The latter, an Andre Previn-Betty Comden ballad from "All American," features perhaps the most strikingly beautiful ballad performance of Darin's career.

Darin pulled out all stops for the "Funny Girl" tune "Don't Rain On My Parade." Shorty Rogers' arrangement swung furiously, and Darin took the opportunity to deliver one of his most dynamic vocals. The song suited Darin's swinging style so well that it appropriately became the opening number in his nightclub act shortly after the release of the album.

With a superb selection of songs, tasteful arrangements, and utterly brilliant singing, **In A Broadway Bag** was consummate Bobby Darin. Though some Darin fans favor his rock'n'roll, Top 40 or folk records more than his recordings of standards, this album is essential listening to grasp the essence of Darin's art. This is the style that many people remember Bobby Darin for, and he never did it better. Few have.

On August 1, 1966, Darin recorded thirteen tracks in Los Angeles including "Danke Schöen," "On A Clear Day," "What Now

My Love" and "Mountain Greenery." No tracks were ever released, and it is believed that these tracks (as well as three dozen additional unreleased Darin cuts spanning 1958-1967) were destroyed in a fire in Atlantic's warehouse.

August also saw the publicly-revealed ending of the Darin-Dee marriage. On August 12, Dee filed for divorce in Los Angeles Superior Court, charging extreme cruelty and mental suffering, and asking for custody of Dodd, five.

According to the UPI news report, Dee testified that Darin "woke up one morning and didn't want to be married anymore," then packed his belongings and left the family home.

A report surfaced that Dee's mother had moved into their home, much to Darin's displeasure, but when asked why the marriage ended, Darin only replied "I don't know. Sandra doesn't know. Nobody knows."

The divorce was finalized on March 7, 1967, with Darin paying a monthly support of $1,200 for Dodd.

CHAPTER 18

"If I Were A Carpenter"

The Folk-Rock Era

On August 15, 1966, three days after Sandra filed for divorce, Bobby Darin recorded two songs in Los Angeles. Both were written by Tim Hardin, a singer-songwriter attracting attention on the post-Dylan folk circuit. Hardin's debut album had gained critical notice, but few sales.

His songs were gentle, and poetic in a somewhat mysterious way. They did not adhere to the traditional pop song structure, yet they were in neither the protest nor stream-of-consciousness veins that marked the work of many of Dylan's disciples. As a lyricist, Hardin eschewed clever wordplay; his rhymes were often obvious, sometimes even awkward. Yet there was a beauty in the subtle way they conveyed a feeling rather than a message. You could always empathize with Hardin, even when you couldn't completely understand his songs.

The first Tim Hardin song Darin recorded was "If I Were A Carpenter." It would change the course of Darin's career.

Obviously, Hardin material was quite a departure for Darin, especially coming off his **Shadow Of Your Smile/In A Broadway Bag** recordings. A few years earlier, Darin and Nik Venet had gone to see Hardin perform at the Tin Angel in Greenwich Village. Venet recalls that Darin and Hardin hit it off well, but Darin apparently never seriously considered recording Hardin songs until he was approached by the men who owned the company that published them: Charles Koppelman and Don Rubin.

Koppelman and Rubin, appropriately enough, started in the business under Don Kirshner. They began as songwriters at Aldon Music in 1962, then learned the ropes of publishing and production. By 1966, they operated Koppelman-Rubin Associates, a record production company which handled the recordings of Tim Hardin, The Lovin' Spoonful, and the Turtles, among others. Faithful Virtue Music, their publishing arm, had a goldmine with the songs of Hardin and the Spoonful's John Sebastian.

The story of how Koppelman and Rubin pitched songs to Darin became a legend of sorts over the years. A 1966 article in the British music publication *Melody Maker* quoted Darin as saying that the pair unsuccessfully pitched John Sebastian's "Do You Believe In Magic," "Younger Girl" and "Daydream" to Darin before they got him to record "Carpenter."

Darin himself incorporated a comic take on the story into his seventies nightclub act, adding "Summer In The City" (another Spoonful smash) into the tale. Darin joked about how he turned down million sellers, and how the publishers' approach to him would change every time they returned with new material. They first addressed him as "Mr. Darin"; then, as they became cockier, they greeted him as "Bob," then "B.D."

While these stories made for good copy (and comedy), they exaggerate the truth. "Do You Believe In Magic," an energetic pop-rock masterpiece, was the Spoonful's first hit, and Koppelman and Rubin were not about to give it away while they were trying to break the band.

When asked about Darin's story that "Magic" was part of their original pitch to him, Don Rubin said, "That does stretch it a bit. 'Magic' was the Spoonful's first hit, and it was only after that success that we could pitch John Sebastian songs to other singers."

Rubin confirmed that "Daydream" was offered to—and turned down by—Darin: "He kind of looked at us crossed-eyed and shook his head and said 'That's not for me.'"

Though neither Koppelman nor Rubin remember for sure, it's likely that the "Younger Girl" part of the story is also true. If so, Darin's rejection of the song is much more understandable than his nay to "Daydream"—the former song's lyric would not have been credible coming from Darin, and it never became a Top 40 hit despite attempts by The Spoonful, The Critters and The Hondells.

Still, Koppelman & Rubin's increasingly successful track record was enough to convince Darin to accept their next song offer. "I'll record anything you tell me to record," he told them the next time they visited his office. When they played him "If I Were A Carpenter," he said "This is the song. I'm not letting this one get away."

In a *Melody Maker* article titled "Darin Bounces Back—Thanks To The 'Younger Guys,'" Darin gave credit to Koppelman and Rubin for pointing him in the new musical direction. (The article's title aside, K&R were hardly from a new generation; Don Rubin was only four years younger than Darin.)

"I was still hipped on big bands and strings and all that," Darin told the publication. "I'd gotten to think that was my bag."

"Bobby was kind of going through his own metamorphosis at the time," recalled Don Rubin. "He kind of changed his mind-set. He wanted to shed his cabaret image and get with the music of the sixties."

Darin insisted that K&R produce his record themselves, though they usually relied on producers Erik Jacobsen (The Spoonful, Hardin) and Joe Wissert (Turtles). Perhaps because he was trying a different direction, Darin agreed to be less involved in the production than usual. Still, despite the fact that he decided to leave the producing and arranging to others, Darin's musical instincts wound up as a significant factor in the success of "Carpenter."

While working on the song with the musicians, Koppelman & Rubin and arranger Don Peake were having problems coming up with the right bass arrangement.

"Darin walked over to the bass player," said Rubin, "and within a few minutes, Darin sang what he thought the bass line should be. It turned out to be the bass line we used, and the main lick in that record is the great bass line."

After the session, Koppelman, Rubin and Darin felt they had a special combination of top-notch song and inspired vocal performance. Rubin flew to New York to play the track for Atlantic's Ahmet Ertegun and Jerry Wexler. Both Koppelman and Rubin recall that the Atlantic brass was taken aback.

"Ahmet and Jerry were very set on Bobby's cabaret style, and very locked into that," said Rubin. "They couldn't see this change. They kind of rejected this weird notion that Bobby was now going to be a folk-rock singer."

Undaunted, Koppelman and Rubin decided to take their case to radio directly. Their promotion man took the tape to KHJ, then the top radio station in Los Angeles. KHJ played the tape, which put pressure on Atlantic to release the track as a single. Once that decision was reached, the label put its full promotional muscle behind the record.

Another Hardin song, "Misty Roses," was recorded the same day as "Carpenter," but was temporarily held from release. Atlantic issued "If I Were A Carpenter" backed with the Darin-composed "Rainin'," the lone track from **The Shadow Of Your Smile** which could pass for contemporary pop.

Despite the initial KHJ acceptance, "If I Were A Carpenter" was initially a tough sell to radio. It had been three years since Darin's last Top 40 hit and in the interim, the pop revolution ushered in by The Beatles virtually swept away all performers who had roots in the 1950s. The fact that the overwhelming majority of Darin's previous mid-sixties singles were aimed at the "adult" market didn't help either.

Ironically, those same "good music" stations which had spun Darin's "Hello, Dolly!" and "Mame" emphatically rejected "If I Were A Carpenter." Though the song now seems a perfect example of a record which could be appreciated by both the Sinatra and Donovan crowds, it was then considered too left-field, and the release never dented *Billboard*'s "Easy Listening" chart.

But more importantly, Top 40 radio soon came around, and "Carpenter" entered the charts on October 8, 1966. It eventually climbed all the way to #8. (The song also clicked in Britain, reaching #9.)

Considering the obstacles, the success of "If I Were A Carpenter" stands as one of the greatest triumphs of Darin's career as a recording artist, testament to both a great song and a brilliant interpretation. Though it has since been recorded by literally scores of other artists, from the Four Tops to Johnny Cash and June Carter to Bob Seger, Darin's version still stands as the first, and the definitive, cover.

Darin himself had such regard for the song that it remained in his repertoire for the rest of his life. That is no small indication of how important this particular song was to Darin. "Splish Splash" drifted in and out of Darin's concerts over the years. Darin even became briefly disenchanted with "Mack The Knife" and dropped it from his set for a short period. But "If I Were A Carpenter" was performed at every full-length concert Darin gave from late 1966 until his death.

"If I Were A Carpenter" earned Darin a Grammy nomination in the "Best Contemporary [Rock and Roll] Solo Vocal Performance" category, but the award was won by Paul McCartney for "Eleanor Rigby."

The success of "If I Were A Carpenter" again prompted some criticism of Darin for "bandwagon jumping" in order to resuscitate his career. But, as Charles Koppelman pointed out, "There really wasn't a bandwagon. It wasn't as if Tim Hardin were a household name."

Folk-rock was certainly "in," but its most popular forms were the electrified guitar jangle of The Byrds or the psychedelia-enhanced style of Donovan. The Spoonful had delved into some softer material, but they were still better known for their "good time" pop sound.

While "Carpenter" now seems to go hand in hand stylistically with other '66 hits such as "Monday Monday" or "Elusive Butterfly," at the time of its release, it was certainly far from a sure-fire hit. While the fact that Darin had nothing to lose made it an easy gamble, it nevertheless was a gamble, and not a bandwagon-hop. When so many performers of Darin's generation were criticized, often justifiably, for not keeping up with the times, it seems ironic that Darin was criticized for the very opposite—the sin of keeping up with the times, and succeeding at it.

With the single riding high, an entire album in the loosely-defined "new folk" style was planned. Darin had no intention of framing "Carpenter" in an MOR album, and not just because of commercial considerations.

"He was very committed to the new style," said Don Rubin, "and not from the standpoint of 'this is a new gimmick I'm going to cash in on.' He felt it. He started wearing jeans and boots. I think he went through a change in his whole being, that made him want to feel part of that time period, and the music that was becoming symbolic of that time."

Twelve more songs were recorded on October 31 and November 1. Not surprisingly, considering Koppelman and Rubin's involvement, that music included a fair number of Tim Hardin and John Sebastian copyrights. But business aside, it's hard to argue that the choices weren't correct, given Darin's superb readings.

Much as he had done on **Earthy** back in 1962, Darin took the "show" out of his voice and sang in a soft, subdued, even pained voice which suited the material perfectly. In addition to "Carpenter," "Misty Roses" was included on the album, along with three more Tim Hardin songs—"Reason To Believe," "Red Balloon," and "Don't Make Promises."

With the exception of a few very hip music critics, Darin was the first person to call attention to Hardin's considerable songwriting talent, showcasing it to both the industry and the general public. His interpretations showed that he had an artistic understanding of Hardin's songs.

"He related to the lyrics," said Charles Koppelman. "Bobby was a very honest, compassionate person, and I think those lyrics and that genre of music struck a chord."

Don Rubin concurred: "Timmy's very poetic sort of way of expressing himself just got to Bobby. The lyrical approach that Tim took was kind of the opposite of the show material Bobby had done previously. He adapted to Timmy's material incredibly."

Darin's renditions of these songs never veered far from Hardin's own recorded versions (which were produced by Erik Jacobsen). Don Rubin acknowledged that Hardin's originals were used as a blueprint for Darin's covers.

"Bobby heard these songs originally via Timmy's versions," he said. "It was common of the way records were made then. You had very talented songwriters who made great demos. When you recorded one of their songs, it was almost impossible to get away from their interpretation. It's part of what sold you on the song in the first place."

For example, Darin's "If I Were A Carpenter" was sweetened only slightly by K&R. In addition to the Darin-arranged enhancement of the bass part, Darin's hit features strings and a pretty, string-led instrumental break not featured in Hardin's version. Likewise, the difference in the versions of "Misty

Roses" is only a string arrangement, which is absent from Hardin's record, but comes in during the second verse of Darin's.

While Hardin's "Red Balloon" was accompanied only by acoustic guitar, Darin's features a bass and drums from the start, and strings shortly thereafter. Conversely, Hardin's "Don't Make Promises" is a full upbeat electric production from the start, while Darin's opens acoustically, then gradually incorporates a bigger beat.

Though not exactly carbon copies, the similarities of the versions, combined with the fact that Darin was a Vegas star who appeared to be appropriating the style of this hip Village folkie, led some to level the charge that Darin "ripped off" Tim Hardin. Darin himself would joke that he heard of people telling Hardin "Bobby Darin stole your song."

Nik Venet, who knew both men and had accompanied Darin to the Tin Angel to see Hardin years earlier, said such comments came from members of a self-appointed "in crowd" who couldn't accept that Darin beat them to the punch.

"I think that so few people knew of Tim Hardin," Venet said, "that in order to prove you knew Hardin, you had to say that Darin ripped him off. That way, you'd show you knew who Tim Hardin was before Darin did his songs."

Unfortunately, the Hardin tracks were passed over when it came to choosing a follow-up to "Carpenter." "Reason To Believe," perhaps Hardin's greatest song, would have been the best choice, but instead Jeffry Stevens' "The Girl That Stood Beside Me" was selected as the second single. The track was the album's most ambitious production job with a backward-tape kind of effect similar to the sound heard in The Beatles' "Rain." It was an odd choice, and the record reached only #66.

Darin got back in the Top 40 with a third single, John Sebastian's "Lovin' You," which climbed to #32. (It would be Darin's last Top 40 hit.) Darin treated Sebastian's songs a little less reverentially than he treated Hardin's, and he put a little more show-business into his reading of "Lovin' You." Ironically, considering the cold shoulder adult radio stations gave to "Carpenter," "Lovin' You" became an Easy Listening hit, reaching #18.

The album also included Darin's cover of the song he turned down earlier that year, the Spoonful's "Daydream." Another

BOBBY DARIN's

great new album...

IF I WERE A CARPENTER

is on Atlantic Records

Produced by
KOPPELMAN & RUBIN

Bramanti

Sebastian song, "Younger Girl," was recorded for the LP, as was a cover of The Beatles' "Good Day Sunshine"; neither was released.

The album also featured John Denver's early "For Baby," Buffy St. Marie's "Until It's Time For You To Go," and Darin's own "Amy," a ballad (from his forthcoming film "Gunfight In Abilene"), which though not folk, was "sensitive" enough to fit in with the rest of the album.

Start to finish, **If I Were A Carpenter** is perhaps the most consistently enjoyable album Darin ever recorded. The arrangements and song choices are entirely tasteful, and Darin's performance was more than merely credible, it was inspired.

Atlantic was pleased; the album finally hit the chart in early 1967, a feat which eluded both **Broadway Bag** and **Shadow Of Your Smile**. The LP reached #142 and was Darin's last album to dent the *Billboard* LP chart.

As all parties appeared satisfied with **Carpenter**, a follow-up album was recorded in March 1967 and released that spring as **Inside Out**. Hoping to repeat the hit magic, Tim Hardin's "Lady Came From Baltimore" was released as the first single. It is one of Hardin's most fascinating and moving compositions, an entire short story told within two-and-a-half minutes. But from a commercial standpoint, it lacked even the mysterious pop appeal of "Carpenter," and the single stiffed at #62.

Darin gave a terrific reading of John Sebastian's most beautiful love song, "Darling Be Home Soon," but given that the Spoonful took it into the Top 20 only a few months earlier, it was doomed as the second single, making only a token chart appearance at #92. The only logical reason for its choice as a single may have been hope that it would reach the "Easy Listening" audience the Spoonful hit had eluded, but it wasn't to be.

The album was fine, but it lacked the spark of the **Carpenter** collection. There were far fewer up- or mid-tempo selections, and you could almost hear the concept grow increasingly tired as the album progressed. It was almost as if Darin had taken the laid back approach a step too far.

While little on the album could be called exciting, there was plenty that was interesting. The two Hardin songs, "Baltimore" and "Black Sheep Boy" were almost note-for-note copies of Hardin's originals. Darin also tackled three songs by a new pair of writers in the Koppelman-Rubin stable, Gary Bonner and Alan Gordon. Earlier in '67, the pair struck paydirt with the Turtles' "Happy Together." Of their contributions to **Inside Out**, the most interesting was "About You," which both the Turtles and Spoonful would later record as "Me About You" with completely different arrangements.

Darin was one of the first of many singers to cover "I Think It's Gonna Rain Today," by his old "Look At Me" collaborator Randy Newman. And, in perhaps the most daring cover choice of his career, Darin closed the album with a rendition of The Rolling Stones' "Back Street Girl." Considering that both albums passed over the by-then obligatory Beatles and Dylan covers, the choice of a Jagger-Richards number is indicative of how Darin was open to new material which ran counter to expectations. Darin pulled off the pretty-but-not-tender Stones ballad quite effectively.

Inside Out also included Darin's most autobiographical composition to date, "I Am," a well-written navel-gazing rumination which pre-dated Neil Diamond's "I Am I Said" by four years.

As neither the album nor its singles succeeded commercially, the direction would not be pursued any further. The next, and final, Darin-Koppelman-Rubin collaboration would be a single of Bonner and Gordon's "She Knows," recorded in July 1967. The production was patterned after "Happy Together" and, though a fine pop effort, the song lacked the glorious hook which made the Turtles' record a classic. "She Knows" got a smattering of airplay and sales, but only "bubbled under" the charts at #106.

"I remember 'She Knows' as being a turn to the right at the time," said Don Rubin. "It could have been the beginnings of the next album, but I don't think anyone involved, either ourselves or Bobby, was that pleased with the outcome."

With that, Darin's second "folk phase" came to an end. "It only lasted for two albums, as far as encapsulating that particular mood and that style of music," said Rubin. "But it was great. He was a joy to work with. Every time he walked into the studio, he was prepared and right on, and gave you a great performance."

Like Darin's 1962-63 folk phase, the "If I Were A Carpenter" era was a surprise to many. By the time Darin would get to the third phase, he would not just surprise, but shock.

Darin at The Flamingo, 1967.
(Las Vegas News Bureau)

CHAPTER 19

"At The Crossroads"

1967-1968 (Pre-RFK)

Despite his new musical direction on record, Bobby Darin retained his swinging, Vegas image on stage and on television throughout 1967. While "If I Were A Carpenter" and "Lovin' You" were added to his club act, the show was still stacked with big band-accompanied standards such as "Don't Rain On My Parade," "Charade" and "The Shadow Of Your Smile."

The Cole Porter standard "I've Got You Under My Skin" was livened up with a Motown-ish arrangement, and Darin returned "18 Yellow Roses" (for which he played guitar) and Ray Charles' "What'd I Say" (for which he played piano) into the set list.

Calling Darin "one of the youngest senior statesmen in the entertainment business," *Billboard*'s Aaron Sternfield lauded Darin's March 1967 stand at the Copa: "As a singer, mimic and purveyor of light banter, Darin goes to the head of the class. He's all showman."

While Darin's admiration of Tim Hardin proved that he appreciated contemporary songwriting, he made it known that he was not abandoning the standards of the pre-rock decades. To emphasize the point, Darin joined The Supremes, The Mamas & The Papas, Petula Clark and Count Basie in an amazing television musical special called "Rodgers & Hart Today," which aired on March 2, 1967.

Under the musical direction of Quincy Jones, the show opened with Darin performing "The Lady Is A Tramp." Over the course of the hour, there was some terrific musical teamwork. Darin and Pet Clark sang a long medley of R&H classics. Darin and Diana Ross and The Supremes, backed by the

Darin's final starring role, 1967's "Gunfight in Abilene."
(Universal Pictures publicity photo)

Count Basie Band, performed "Falling In Love With Love." Later, the Basie band swung behind Darin on "I Wish I Were In Love Again."

In May, "Gunfight In Abilene," the last film in which Darin would have a starring role, opened. It was a Western, with Darin playing an ex-Confederate officer who was appointed sheriff. Not surprisingly, it bombed, both critically and commercially.

Even before the film opened, Darin suggested that he was unhappy with the way his once-promising movie career was progressing. He told *Variety* that of all his films, he was only proud of "Captain Newman" and "Pressure Point" and vowed, after "Abilene," to take on roles with "extreme caution."

His next film, "Stranger In The House," opened in Great Britain in July 1967. In his smallest role since "Hell Is For Heroes," Darin received third billing after James Mason and Geraldine Chaplin. The film was not released in the U.S. until January 1968, under the name "Cop-Out."

Darin continued to write music during this time, copyrighting eight songs on April 14, 1967. Although the fate of titles such as "Face To Face," "Ballet Dance" and "The Greatest Lover In The World" is not known, it is possible that some of them are instrumental pieces used in the score of "Gunfight."

That Fourth of July, Darin performed at the Melodyland Ampitheatre in Anaheim, with the British duo Chad & Jeremy as opening act. "Born Free" and "I've Got The World On A String" were added to the Darin repertoire.

Darin was soon back in the studio for a project which still puzzles those who were enamored with his "Carpenter" direction. Released in August 1967, **Bobby Darin Sings Dr. Dolittle** found Darin singing ten Leslie Bricusse songs from the movie musical.

Though a few of the score's softer, contemporary ballads such as "After Today" wouldn't have sounded out of place on the earlier albums, for the most part, the entire first side of the album featured slow melodies which tended to run together. Side 2, which featured uptempo melodies and more inspired lyrics, was better.

Songs like "Beautiful Things" and "Talk To The Animals" provided Darin with material he could sink his teeth into,

BOBBY DARIN
Sings the sound-track songs from the
20th Century-Fox Motion Picture . . .

DOCTOR
DOLITTLE

ATLANTIC 8154/SD8154

albeit in the old style. As ridiculous as it seemed as a follow-up to Tim Hardin and John Sebastian songs, "Talk To The Animals" is classic Bobby Darin, a show-stopper which he played to the hilt.

Contrary to what might be believed, the album was indeed Darin's idea, and not encouraged by Atlantic Records. Ahmet Ertegun still refers to the collection as "those animal songs," and says that he tried to talk Darin out of the commercially unsuccessful project. Even Easy Listening stations declined to play "Talk To The Animals."

"It wasn't a very good idea," Ertegun said of the entire **Dolittle** album. "Bobby would get an idea, and it was hard to get him off it."

Darin did return to the studio later that year to record six more tracks, including Jerry Reed's "Tupelo Mississippi Flash" and a song called "Natural Soul Loving Big City Countryfied Man." None of the tracks was ever released.

Darin became hot news that August, but not because of his record, film or stage efforts. He was linked in press reports to Diane Hartford, the twenty-five-year-old wife of A&P heir Huntington Hartford. The millionaire accused Darin of "monopolizing" his wife.

Darin, who claimed the relationship was platonic, quipped "I don't play monopoly. Hartford does. He has enough money for that."

The press, notably the *New York Post* and *New York Daily News*, treated the situation as a juicy scandal, trailing Darin and reporting on his every move in and out of New York for weeks.

On one of those trips, Darin went to Monaco at the invitation of Princess Grace to headline at her annual Red Cross gala. "She was an excellent dancer, in addition to being a charming princess," Darin graciously said of the monarch.

That October, Darin returned to network TV to host the "Kraft Music Hall" special "Give My Regards To Broadway" on NBC. Set in 1917, the show was a tribute to vaudeville, with Darin portraying the legendary George M. Cohan.

Never having seen Cohan work, Darin went to George Burns for advice on his portrayal. "Cohan worked like you work," Burns told Darin. "He was sure of himself, creative,

Bobby Van (left) joins Darin on "The Kraft Music Hall" production, "A Grand Night For Swinging."
(NBC publicity photo)

wrote all his own material. He was a down front performer."

Rather than imitating Cohan, Darin tried to capture the spirit of his songs such as "Yankee Doodle Dandy." The performance didn't satisfy everyone. "A competent performer in his own right, Darin lacked any authenticity or warmth in aping the famed songwriter and vaudevillian," said *Variety*.

Darin opened 1968 by hosting yet another "Kraft Music Hall" program, "A Grand Night For Swinging," performing "Mack The Knife" and "Talk To The Animals." He also performed a vaudeville routine with Bobby Van and sang a new original composition, "Long Time Movin'," as a duet with Bobbie Gentry. It was one of four new songs Darin copyrighted that January, none of which he ever recorded.

On stage, Darin used "Talk To The Animals" as a springboard for his impressions routine, which now included Rex Harrison, James Cagney, Cary Grant, Clark Gable, Jimmy Stewart, Tony Bennett, Robert Mitchum, Dean Martin, W.C. Fields and Al Jolson. In a concert review, *Variety* noted that "Mack The Knife" was "unfortunately parodied and tossed around like a bit of fluff," but called Darin "a completely authoritative saloon star."

But, speaking to columnist Earl Wilson that March, Darin hinted at a restlessness with his supper-club star success. "To be called the greatest entertainer may mean being paid more than anybody, or having four limousines," he said. "These are not essential to me anymore. Being accepted as an entertainer and human being are."

Darin was looking for—and finding—a new outlet for his energy: politics. Early in 1968, he joined Jimmy Durante in Indiana to entertain at a Democratic rally for U.S. Senator Birch E. Bayh. By May, he would place his support behind the man he believed would be the next president of the United States—Robert F. Kennedy.

Chapter 20
"A Reason To Believe"
RFK

"He was someone I could believe in," Bobby Darin said about Robert F. Kennedy.

Armed with the belief that RFK could help heal a racially-divided and war-torn America, Darin threw his support behind Kennedy's presidential bid and joined the campaign in the spring of 1968. "I stepped out for a man I thought could help re-direct the system," Darin explained.

Darin was a believer, not a show-biz friend of Kennedy. He had only met RFK a few times, and their most lengthy meeting was during the campaign, on a plane along with fifty other people. "In that short time, everything I felt about the man was confirmed," Darin would say.

Darin was part of the official traveling campaign for only a brief time, probably about ten days. He kept a low profile, so low that Frank Mankiewicz, Kennedy's press manager, would say twenty years later that Darin had "no role of any significance in the campaign."

Although aware that Darin was on the campaign "briefly," singer-songwriter John Stewart, who had just left The Kingston Trio to act as "resident campaign singer" at RFK rallies, also never crossed paths with Darin. Still, Stewart (who as a Trio member recorded for Capitol the same time Darin did) said that at the time, he was not surprised to learn that Darin was helping their cause.

"He went through so many surprises that he ceased surprising me," Stewart said of Darin. "I wasn't surprised; it seemed very Darin-like."

Nik Venet believes that Darin contributed to RFK's campaign in a behind-the-scenes capacity. "Darin was talking to very big businessmen about big bucks for the campaign," Venet said. "He was hitting a lot of TV producers, movie producers. He was raising money personally, meeting people one on one."

When publicly visible on the campaign, Darin would warm up crowds with a few words and a song before Kennedy would speak. "RFK was a great fan of his," recalled Fred Dutton, who was in charge of the campaign's "road show."

Accompanying himself on guitar, Darin would sing the campaign's theme song, Woody Guthrie's "This Land Is Your Land" (reworked as "This Man Is Your Man"), and then exchange a small amount of banter with RFK before leaving the microphone to the candidate.

Music was an integral part of the Kennedy campaign, for tension relief if nothing else. On one occasion, Darin had the opportunity to sit down next to RFK on a plane and sing for him.

"There was a party atmosphere on the plane," recalled John Stewart. "Kennedy loved to hear people sing. Requests would come from RFK, the press, or campaign workers. Having someone with Darin's talent on the plane, it was inevitable that someone would request him to pull out his guitar."

During that performance, Darin was at least partially responsible for opening RFK's eyes to the musical poetry of Bob Dylan. Young journalist Jack Newfield, who superbly chronicled the RFK campaign in the 1969 book *Robert Kennedy: A Memoir*, had tried, but failed to turn Kennedy on to Dylan earlier.

"I had this running attempt with Kennedy to try to get him to appreciate Dylan, because he hated his voice," said Newfield, who was a Darin fan and fellow alumnus of Hunter College. "Darin was the perfect transition."

The following day on the plane, Kennedy made a point of stopping Newfield and telling him that after hearing Darin sing "Blowin' In The Wind," he was impressed with Dylan's lyrics.

"Now [Kennedy] had heard a more traditional singer sing Dylan's words," wrote Newfield, "and it had registered on Kennedy's contemporary sensibility."

On May 30, Darin began a week's run as the first performer at a new San Francisco nightclub called Mr. D's. While there, he learned of the events of June 4, 1968. After winning the California primary election, Kennedy was shot at the Ambassador Hotel in Los Angeles, and died a day later.

Darin attended the RFK memorial service in New York, and the funeral at Arlington National Cemetery on June 9. Stunned, he stood at the gravesite for almost seven hours. Still there when the guards lowered the coffin and filled the grave, Darin was the last person to leave.

"With him in the ground, part of me went, too," Darin said. Later, he would explain that he had a "spiritual revelation" that night.

He told columnist Earl Wilson: "It was as though all my hostilities, anxieties and conflicts were in one ball that had been flying away into space, farther and farther from me all the time, leaving me finally content with myself."

Watching a television report about Kennedy's funeral, John Stewart noticed that the cameras caught Darin leaning on a fence in a crowd shot.

"I thought it was a very poignant picture of how committed Darin was," said Stewart. "He didn't ask for VIP treatment; he went down with the crowd. He was up against the fence with the populous, looking at the funeral."

Though Darin said the gravesite vigil left him with a "peace and calm I've never had before," the pain stayed with him for years. As late as 1972, he was still talking about Kennedy's death in interviews.

"In some way, I felt I contributed to his death," he told Estelle Changas of the *Los Angeles Times*. "I was one of those who said 'I'm going to work for him,' and through this encouragement to his candidacy, helped make him publicly vulnerable to tragedy."

"Most people took four days to get over his death," he told *TV Guide* later that year. "It took me almost four years." Indeed, Geoff Edwards, who worked with Darin in 1972-73, recalled that Darin was distraught about RFK even then. "It was on Darin's mind until he died," Edwards said.

The new look: Bob Darin, 1969.

CHAPTER 21

"I Guess I'll Have To Change My Plan"

Post-RFK

June 1968: In the previous two months, both Martin Luther King, Jr. and Robert F. Kennedy had been assassinated. And the United States was still knee-deep in Vietnam.

Suddenly, Bobby Darin felt that merely entertaining people in hotel showrooms and supper clubs had lost its relevance. Making an audience smile with a song, a dance or a joke was not enough for him anymore. He had to say something about the world, try in some small way to make things better. He set about to do it the only way he knew how—through his music.

Many previous reports and articles about Darin have suggested that he stopped performing and dropped out of sight after RFK's death. In truth, he was back at the Frontier in Las Vegas about a month after the assassination, and initially, little changed in his show. One number that he hadn't performed in a while was back in his set list: Alone on stage, sitting on a stool with guitar in hand, Darin sang the spiritual "I'm On My Way," the same song he performed on "The Judy Garland Show" days after President Kennedy's death.

By early October, Darin added Otis Redding's classics "Try A Little Tenderness" and "Dock Of The Bay" to his live repertoire, plus Bob Dylan's "I'll Be Your Baby Tonight." But Darin saved the biggest surprise for his October 30 opening at L.A.'s Cocoanut Grove in the Ambassador Hotel—the hotel where Bobby Kennedy had been gunned down.

The show opened traditionally. Backed with a twenty-one-piece orchestra, Darin started with the bluesy "Let The Good Times Roll," "Mack The Knife," "Try A Little Tenderness" and "Talk To The Animals," still replete with his celebrity impersonation routine.

Then the orchestra left the stage, as did Darin, who changed out of his tuxedo and into a blue denim jacket. Upon his return, backed by only his four-piece combo, Darin debuted a new original song called "Long Line Rider." It was a hard-hitting rock number whose lyrics referred to an incident at an Arkansas prison where a number of skeletons were uncovered in the ground, and the subsequent cover-up by officials.

"All the records show so clear / Not a single man was here / Anyway, Anyway / That's the tale the warden tells / As he counts his empty shells / By the day," Darin sang. It was hardly "Mack The Knife" and the audience was a bit taken aback.

Darin continued, accompanying himself on guitar for "If I Were A Carpenter" and "I'll Be Your Baby Tonight." Darin then pulled out his harmonica and the band tore into some electric blues for "Got My Mojo Working." Finally, he sat down at the piano for a long, wild rendition of "What'd I Say," during which Darin also threw in bits of the Aretha Franklin/Otis Redding r&b classic "Respect." Darin's new act went over quite well with the entertainment critics in attendance.

"If the mitts were not exactly torrid, it is because the new Darin comes as something of a surprise," said *Variety*. "There is now a far more appealing, grown-up image. He definitely is headed in the proper direction."

"Bobby Darin is developing into a social commentator in his nightclub act," proclaimed *Billboard*'s Elliot Tiegel, while the *Los Angeles Times*' Leonard Feather wrote "Leaning on his own special and highly-charged R&B rhythm section, he is first and foremost a rhythm singer of exceptional power and conviction."

The changes in Darin were not confined to the stage. In fact, his change in direction in the recording studio would be even more radical. In late July, Darin announced the formation of his own label, Direction Records.

The label would release Darin's own recordings, which would now, he announced at a press conference, reflect his thoughts and concerns about a troubled society. In addition to his own music, Darin intended to cultivate a roster of "statement makers," other artists he believed in.

In late September, Darin released his first Direction album, **Bobby Darin Born Walden Robert Cassotto**. Not only was it unlike anything Darin had done previously, it was unlike any record ever made by a major mainstream entertainment figure.

The Bobby Darin who wrote and performed these songs essentially had no ties to the Bobby Darin who had been a pop star for ten years. It was as if Darin had wiped the slate completely clean—starting with the "Bobby Darin" persona, as the album's title and cover art made clear.

The cover featured a blurred photo of a tuxedoed Darin to the left, with a grainy boyhood photo of young Walden Robert Cassotto superimposed to the right. As the *Los Angeles Times*' Estelle Changas noted, "The feeling is of the artist searching for his origins, attempting to return to the most essential part of himself, an identity obscured and distorted by the slick superficiality of his celebrity image."

For the first time on a Darin LP, lyrics were printed on the album's gatefold. Stream of consciousness poetry graced the album's back cover, and the credit read "This album was Written, Arranged, Produced, Designed and Photographed by BOBBY DARIN." But the most shocking thing about the package was the music inside, a surprise to both those who adored Darin and those who dismissed him as irrelevant in the post-**Sgt. Pepper** pop world.

The album showcased the songwriter rather than the singer; the songs demanded little vocal effort and Darin's trademark vocal personality never encroached on them. Instrumentally, the arrangements were sparse, with simple guitar, bass and drums dominating.

Thematically, the album was certainly "heavy." "Long Line Rider" was included and released as a single, reaching #79, a far better showing than "safer" efforts such as "Talk To The Animals." Darin also tackled environmental pollution in "Questions" and questioned the validity of organized religion in "Sunday."

On a more personal note, the song "Change," a musical cousin of Dylan's "Don't Think Twice," explored Darin's personal and musical evolution ("Music that used to seem hollow now seems to fit in your range ...Damned if what you're feeling isn't change").

The album was more interesting lyrically than musically. Many of the melodies were basic and most songs contained no outright chorus or bridge. But the lyrics never failed to be intriguing, as Darin displayed a previously undeveloped knack for rhyme and wordplay.

He also displayed a biting wit. "The Proper Gander" was an allegory about the cold war, told via the story of a community of mice who are fleeced by their leader into being afraid of a mythical three-eyed Siamese cat ("They sang this land is mice land/Mice country tis of thee").

The album's peak was its final song, in which Darin put his feelings about Robert F. Kennedy's life and death into music. "In Memoriam" featured only Darin's whispered vocal and his acoustic guitar in a quiet, mournful performance which seems to be mixed at a lower volume than the rest of the album. Although the melody is only rudimentary, the song's painful honesty makes it one of Darin's most compelling compositions and performances.

"In Memoriam" opens with the words of Bobby Kennedy's enemies—"He's a ruthless opportunist"—and proceeds through Darin's observations of his own Arlington cemetery vigil. At the end, Darin comes to terms with his own belief in Kennedy—"Now no man has the answers and he was just a man / And yet I can't help feelin' that he knew a better plan." Darin's conclusion about the RFK tragedy, repeated at the end of the song's six verses was, "They never understood him, so they put him in the ground."

Born Walden Robert Cassotto was an absolute artistic triumph for Bobby Darin. It would have been a commendable effort from any artist, but the fact that it was the product of a man so ensconced in the traditional show business world made it that much more compelling. No Las Vegas artist, before or since, has spoken out so eloquently in protest of mainstream corporate and political America.

Unfortunately, but not surprisingly, the album was largely overlooked. Though it seemed to be an obvious effort to reach the *Rolling Stone* audience, that publication did not acknowledge its existence. The *Los Angeles Times*' Robert Hilburn, who would come to be regarded as one of the most respected pop music critics, was the first of the new generation of pop journalists to recognize Darin as a serious artist, but even he would wait almost nine months to chime in with praise of the album.

Later, in a profile of Darin, *Times*' writer Estelle Changas would say of the LP, "The songs convey an urgent sense of someone beginning absolutely fresh. They offer what is unusual in recorded music, an opportunity to glimpse the artist at a key transitional stage in his life. These compositions are a striking contrast to what many would identify as the public image of Darin the nightclub performer."

During the LP's production, Darin hooked up with a new, younger group of musical mates. The album's basic tracks were originally recorded in Los Angeles, then mixed in Las Vegas by engineer Brent Maher, who in the eighties would become one of the hottest and most respected producers of country music (for The Judds, among others). Maher recalled that Darin's reputation preceded him in Vegas studios.

"I was with another engineer in the studio," Maher said, "and when he heard I was going to work with Bobby, he said 'Oh, you poor soul. The guy's known to be a terror. You can't please him.' So I wasn't really looking forward to this, and when Bobby brought in the tape, I was kind of dubious about what I was going to be in for.

"What I found out about Bobby," Maher continued, "was that he just wanted people to work as hard as he worked. He didn't have much patience with people who didn't give 100%. If you gave more than 100%, he was more than appreciative, and was really a great guy."

When Darin gave Maher the tape, the engineer felt that a couple of the tracks weren't quite right, and asked Darin if he could re-cut the songs using a Nashville group he was working with. Darin agreed and liked what he heard of Maher and the group's work. So much so, in fact, that he hired the Nashville band—pianist Bill Aikens, bassist Quitman Dennis, drummer Tommy Amato, and guitarist Bubba Poythress—as his own group.

Darin grew quite close to Amato (who would remain as the band's drummer until Darin's death) and Dennis (at whose wedding Darin stood as best man). Dennis recalled that in the summer of 1968, the young band members, all into rock'n'roll,

Sailin'.

had no concept of Bobby Darin, Vegas superstar. Darin appreciated that fact.

"He was just being a guy like the rest of us, and we just started clowning around and doing stuff in the studio," Dennis recalled. "I really didn't know this 'other' Bobby Darin, and neither did the rest of us, so he loved that. We weren't afraid of him; that's what he liked. Everybody else was intimidated by him, or wanted something from him. All we wanted to do was play music, and we liked the guy. He was just trying to be one of the guys, and play rock'n'roll."

In hooking up with the new band, and in concentrating on new music, Darin was breaking ties with his former manner of doing business.

"I'm bailing out of what I'm doing at the Frontier," Darin told Quitman Dennis at the time. "I work and I make forty grand a week, and I've got a manager, an agent, this person, that person, and by the time it's all said and done, I got zip. So I told them all to go away."

In August 1968, Darin sold T.M. Music to Commonwealth United Corporation. Earlier that year, Commonwealth had purchased Koppelman-Rubin Associates, and Darin's former producers were now running the corporation's expanding music publishing and production subsidiary. Darin received his reported $1 million take in Commonwealth United stock. (Eventually, the corporation collapsed, and Darin lost his million, in addition to his copyrights.)

Darin began 1969 with a January 2 opening night gig at the Copacabana. His stage show had changed little from the one he presented at the Cocoanut Grove the previous October. He played his opening four songs, including "Mack The Knife," with a big band, then introduced "Long Line Rider" as a song "that has a little something to say which I'm proud of." He concentrated on the folk-rock material from that point.

But there were some obvious changes in Darin's appearance. He now sported a moustache. He did not wear his toupee. He wore denims from the beginning of the show. And dispensing with the big show-biz introduction, he simply walked on stage and began to sing.

"Introductions are part of the phony," he told columnist Earl Wilson. "I figure they must all know who they came here to see."

Open-minded critics were digging the new Darin: "Bobby Darin is a study in the musical evolution of an artist," wrote *Billboard*'s Claude Hall in a glowing review of the Copa performance. "He exhibited an attitude of involvement with today's serious music—progressive rock."

Even *Variety*, often less concerned with the artistic merits of a show than its ability to draw customers, gave Darin a good review and did not mention any audience dissatisfaction. But some of the Copa clientele was far less receptive of the new Darin than the critics. Some walked out, and some others that stayed voiced their dissatisfaction to the Copa brass.

Darin's new act was not the kind of entertainment the conservative Copa crowd wanted to see, and after this engagement, Darin became *persona non grata* at the club where he established himself as a top nightclub star.

It wasn't just nightclub management or patrons that did not appreciate the new Darin. Some other musicians were mystified. Darin's old friend and arranger Bobby Scott, never a fan of rock music, saw the Copa show and did not understand what Darin was trying to accomplish.

"It wasn't in keeping," Scott said Darin's change. "The fans who came out and paid a hell of a lot of money did not come for that guy. They might have taken that guy if he had also done some of the other things. But he was already making fun of some of the hits he had. He had kind of passed it by, but the audience hadn't."

While Scott thought the 1969 Darin was "a vestige of his former self," he could tell that Darin was content when they met backstage. "I did detect that he was at peace, exuding a non-characteristic relaxation, miles away from the Darin of '59," Scott said.

Indeed, Darin did not appear terribly concerned about anyone's dissatisfaction with his new act. During his Copa engagement, he told Earl Wilson he wanted to give up nightclubs. "I want to get into college concerts," Darin said. "I don't want business or politics. You can't tell the truth."

Darin butted heads with the entertainment establishment again in late January, when he was scheduled to appear on the "Jackie Gleason Show." For his solo number, he chose "Long

Line Rider." On the night of the taping, CBS' Programming Practices Department ordered him to cut the lines "This kind of thing can't happen here / 'Specially not in an election year." Rather than censor himself, Darin walked off the set.

While absolving Gleason of any responsibility for the decision, Darin told the press he would sue CBS: "I don't care if I never do another TV show in my life, they are not going to interfere with my right to express myself," he said.

Darin didn't have to wait long before experiencing the crowning moment of this stage of his career. In May, he opened a six-night stand at Los Angeles' Troubadour. The club generally showcased the hippest folk and rock acts, and would never have booked the old Bobby Darin. But some other artists with mainstream pop images, such as Rick Nelson and Neil Diamond, had successfully used 1969 appearances there to showcase their growth as artists. The Troubadour audience was open to anyone who performed with integrity.

For the Troubadour gig, Darin was accompanied solely by the four-piece band of Dennis, Amato, Aikens and Poythress. Additionally, Darin played acoustic guitar for much of the set and chimed in on harmonica often. "Mack The Knife" was dropped. Darin debuted a number of new original songs, and besides the Hardin and Dylan holdovers, added new songs to his set: The Beatles' "Lady Madonna," Joe South's "Gabriel," Hank Williams' "Lonesome Whistle" and Leadbelly's "Midnight Special."

A few new originals such as "Distractions" and "Me And Mr. Hohner" were previews of Darin's next Direction album. But the Troubadour gig's set list was most noteworthy for the debut of a new Darin composition, "Simple Song of Freedom." It was the zenith of Darin's move into composing topical, meaningful songs, validation of the entire move into folk-rock.

The song neatly summed up Darin's newfound belief that music—the simple act of singing—could be the forum in which people could stand up and demand peace. In the lyric, Darin reached his hand out to black Americans, and to Alexander Solzhenitsyn in the Soviet Union ("Tell me if the man who is plowing up your land / has got the war machine upon his mind").

He lashed out at governmental lies and war-mongering

leaders, singing "Let's all build them shelves and let them fight it out among themselves / And leave the people be who love to sing."

The last line of the chorus summed up Darin's most pressing concern, one shared by millions of Americans at the time—"We the people here don't want a war."

Just as "Simple Song Of Freedom" was the new Darin's high water mark as a songwriter, the Troubadour concerts were his high point as performer. He was completely accepted on his own terms—simply on the quality and integrity of his new music.

Reviewing Darin's opening night at the Troubadour, Pete Johnson of the *Los Angeles Times* wrote "This latest transition is remarkable and seems to have left Darin nearly as surprised and delighted as it left his opening night capacity audience. The overflow crowd loved him and his newly-assembled combo."

That summer, Darin and the band embarked on a series of dates playing at outdoor fairs. It succeeded at getting Darin off the supper club circuit, but it failed at finding audiences even remotely as accepting as the Troubadour's. For these dates, there was one more, not so minor, change: Darin's name.

To completely connote the break from his previous persona, he now wished to be known as "Bob" Darin: more adult, more serious, and distanced from the show-biz swinger. But Darin found that audiences couldn't wipe the slate clean nearly as easily as he could himself.

"People were eminently dissatisfied with what happened on stage," Quitman Dennis said of those fair dates. "It was the four-piece band, with Bobby playing acoustic guitar. He was still a good entertainer, but the material was going over their heads. He would not do the things they wanted him to do. Zero."

Ironically, Bob Darin received a much warmer reception in Las Vegas, when he stopped there for a one-night stand at the Bonanza on July 16. "Bob Darin has Vegas buzzing and favorably so," wrote *Variety*. "Obviously deeply committed to his new songbag, he makes believers out of cynics here."

Also in July, Darin released **Commitment**, his first and only LP released under the name "Bob Darin." While a hatted Darin's back was turned on the album's cover, the inside sleeves showed a non-toupeed Darin replete with moustache and denim jacket.

Like **Born Walden Robert Cassotto**, the second album showed no trace of the dynamic Darin voice and its songs, again minus choruses and bridges, were not crafted for the pop market. Unlike the first record, where at least every lyric was interesting, there were a couple of songs on **Commitment** which lacked even curiosity appeal.

But the highlights of **Commitment** rose above even the best tracks from the first album. "Me And Mr. Hohner" stood out, with Darin delivering some clever rhyme schemes in a manner similar to the fast-talking style John Sebastian used on some Lovin' Spoonful records such as "Jug Band Music" and "Pow." The track was released as a single, but only reached #123 nationally. It received significantly greater airplay in select markets such as New England, which caused it to "bubble under" the *Billboard* Top 100 chart for five weeks, an unusually long time for a non-hit.

Though Darin associates have no recollection of him using drugs, on **Commitment** he at least philosophically aligned himself with the drug-accepting counterculture. Not only are "pot" and "hash" referred to in "Mr. Hohner" (a large reason for radio's resistance to the song), but in "Water Color Canvas," Darin sings of "frying pans of coffee 'cause the only pot we had would not oblige." In "Jive" (the LP's second single), he sings of being "stoned since half past one."

Darin's knack for wordplay and personal insight came to the forefront on "Song For A Dollar," an autobiographical tune in which Darin confronted his own motivation for making music. A superb bass line propelled the song, and Darin found fresh ways to combine rhyming words such as "moral quarrel."

Another noteworthy song was "Sausalito (The Governors Song)," significant in that Darin was at least a dozen years ahead of most in coming out with an anti-Ronald Reagan song. "Sounds from Sacramento shouldn't be heard," he sang of the then-governor of California. Alluding to the Mamas & Papas 1966 classic "California Dreamin'," Darin sang, "To paraphrase Papa John, we're living in a California nightmare."

Again ignored by record buyers, **Commitment** did receive notice from critics. In fact, Darin's whole musical evolution was the subject of an insightful article by *L.A. Times* pop critic Robert Hilburn.

Noting that some cynical listeners might now consider Darin a trend-follower, Hillburn wrote "Maybe the real Bobby Darin is beginning to stand up. I hope so...Darin seems to be involved in a painful search for identity. It is a search that holds promise of rich rewards."

Cashbox magazine covered **Born Walden** and **Commitment** in the same glowing review: "Both belong among the dominant social documents of our time...They are shattering songs of social consciousness that belong in the mainstream of our new American revolution."

Darin also wanted to make sure his new messages were recognized in the music industry. To this end, Direction Records took out full-page ads in trade publications. With small white lettering against a black background, the message simply read "Peace...Bob Darin." Direction and Commonwealth United also took out a two-page *Cashbox* spread reprinting the lyrics of "Me And Mr. Hohner" in full.

However, even the people Darin was working with were not necessarily tuned into his lyrics.

"I really didn't agree with a lot of his politics," said Brent Maher, who had contributed significantly to the production of **Commitment**. "I was a lot more conservative, after putting in four years in the air force. Of course, as history proves, he was right. Bobby was dead on about some of these issues."

"At the time, a lot of it went over my head," said bass player Quitman Dennis. "He was coding things into those songs, and if you didn't have the insight into the politics of the time, you might miss part of it. I was in my twenties and I didn't have the awareness to be on the same train as him."

During his work with Darin in the studio and on stage, Dennis did observe Darin's *modus operandi* as a songwriter and musician.

"He understood the craft of songwriting," Dennis said. "He'd keep crankin' them out, and every now and then, he got hold of something. He understood the process—that some of them will be good, some of them will be not so good, and every now and then, you get one that really flies.

"He was a very good musician, a natural musician in his

own way," Dennis said. "He didn't have the patience or the discipline to develop any considerable skills on an instrument, but he could tackle an instrument and learn to do a tune or two with what appeared to be authority. That's a very unique gift. He could do that with drums, vibes, and piano, but his repertoire in each of those was limited. I appreciate his musicianship in that regard."

Although record buyers and radio stations shied away from Bob Darin's records, he did hit the chart as a songwriter. In August 1969, none other than Tim Hardin, the writer of "If I Were A Carpenter" charted with a version of "Simple Song Of Freedom."

Hardin was still under contract with Koppelman-Rubin Associates, and was recording his first album for Columbia Records. Though generally pleased with the album, the label wanted a single it could push to radio. Darin told Koppelman and Rubin that "Simple Song Of Freedom" might work for Hardin. Because Hardin did not usually record other songwriters' material, it was a tough sell, recalled Don Rubin.

"Timmy didn't really want to do it," said Rubin. "We played it for him and used the angle that it's Bobby's payback and it could be a big hit. He finally relented and agreed to do it. It was a little more to the pop side, not something Timmy was noted for. I think he agreed to do it because of the lyric. It didn't compromise his own feeling."

Hardin's record reached #50 nationally, although it was a larger hit in many regional markets. Ironically, considering Hardin's own gift as a writer, it was his only hit single.

The record was a bit over-produced, with a full band sound and female background vocalists. Even omitting Darin's verse about Solzhenitsyn, it still clocked in at 3:49.

The recording probably did more for Darin than Hardin. It gave Darin a bit of hip credibility, and he was very proud that a songwriter of Hardin's reputation recorded the song. For years, before performing the song himself, Darin would always mention that Hardin had the hit with it.

"Bob" Darin made his prime-time network TV debut that October with a guest appearance on the "Tom Jones Show," singing "Distractions" (a **Commitment** track) and joining Jones for a medley of "Aquarius" and "Let The Sunshine In."

Darin's final single of 1969 was an impressive one. "Baby May" expanded his sound to include a Memphis soul feel, with Steve Cropper-like guitar licks and a horn section. The song called for—and Darin delivered—some of the vocal dynamism he suppressed on the two previous albums.

The song was inspired by the suicide death of Art Linkletter's daughter. In the record's publicity material, Darin said he felt Linkletter could have assumed more responsibility, and the lyric included the line "Baby May had to pass away to hear her daddy say 'I was wrong'." Although the song is quite good and Darin's intention was to promote inter-generational communication, calling attention to the Linkletter tragedy may have been a mistake, as it made Darin come across as somewhat judgmental.

The single's flip side was another gem, a quiet acoustic ballad called "Sweet Reasons." It was the first song in which Darin lyrically addressed his own mortality, with lines such as "Oh, Sweet Reason, please be kind/ I haven't much time/ And I just want to be."

Darin had begun the composition back in 1963, after a conversation with Nik Venet in which Darin confided his concern about his health.

"That was the first time we really discussed the possibility of his passing away," Venet said. "That song was very special to him, because he wrote it in that mood. A lot of people didn't realize that he had so little time. And that was the first time he discussed it at length with me."

Musically, this melancholy, beautiful song proved that Darin had been listening to Simon & Garfunkel, and it's a shame that neither it nor "Baby May" was ever included on a Darin LP.

The single's label told of a few changes. First, Bell Records, which had distributed previous Direction product, was no longer in the picture. The record was distributed by Commonwealth United Records, Koppelman & Rubin's label. Secondly, the production credit had changed; both sides were produced by "Maher, Dennis and Amato for ABQ Productions."

"What he wanted to do there was give us a little to run with and see what we could do," Dennis said of Darin's decision to remove himself from the producer's chair. "I think he felt that when he was trying to control everything, he was limiting himself. He wanted to see if we could make some records that would wind up on the charts, but still have his message coded into the lyrics."

As 1969 wound down, Darin wanted to make sure that even the motion picture industry knew that he had changed. For a small role in "The Happy Ending," released late that year, he was billed as Robert Darin.

Even after all these changes, Darin still had one surprise up his sleeve. He would do the one thing he had never done before: Stop working.

Bob Darin, late 1969, in photo promoting/warning about his December engagement at The Sahara.
(Las Vegas News Bureau)

CHAPTER 22
"Nature Boy"
Big Sur

Although there was intermittent, interesting work, Bob Darin took a sabbatical from the fall of 1969 through the spring of 1970. For about nine months, work took a back seat to Darin's desire to sort things out, relax, and get in touch with himself.

He chose Big Sur, California. Darin bought a trailer and parked it in the back of a friend's seventy-acre farm.

So that he would be completely unencumbered by any previous ties, before the move, Darin divested himself of vast quantities of his belongings, including his cars, homes and wardrobe. To Big Sur, he took only a few denim jackets, dungarees, some slacks, books, and tapes of music.

"I just decided I didn't want to be owned by anybody," he told *Melody Maker*'s Bernard Barry later. "I felt myself losing touch with a great many things: life, the earth, everything."

Darin spent his days reading, listening to music, chopping wood and even working on the farm to pay for his trailer space. "I know it sounds mundane," he explained, "but I just felt things closing in on me."

"He wasn't secluding himself," opined Nik Venet. "He was just trying not to be 'Bobby Darin, Entertainer.' I think Bobby thought he was going to die. He couldn't deny the fact that he was not going to live to be seventy or sixty or even fifty. I think that weighed heavily on him. He just didn't know what he wanted to do for the last couple of go-rounds."

Darin did re-emerge temporarily in December 1969 for another confrontational Bob Darin gig, this time for two weeks at The Sahara in Las Vegas. Many Vegas showrooms simply went dark for the pre-Christmas season, but the Sahara took a chance on Darin—at $40,000 a week.

It was Darin's first Vegas showroom date in fourteen months (the Bonanza was a one-night stand), and he wanted to make sure the audience knew what they were in for. He had a full-size cut-out picture of himself (with moustache, Levi jacket, Levi jeans, and a cowboy hat) placed in the showroom's entrance.

The warning didn't stop people from walking out. During the engagement, boos, catcalls and heckling were also heard, especially when Darin turned down requests for "Mack The Knife."

Darin's show was essentially the same one he had performed at the Troubadour and Bonanza. Between songs, he would comment on topics such as the Santa Barbara oil spill, or knock the Nixon-Agnew administration, referring to "Slicky Dick and Zero Agnew."

Again, critics were kinder to Bob Darin than audiences were. While noting that Darin was "certain to lift the young establishment enemies into ecstacy," the *Variety* review noted, "He makes his point in a profound, interesting, musical manner."

The *New York Post*'s Alfred G. Aronowitz, long a Darin fan, noted the absurdity of the Vegas conservatives' reaction to Darin's protest songs: "Is there a more revealing commentary on Las Vegas than the fact that it considers Bobby Darin's appearance here its first major confrontation with the youth underground?"

The reaction to Bob Darin in Vegas wasn't always negative, recalled Brent Maher, who recorded the Sahara dates for a potential live album which never materialized.

"It would depend on the crowd," Maher said. "Sometimes the people went there and expected to hear Bobby Darin and what that represented in their minds. Those people weren't willing to listen. Especially on weekends, the demographics of the people were age thirty-five to forty or older. They were probably on the conservative side.

"Some other nights, you'd have people standing up and yelling 'Right on'," he said. "People were really in his corner, respecting where he was at and digging the music."

Darin appreciated the Sahara's decision to book him: "It took a lot of guts on the Hotel Sahara's part to try me out doing what I'm doing now," he said from the stage on his final night. "They pay me a lot of money for something I would have done for nothing."

But the Sahara's motives weren't purely altruistic. Darin could still draw in a crowd of big-spenders, and Aronowitz reported that during Darin's engagement, the Sahara casino "reported some of the briskest handles on The Strip."

Darin spent a fair amount of his $80,000 paycheck by bringing in a film crew to tape a couple of shows for a potential TV special.

"None of it worked technically," recalled Quitman Dennis, who said Darin refused to alter the stage lighting to accommodate the cameras, rather than the live audience. "He had a couple of rolls processed and it was all too black to print."

Darin would also return to Los Angeles from Big Sur periodically to work on a movie he had written, and would produce and direct, called "The Vendors." The plot centered on the relationship between a heroin addict and a prostitute, and the cast reportedly included Mariette Hartley, Gary Wood, and Dick Lord. (Dick Bakalyan has also previously been reported to be in the cast, but he was not.)

Darin had actually been tinkering with "The Vendors" since 1966, going as far as to set up a shoot that year, with his old guitarist, Jim McGuinn (then flying high with The Byrds) cast in the lead role. Back in the early sixties, McGuinn had told Darin that he wanted to get into movies and Darin gave him this advice: "Become a rock'n'roll star and then you can do anything you want."

McGuinn initially agreed to play the "Vendors" role, but backed out. "I read the script and liked it," he said. "Then I showed it to a friend who said, 'Jim, you're going to get typecast in this junkie role and it's not a good way to start out.'

"I was doing drugs at the time, and I got a little paranoid," said McGuinn. "So, the day of the shooting, Bobby was there with the camera crew all set up, and I called him and said 'I don't want to do it.' I told Bobby I'd pay for the crew, and he sent me a bill for the shoot."

Darin was more successful at getting the movie filmed in

1969-70, but not in getting it in condition to be released. As late as 1972, he still intended to put the film out, and the *L.A. Times* reported that "The Vendors" would be released in late 1972. However, the film never surfaced.

In early 1970, while Darin was editing "The Vendors," Terry Melcher, his old T.M. Music associate, approached him with a song he thought would be great for Darin, Jackson Browne's "Federal Review." Melcher offered to produce it and thought the song's anti-war message would fit in nicely with Darin's new image. Darin liked the song, and Melcher went ahead and cut an instrumental track, but the record was never completed.

Darin's next Direction single, "Maybe We Can Get It Together," would be his last for his own label. It was a gospel-oriented song which featured background vocals from three young black girls Darin and Brent Maher recruited from a Las Vegas choir.

Darin enjoyed his occasionally-interrupted Big Sur sabbatical, telling reporters it was "absolutely necessary for my spiritual survival." But by May 1970, he was ready to go back to work. And, as much as he believed in his new music, he was bothered when people walked out of his shows. Alienating audiences ran counter to everything he had ever strived for.

For his return, Darin decided to compromise. He would go back to being "Bobby Darin." Not the Bobby Darin that was king of Vegas supper-club standards. But not the Bob Darin of hard-core protest either.

He tried to find a happy medium. He would still play "Long Line Rider," "Simple Song Of Freedom," and of course, the Hardin and Dylan set staples. But he would also re-insert "Mack The Knife" into his show, and throw in some contemporary songs which were pop hits, such as "Everybody's Talkin'," and Blood, Sweat & Tears' "Spinning Wheel."

In 1972 interviews, Darin reflected on his reasons for making the compromise. "I thought I could present myself differently," he told the *Los Angeles Times*' Estelle Changas, "and that by this change in appearance, I could be closer to my own personal statement. But I turned off so many people, they didn't hear me, and those whom I've known for years swore to me that I had tried to be a hippie."

But the bottom line was that Darin genuinely missed the thrill of turning on an audience. "As much as I needed to divest myself of all these games and toys and possessions," he told *Melody Maker*'s Loraine Alterman, "I accumulated all that by doing something I really enjoyed. I did not have to divest myself of performing. I said I'd like to work in places where they'll accept the compromise that I'm willing to make."

The compromise may have been away from protest, but Darin didn't want to "soften" his sound musically. Before his "comeback" at the Landmark Hotel in May 1970, Darin appointed bassist Quitman Dennis as his "musical director" and instructed him on the sound that he wanted.

Darin would still perform with his four-piece band, but he decided to augment them with a seven-piece horn section. He told Dennis he wanted four saxophones and three trumpets, and arrangements to make them sound like a Little Richard/rock'n'roll horn section. "He wanted a rock'n'roll band," Dennis said.

"It was still not what people expected," Dennis recalled. "But it was strong musically and it was entertaining. I didn't notice any dissatisfaction from the public."

Indeed, upon his return, Darin found Vegas waiting with open arms: "Bobby Darin is back, and he brought 'Mack The Knife' with him," proclaimed *Variety*. "This time around, Darin compromises—but not enough to sacrifice his integrity. The slight surrender results in a strong, excellent turn."

It wasn't just the Vegas establishment that was glad "Bobby" was back in town. Many of Darin's friends and musical comrades believed that he sacrificed too much of his unique performing charm during his protest phase.

"No one was happier when he went back to being Bobby Darin," said Darin's old Capitol co-hort, saxophonist Steve Douglas, who had seen Darin's protest act. "Bobby wasn't a folkie. He seemed to be a guy pretty lost, searching for something. He didn't seem comfortable. Bobby was at home on a stage in Vegas, entertaining the folks. That's what he was—a great entertainer."

All in all, Darin's retreat to Big Sur and subsequent return to Vegas has been greatly exaggerated, even by people who should know better.

For example, in his autobiography *Once Before I Go*, Wayne Newton writes of Darin becoming a recluse immediately after Robert Kennedy's death, and of a Darin "comeback" performance in Reno, saying, "This was the first time in three years Darin had stood in the spotlight of a nightclub stage."

Even if the Bonanza gig is not counted because it was a one-shot, the longest Darin was away from Vegas was slightly more than a year. And even if the two week "experiment" at the Sahara is not counted, the span between Darin's regular Vegas engagements—the Frontier in late 1968 and the Landmark in mid-1970—was only eighteen or nineteen months.

Newton also writes that after the Big Sur retreat, none of the Vegas showrooms would touch Darin, and that Newton had to pull strings to get him booked at the Desert Inn in 1971. Again, this story appears pretty dubious after examining Darin's Vegas performance record. If the Desert Inn hadn't grabbed Darin, it's hard to imagine that another hotel wouldn't have.

CHAPTER 23

"The Breaking Point"

The "Comeback"

Just because Bobby Darin was back in Las Vegas, it did not mean that he was keeping his political opinions to himself. In May 1970, Darin took out newspaper ads denouncing President Nixon's decision to invade Cambodia.

On May 12, in the wake of the U.S. military action, Darin participated in an anti-war demonstration at Los Angeles City Hall. A number of speakers, including future L.A. mayor Thomas Bradley, addressed a crowd of about six hundred, consisting mostly of USC students.

When Darin took the mike, he announced a project called "Phone For Peace" and urged the crowd to telephone the White House and leave a peace message for Nixon. He said he hoped a tie-up of the White House switchboard would cause the President to take notice. Darin's comments and participation in the protest were duly noted by the FBI.

Back in Las Vegas, Darin continued to refine his new stage show at the Landmark. He added a Beatles medley and Neil Diamond's "Sweet Caroline" to the act. With the exception of "Mack The Knife," "If I Were A Carpenter" and "Splish Splash" (part of a closing rock'n'soul medley), he eschewed performing his own hit records.

"He didn't want to do his previous hits," explained Quitman Dennis. "He wanted to keep moving forward, and experience the buzz of doing new, exciting material, rather than reiterating the past."

Sometimes that new material would be a classic associated with another artist. Television actor Alan Thicke, who would later work with Darin, recalled being knocked out by Darin's

Darin and Mike Douglas (right) during Darin's week as guest host on "The Mike Douglas Show," July 1970.

early seventies rendition of Jackie Wilson's "Higher And Higher."

"I think Bobby did the definitive version of 'Higher And Higher,'" Thicke said. "It had real rock'n'roll credibility, even in his Vegas presentation. It was as authentic rock'n'roll as Vegas had seen at the time."

Darin also decided to get back to mainstream audiences via television. Shortly after leaving Big Sur, and only months after denouncing Nixon, Darin went about as middle-America as you can get when he co-hosted the daily "Mike Douglas Show" the week of July 27.

Darin, still without his toupee and sporting his moustache, chatted, sang and danced with Douglas, whose show was broadcast during the day in most markets. The guest list for the week reflected no counterculture, but both Little Richard and Wilson Pickett appeared, giving the show an unusual r&b punch for the week.

That fall, Darin also became something of a semi-regular guest on the "Flip Wilson Show," appearing on four shows between September and January. He sang songs from his act such as "Gabriel," "Higher And Higher" and "If I Were A Carpenter" and even revisited, for the first time in years, "Lazy River." A song that he performed in September, "Melodie," would be his new single for a new record label—Motown.

Motown seemed an unusual home for Bobby Darin, but in '71, the label had also signed other white sixties pop stars such as The Four Seasons and Leslie Gore. Although Motown planned to make Darin's first LP a live recording (with the tentative title of **Finally**), "Melodie," which was held from release until April 1971, was not a live track (despite the fact that its label credit reads "In Album 'Live At The Desert Inn'"). Quitman Dennis does not recall the song ever being performed live.

The record's sound was definitely more Motown than Darin. Darin was a fine r&b singer, but he was no soul shouter, and the production of "Melodie" was tailored for a singer more along the lines of the Four Tops' Levi Stubbs. "Melodie" was far from sensational, but it certainly deserved more attention than the total indifference with which it was greeted by radio.

Its flip side, a cover of the Supremes' swan song hit "Someday We'll Be Together," ranks as perhaps the worst track

Darin on stage at Desert Inn,
shortly before undergoing heart surgery.
(Las Vegas News Bureau)

Darin ever recorded. From background vocalists warbling "Sing It Bobby" to Darin's strained vocal which never stays on the melody, this Motown debut was quite a disappointment after the always-interesting original material Darin waxed for Direction.

In October 1970, Darin went to Toronto to tape a Canadian TV special called "The Darin Invasion." The hour-long program was syndicated in the U.S. a year later. The show was a curious, yet effective mix of old and new Darin.

Guests from the contemporary pop world included The Poppy Family and Linda Ronstadt. (Darin accompanied Ronstadt on guitar during her performance of "Long Long Time.") George Burns also guested, and he and Darin reprised their old Vegas "I Ain't Got Nobody" soft-shoe routine.

Darin also presented himself as an actor. He and actress Pat Carroll performed a sketch about a working class couple in a kind of updated "Honeymooners" style. And Darin, in full costume and makeup, performed "I'm Reviewing The Situation" from "Oliver."

But the highlights were Darin's own musical numbers—"Higher And Higher," "Hi-De-Ho" and "If I Were A Carpenter." To close the show in grand fashion, Darin picked up his guitar and began "Simple Song Of Freedom." As the song progressed and the arrangement built, Darin's performance grew more intense and joyous. His face exhibited a look of complete musical satisfaction, and he reveled in the audience's warm reaction.

In January 1971, Darin began an engagement at the Desert Inn in Las Vegas. By this point, Darin dropped "Long Line Rider" and all his original protest songs from the act, save for "Simple Song Of Freedom." Joe South's "Gabriel" was replaced as set opener by Laura Nyro's "Save The Country," an attractive composition to Darin because of its references to "We Shall Overcome" and "the dream of the two young brothers." (His politics were also advertised when "Mr. Agnew" took the place of the devil in "Hi-De-Ho.") A superb acoustic version of James Taylor's "Fire And Rain" was also added.

During his run at the Desert Inn, Darin struck up a friendship with the Inn's *maitre d'*, Georges LaForge. Darin spoke fluent French and often conversed with LaForge between shows or over dinner.

"He was a very down to earth person, no pretensions whatsoever," LaForge recalled. In one of their conversations, Darin told LaForge he had always dreamed of opening a French restaurant and proposed that LaForge join him in this business venture.

Darin offered to finance the restaurant, which LaForge would run, on two conditions: that it be located in Beverly Hills, and that it be named "Pamplemousse" (the French word for grapefruit). LaForge inquired about Darin's insistence on that name.

"All my life, I have thought it was the most beautiful word in French," Darin told him. "I love the sound of it. With a name like Pamplemousse, it can do nothing but succeed."

The two never got their restaurant open, but years later, LaForge himself opened a restaurant in Las Vegas. In tribute to Bobby Darin, he named it Pamplemousse.

Also during Darin's Desert Inn stand, Motown brought in an eight-track mobile unit to record the shows for a scheduled live album release (one which did not reach the public until more than a dozen years after Darin's death).

The live recording showed Darin in fine form. The presentation was unmistakably Vegas, and surprises in the song selection were few and far between. However, Darin's version of "Simple Song Of Freedom" was both stronger and more commercial than Tim Hardin's. Motown released it on a promotion-only single to radio, but strangely, not to the public. And Darin's closing rock and soul medley of "Chain Of Fools," "Respect," "Splish Splash" and "Johnny B. Goode" proved that he and his band could cook with the best rock ensembles.

Darin's Desert Inn performance was top-notch. Usually, that was a given, but it was absolutely remarkable in light of the fact that Darin entered the hospital the day after his closing night—for major heart surgery.

In 1970, Darin's damaged heart finally caught up with him. Darin's old friend Harriet Wasser saw the evidence first-hand when she visited the set of the "Darin Invasion" special.

"That was a horrible scene," she said. "After that show, he was so sick that he sat in front of his dressing room door. He could not get up. They put him in bed. He said to me, 'I feel like

I'm running a hundred miles an hour around this room'."

Oxygen masks and avoidance of stairs were no longer enough to keep Darin going. Six times, he went into intensive care for electroconversion. His heart would beat 140 to 160 times a minute, instead of the normal 72 to 80.

Open-heart surgery was the only option he had. "My valves had deteriorated to the point where if [surgery] was not now, then it would have to be the next year, and in the meantime, I'd have to curtail my activities," he explained.

Doctors had actually advised him to undergo surgery earlier, but Darin was committed to his Desert Inn gig for the first six weeks of 1971. "You give me these six weeks to work," he told his doctors. "Somehow, you keep me alive by remote control, and the moment I close, I'll go home, check myself into the hospital and give myself to you."

During a nine-hour open-heart surgery procedure at Cedars of Lebanon Hospital, two plastic valves were inserted into Darin's heart. Darin came precariously close to death. He was in intensive care for five days, and (he later told writer Alfred Aronowitz) he remembered nearly dying three times. He spent six weeks in the hospital.

Darin was advised, and agreed, to take it slow upon his release and allow enough time for adequate recuperation. Even accepting summer work would be rushing it.

Darin tried to reassure worried friends and associates by throwing a party that summer to celebrate the success of the surgery. On his property, he imported a carnival, and set up tents and carnival games. He introduced everyone to his surgeon, Dr. Josh Fields. "He was that happy to be alive," recalled Darin's old friend from "Pressure Point," actor Dick Bakalyan.

"I had expected to kick off by the time I was thirty," Darin told reporters upon his re-emergence. "So I bought a few extra years."

Darin at The Hilton, September 1972.
(Las Vegas News Bureau)

CHAPTER 24

"Everything's OK"

Post-Surgery

Although Darin considered it a long recuperation period, it was only seven months after open-heart surgery that Bobby Darin resumed performing activities. He opened at Harrahs in Reno on September 1, 1971.

Post-surgery Bobby Darin would be very similar to pre-RFK Bobby Darin. The denim tux was gone, replaced by the standard nightclub tuxedo. The toupee went back on. More comedy, and even the celebrity impersonations, returned to the act. Darin seemed resigned to the fact that he was at his best as a Las Vegas-style entertainer. He seemed to care not a whit if he would appear unhip, even irrelevant, to the under-thirty crowd.

He had thought all this out completely during his recovery, he told the *New York Post*'s Alfred Aronowitz. "I had tried to put my street self on stage," he said of his denim phase. "But then I began to think...What they want is an actor on the stage.

"I'm an actor," he continued. "An actor wears a costume and makeup. There's nothing wrong with that. You go out and you entertain them. If what they hear is what they see, then indeed, let me put on my tux. I'm comfortable in it. I don't have any inner arguments anymore."

Darin did take a renewed interest in acting upon his return, guesting on a number of television series. Within a four month span, he appeared in dramatic roles in episodes of "Night Gallery," "Ironsides," and "Cades County." And, back on the "Flip Wilson Show," he displayed the best of his new-old act by performing "Mack The Knife" and "Simple Song Of

Freedom."

As 1972 dawned, Darin was back on the nightclub scene with a vengeance. Critics again greeted him warmly. "Making a triumphant return to the Strip after open-heart surgery, the old-new Bobby Darin was relaxed, happy and great," wrote *Billboard*'s Laura Deni in a review of his February show at the Desert Inn.

Variety concurred: "The 'new' Bobby Darin is the 'old' Bobby Darin; he's dumped the jeans and is back in a tux singing tux-type songs." To prove this point, Darin returned "That's All" and "Beyond The Sea" to his act. However, he didn't abandon folk—the triumvirate of "If I Were A Carpenter," "I'll Be Your Baby Tonight" and "Simple Song Of Freedom" still closed the show.

While Darin had little doubt that he would succeed at the Desert Inn, he was challenged by a return to the Copacabana. Neither he nor the Copa brass had forgotten his disastrous 1969 gig there. Darin asked for another chance, and offered an olive branch. He had an intermediary call Jules Podell.

"Tell Julie I want to play [the club] and settle the situation," were his instructions. "I did a bad thing last time. One thing I know now is that I'm a saloon singer." He opened at the Copa on February 24, slightly more than three years after the '69 debacle.

This time, he went over like gangbusters, with both the audience and Podell. Darin was asked to come back to the club eight months later.

New York Times writer Don Heckman tried to be as hard on Darin as possible in his review of the February Copa show. Heckman accurately reported Darin's step back to show-biz traditions, noting that he "is clearly more comfortable with the Frank Sinatra-Dean Martin style." Along the same line, the writer opined that Darin's act of whipping off his tie during a hot number was "a routine that now looks as humorously antiquated as Al Jolson getting down on one knee to sing 'Mammy.'" While Darin might have been upset with that interpretation three years earlier, he probably regarded it as a compliment in 1972.

Despite his reservations, Heckman found that Darin was a hard act to dislike: "Elusive though his style may be—folkyhumble at some points, Vegas-flashy at others—Darin is still a first class performer."

Darin found himself back in the media spotlight during his Copa engagement, although by this time he grew tired of questions about his heart surgery.

"I don't want to talk about that," he testily told *New York Daily News* reporter Patricia O'Haire. "Yes, I did have such an operation one year ago, and that's all I wish to say about it. We can talk about the future, we can talk about the past, we can talk about my work, or we can talk about the weather, but I don't want to talk about the surgery."

Darin also took his act to the West Coast, returning to the Grove for the first time since shortly after RFK's death. Longtime Darin admirer Robert Hilburn, the *Los Angeles Times* critic, liked what he saw: " He's better than ever, a consummate nightclub performer," Hilburn wrote. "As with the best entertainers, he makes it look effortless. Darin moves with the grace and confidence of a superbly trained athlete, one who knows he is in control of the situation."

Darin won over more fans that summer with a concert in New York City's Central Park. "A lot of kids there hadn't come out to see Bobby Darin so much as they just wanted to come out to the park," wrote Alfred Aronowitz, "but when the show was over, the crowd was screaming for more. He can still sing, but more than that, he can make you have a good time."

Indeed, Darin's act now featured so much comedy that many considered it the highlight of his show. "There is a tremendous amount of comedy and talk in his turn," wrote *Variety*, reviewing his October Copa show. "In all, Darin impresses as a performer who has gone beyond the singing medium."

Moving the act into the multi-media arena, old silent-film clips of car crashes and chases were projected during Darin's drum solo. He impersonated W.C. Fields, Marlon Brando and Dean Martin. And his humor could be very self-effacing; Darin wasn't afraid now to joke about his height and toupee.

"If I can laugh about it," he told columnist Earl Wilson, "that shows it doesn't bug me anymore." Darin reveled in a line Steve Lawrence was tossing off in his act then—"Did you hear about Bobby Darin's accident at the Copa? He fell off his shoes."

In Vegas, Darin moved from the Desert Inn to the Hilton that September, with Shirley Bassey as his opening act. The extensive live work didn't keep him from other activities. Also in 1972, Darin was a presenter at the Grammy Awards. He told the *Los Angeles Times* he would begin work on his first novel. And in August, his first album in three years was released.

Bobby Darin, on Motown, was in many respects a typical early seventies MOR album, which was a bit of a disappointment coming off Darin's previous progressive efforts. The songs were certainly contemporary and relatively modern in their lyrical themes, but they in no sense approached rock, even the "soft rock" then in vogue via Carole King and James Taylor.

Strings and horns added a pop influence to nearly every track, and background vocals, often an intrusion on Darin records, were again overblown here. And the motivation behind some of Joe Porter's production moves was mysterious: "I've Already Stayed Too Long," a fairly interesting country-influenced song, was faded out before even reaching its second chorus.

The album did get off to a great start, with Darin's cover of Randy Newman's "Sail Away," a choice which proved that Darin still hadn't lost his great taste in material. With a relatively unobtrusive arrangement which featured a Darin harmonica break, the track seemed the culmination of everything Darin couldn't accomplish at Direction. Unfortunately, when released as a single, the record stiffed.

Throughout the album, Darin's voice sounded a bit weaker and more vulnerable than it was in the pre-operation days. He appeared to be straining at times, although the effect did not detract from the album.

The chief reason for the album's commercial failure was its lack of a standout, sure-fire hit. A cover of the Everly Brothers' "Let It Be Me" was very overwrought, and Cat Stevens' "Hard Headed Woman" was only slightly more appealing.

In fact, besides "Sail Away," the most interesting track was the only one Darin had a hand in writing himself. "Something In Her Love," written with drummer Tommy Amato, was the most old-fashioned, middle of the road song on the LP, but it was a finely crafted ballad. Vocally, Darin never sounded more like Sinatra than he did on this track.

The fact that Darin co-wrote only one out of ten songs was a disappointing indication of his abdication of any artistic responsibility, save for his singing. He offered an explanation on his lack of writing to Britain's *Melody Maker*, saying his sunken publishing deal with Commonwealth United, in which he lost control of his copyrights, would not end until 1973, and he didn't feel like writing much until then.

Despite his recording, performing and acting activities, Darin still took time to get away and relax. He had a new companion, Andrea Yaeger, a former Beverly Hills legal secretary. In interviews at the time, Darin casually referred to her as "my wife" or "Mrs. Darin," although they were not then legally married. "We've just dispensed with the bureaucratic involvement," he explained.

Darin still found his favorite method of unwinding to be camping. He and Andrea would drive to the California countryside, pull out sleeping bags, sleep in the open air, and cook their own food. They would bring only a few canned goods, some fishing gear, and some cooking equipment for sojourns which would usually last one to three days. According to Terry Melcher, Darin would also drive his motor home to Big Sur on occasion, and spend some time parked on the ranch owned by Beach Boy Al Jardine.

However, there would be less time for relaxation with the advent of Darin's next project, one which would build his popularity, but wreck his health.

Carl Reiner (left) and Darin (as Groucho Marx) on
"The Bobby Darin Amusement Company," August 1972.
(NBC publicity photo)

Chapter 25
"Always Leave 'Em Laughing"
The TV Show

Despite the fact that Bobby Darin was further from "hot" than he'd been at any time since 1958, prime-time network TV came calling in the summer of 1972. The "Dean Martin Show" was going on its usual summer hiatus, and Darin was chosen to star in a short-run summer-replacement variety series on NBC.

Some top-notch talent was associated with his show. Producers Saul Ilson and Ernest Chambers, both TV veterans, had produced Frank Sinatra's 1968 TV special, and The Smothers Brothers' controversial comedy series which had been yanked by CBS a few years earlier. The producers saw potential in a Darin-hosted show with an unusual twist.

"Bobby was certainly a great singer, but that's not an important consideration in a television hit," Ernest Chambers said. "But we felt he had a range and personality, and that properly handled, he could be a success. What we had to do was create some pieces for Bobby to do, and create a supporting cast."

In the same way that CBS' "Sonny & Cher Comedy Hour" was titled to emphasize the program's emphasis on comedy, not music, Darin's program was christened "The Bobby Darin Amusement Company." (Technically, it was called "Dean Martin Presents The Bobby Darin Amusement Company"; the introductory credit didn't sit well with Darin from the ego point of view, said Ilson.)

"We called it 'The Bobby Darin Amusement Company' specifically to tell the audience that it would not just be an hour of a guy singing," said Chambers. Though Darin had done numerous variety shows and some light comedy in films, the weight of carrying a broad comedy show was a new challenge to him. Darin relished the opportunity to show people outside the Vegas circuit that he was more than a singer.

"He was not a great comedian," recalled Chambers, "but he was a good actor. If you gave him a character to play, and some lines, he could do that."

"He did it very well," said Ilson. "I thought he had natural abilities. He could do jokes, sketches, and he was very instrumental in the show. He added a lot."

Some regular characters and bits were set up. One featured comedian Steve Landesberg (later of "Barney Miller") as a Freud-like psychiatrist who analyzed Darin.

"We knew Darin had a reputation for being volatile and arrogant, so we addressed that issue head on by having Landesberg play his psychiatrist and come on stage and talk to him," recalled Chambers. "It was very effective because the fact that Bobby could laugh at that quality in himself helped take the sting out."

One of Darin's best impersonations, his Groucho Marx, was incorporated into many shows. (A picture of Darin and Tom and Dick Smothers as Groucho, Chico and Harpo still hangs in Ernest Chambers' office.) Comedian Rip Taylor appeared as "Skyway Silverman," a goofy helicopter traffic reporter.

Another recurring and silly bit showcased Darin in drag as "The Godmother," an old Italian woman. His sparring partner in these sketches was often Geoff Edwards, an L.A.-area disc jockey who would go on to success as a game show host on programs such as "Jackpot" and "Treasure Hunt." Edwards called his experience on the Darin show a joy.

"Everybody was having a great time and all of us loved him," Edwards recalled. "Working on that show was the happiest six months of my life."

Edwards' "interviews" with the Godmother were loosely scripted, but the segments highlighted Darin's ability to humorously improvise, sometimes to the point of breaking up Edwards on camera. In one sketch, when Edwards, looking at cue cards, stumbled through the question "Are there any telltale signs to indicate that a marriage is in trouble?," Darin shot back "Yes, and there are also tell-tale signs to indicate that you can't read."

"Bobby always surprised me," Edwards said. "He had an incredible instinct for comedy."

Perhaps the most fondly-remembered, and certainly the most consistently good, sketch on the Darin show was "Carmine and Angie" (also called "The Neighborhood"), a weekly segment revolving around the conversations of two friends sitting on the front porch stoop in an old Italian neighborhood. This segment was conceived and developed by Darin himself, who played Angie. For the part of Carmine, Darin called in his old friend from "Pressure Point," Dick Bakalyan. The producers initially balked at Darin's choice.

"They called me in and we had a meeting," recalled Bakalyan. "The producers told me 'your hair's too white.' Bobby said 'put a rinse in it.' They said, 'we need a comic to do this part.' Bobby said 'Dickie's an actor; he'll play a comic playing the part.' Bobby afforded me the opportunity to do a lot of things that I wouldn't have had the opportunity to do."

Darin's casting instincts were correct, as the chemistry between he and Bakalyan worked quite effectively. Darin, dressed in a Mets cap and jacket, played the married, know-it-all cynic with submerged hope and heart. Bakalyan played the less-worldly innocent who still lived with his mother and was easily swayed by the whims of any of the numerous "chicks" he was chasing. Both spoke with a New York-by-way-of-Italy accent, and the bits were laced with ethnic references to the "old country."

"'Carmine And Angie' really came out of a conversation we had with Bobby," remembered Saul Ilson. "He used to talk about sitting on a stoop with his friend, and talking about how they were going to solve the world's problems."

"That stoop was Bobby's neighborhood," said Bakalyan. "That was the front of his place in the Bronx where he grew up."

Like the Godmother sketches, "Carmine and Angie" was scripted, but Darin and Bakalyan used their own instincts often. (In fact, Bakalyan received writing credit for one week's segment.) The sketches were never out-and-out hilarious, but they were not intended to be. They succeeded as heartwarming, humorous characterizations and situations based on real immigrant neighborhoods.

"The thing was, there are real people out there like Carmine and Angie," Bakalyan said. "I still get mail from people from Italy who remember that. We got mail from all over the country, even from people who weren't in cities, because they understood about a pal leaving the neighborhood."

Through the two Italian paesanos, Darin occasionally snuck in some of his own social opinions or ironic humor. In one bit, Darin's Angie scoffed at actors who change their names. In another, Carmine, egged on by a girl, pushed the Sierra Club to a cynical Angie.

"Bobby had a great sense of humor and put-on," said Bakalyan. "I remember being at a screening at his house once. He went into the bathroom for a long time, and we kept waiting for him to come out. We finally went in, and there was nobody in there. He had crawled through this very small window, climbed along the ledge, came in through the kitchen, and was watching everybody look for him in the bathroom. It was hilarious."

Another long-time Darin friend and associate, Dick Lord, was brought aboard as a "comedy consultant" for the show. But some new, younger talent also joined the Darin circle. The youngest member of writing staff was Alan Thicke, who would go on to great television success as the star of the late eighties ABC-TV sitcom "Growing Pains."

"I was a genuine fan of Darin's," said Thicke, a native of Canada who had made several television appearances in his homeland before heading for the U.S. "For my audition piece at the CBC, I did 'If I Were A Carpenter,' ripping off his sound as closely as I could manage. On my very first show, my first professional broadcast number was 'If I Were A Carpenter.'"

The fact that he was such an avowed Darin fan helped Thicke (who later produced and wrote for the cult TV classic "Fernwood Tonight") land a slot writing special musical-comedy numbers for the "Amusement Company."

"I think what got me the job was when I relayed an anecdote to the producers," recalled Thicke. "In 1967, in my last year of college, a buddy and I, after striking out with these two girls at our fraternity prom, jumped in my little Volkswagen at about two in the morning, and in our tuxedos, drove from London, Ontario to Miami Beach.

"I took forty dollars of my last hundred and spent it on one of those 'blue haired lady' bus tours, where you got two hotels and a beverage," he said. "Bobby Darin was at the Deauville Hotel. While my buddy went to pick up girls, I went with a bunch of old ladies, sat in the back of the room, and watched Bobby."

Thicke came up with some special musical material that Darin liked, such as a mock-rock version of "Macbeth," which told the Shakespeare story with parodies of fifties and sixties rock'n'roll songs. (Examples: "Got To Kill The King Tonight Blues" and "Tell Banquo I'm Sorry.") Darin took a liking to the "kid" of the writing staff.

"I think we had a pretty warm relationship for a staff writer-star kind of situation," recalled Thicke. "He was very kind to me, and generally kind to the staff. I was quite honored that he came to my house for dinner one night. We spent the night shooting pool and shooting the breeze. I don't think he saw me as just another writer doing just another job. I think he enjoyed teaching me, and being my mentor in some ways."

All participants were very optimistic about the show, and by all accounts, Darin was very involved in the creative planning for the summer replacement run. In fact, *TV Guide* writer Leslie Raddatz, in a behind-the-scenes preview article, wrote, "Darin seems to be the man in charge, an effect he accomplishes with an air of quiet authority, rather than the brashness that might perhaps be expected."

Darin's decision about the show's music was to play it safe and, for the most part, stay in the middle of the road. He went back into his own standard songbag for material such as "Beyond The Sea," "That's All," and "Artificial Flowers." He also utilized songs from his current club act such as "Can't Take My Eyes Off You" and "Spinning Wheel." Darin's only folk-flavored forays also came straight from his regular act: "Carpenter" and Dylan's "I'll Be Your Baby Tonight."

Each show also featured Darin dueting with female guest stars, ranging from respected contemporary songstresses (Dionne Warwick, Dusty Springfield) to actresses (Debbie Reynolds, Florence Henderson) to an old friend (Joanie Sommers). One duet per show was performed in what Ilson came to call the "mouth-to-mouth resuscitation" format: Darin and his female

Freda Payne and Darin duet on "The Bobby Darin Show," 1973.
(NBC publicity photo)

partner started off facing each other in extremely close proximity, and gradually moved their mouths even closer until, at song's end, they kissed.

The only part of the show where Darin seemed uncomfortable was, ironically, his signature number, "Mack The Knife," which he performed each week as the closing credits rolled. His discomfort was understandable. First, as Darin had to share screen space with the credits, the number lost much of its impact. Also the rote week-after-week reading seemed to bore Darin, who at about mid-song would turn his back to the camera and shuffle down a long corridor off-stage.

"He didn't want to do that," Ilson acknowledged. "I had to talk him into it. He said 'I'm not a dancer, I don't do those things.'"

The show was slated for a seven-week run, but Ilson and Chambers had bigger things in mind. "We don't do summer shows," Ilson told *TV Guide*. "We expect to be back in January."

Despite the smaller summer show budget, the program's sets and production numbers were elaborate, and guest stars were of high quality. George Burns, Burt Reynolds, Donald O'Connor, Joan Rivers, Carl Reiner, The Smothers Brothers, Pat Paulsen, and Debbie Reynolds all appeared.

"The Bobby Darin Amusement Company" premiered on Thursday, July 27, 1972 at 10:00 p.m. on NBC. George Burns, Burt Reynolds (whose booking was quite a coup, coming shortly after his highly-publicized nude pose in *Cosmopolitan*) and singer Bobbie Gentry were Darin's guests.

Variety gave the program a generally favorable review, noting that "the musical portions were generally standout, with the comedic endeavors a trifle spotty, but still promising. Pacing and overall concept were knowingly deft."

The seventh and final episode of the summer series aired September 7, 1972. NBC was pleased enough with the show—and its ratings—to order it renewed for a regular run beginning in January 1973. It would come back with a new concept and a new look.

* * * * * * * *

On Friday, January 19, 1973, "The Bobby Darin Show" premiered at 10 p.m. on NBC. It didn't take a genius to figure out that the change in the title indicated more emphasis on Bobby Darin, less on the former "Amusement Company."

Rip Taylor, whose segments never really hit the mark, was gone. So was Steve Landesberg's psychiatrist bit. Echoing what the *Variety* review pointed out, Darin felt music was the show's strongest element, and decided to give it greater prominence.

"Bobby put his foot down and said he didn't want any of those people; he wanted to do a straight music show," said Chambers. "He got rid of the psychiatrist because he didn't like being insulted every week. As a result, the show lost a lot of its comic energy. It became a softer show, more music. I think that hurt the show's power to hold an audience. It became too narrow."

Looking back, Ilson agreed with Chambers' assessment of the change, but was more understanding of Darin's position.

"It's not uncommon," he said. "If you look at any show, the minute the stars start feeling their oats, they usually take over and try to dictate, and that's where it becomes a conflict.

"He wanted to do certain things on the show," Ilson continued. "Some of it, we disagreed with, some of it, the network disagreed with. But to be honest about it, Bobby contributed a lot to the show. He had a lot of ideas, a lot of good things to say, and he was worth listening to."

Alan Thicke also noted the change in the show's direction, but as a fan of Darin's music, he thought it was a positive step.

"It shifted away from the variety format and got closer to the roots of Bobby Darin, who he really was, and what his music was all about," Thicke said. "I think that when the network got more comfortable with how strong Bobby's music was, they figured they could go with more of that, and less fancy footwork."

Truth be told, Chambers' opinion that the show lost its comic energy is justified. The second go-round did not match the quality of the summer run, though certainly not entirely because of the Darin-directed changes.

The Godmother remained and "Carmine and Angie" continued to be high-quality, heart-warming comedy. But too many of the other sketches were unimaginative. While Darin's musical numbers continued to be superb, the show offered little to those who felt indifferent to yet another hour of a singer, no matter how talented, on TV every week. And the show failed to attract the high quality guests of its summer run. As opposed to the summer debut with Burt Reynolds and George Burns, the winter premier could only offer Burl Ives and Dyan Cannon.

Variety's review of the opening show said, "There is more to being a variety show host than telling a few jokes and singing a couple of songs. Bobby Darin still has not entirely made the transition." The review also noted that none of the comedy sketches "were developed fully enough to get off the ground."

"The Bobby Darin Show" was, unfortunately, very formulaic TV variety for the most part. With the exception of Darin's singing, the program presented little that a viewer couldn't get from a dozen other shows of the day. In particular, the show offered no enticement to a younger, perhaps hipper, audience. Too many of the guest stars were the usual TV faces who had almost already worn out their welcome: Joey Heatherton, Charles Nelson Reilly, Cloris Leachman, Tim Conway, Andy Griffith, Phyllis Diller, Artie Johnson.

The musical guest list fared slightly better, as the program did feature some acts with then-current chart hits—Bread, Seals & Crofts, Bill Withers. But unfortunately few musical bookings were left field, with the exceptions of blues singer Taj Mahal and guitarist David Bromberg. In retrospect, one wonders whether Darin ever considered former associates such as Tim Hardin, John Sebastian, or Randy Newman, all of whom would have been palatable (at least for a couple of numbers) in middle America's living rooms in 1973.

With more emphasis on music, Darin's own song list expanded, though it stayed decidedly middle of the road. His **That's All**, **This Is Darin**, **Oh! Look At Me Now**, **Hello Dolly**, and **In A Broadway Bag** albums were mined. A few contemporary songs were added: "If," "Alone Again Naturally," "Help Me Make It Through The Night." Darin also seemed to take a particular shine to the compositions of Neil Diamond, performing "Brooklyn Roads" and "Shilo" in quite effective semi-acoustic settings, and "Sweet Caroline" and "Song Sung Blue" in more show-biz arrangements.

Strangely, considering his relatively unimaginative song choices, Darin never performed his own hits. "Dream Lover," "Queen Of The Hop," "Things," "Lazy River," "18 Yellow Roses" and many other Darin classics were all conspicuous by their absence. Darin also passed over the more contemporary choices from his albums. While one could not have reasonably expected "Long Line Rider" and its ilk, none of the '66-'67 Atlantic material (save "Carpenter") was performed. Similarly, nothing from the August 1972 **Bobby Darin** Motown LP showed up.

Not that the shows were completely devoid of musical highlights or surprises. Darin and Helen Reddy sang a wonderful duet version of Dylan's "If Not For You," for which Darin returned to his subdued "folk" voice. Darin and Nancy Sinatra heated up the screen in a "mouth-to-mouth" duet on "Light My Fire." And Petula Clark and Dusty Springfield made welcome appearances.

Nine shows had aired when NBC announced cancellation of "The Bobby Darin Show" in April 1973. Four more shows would air that April, then the plug would be pulled. Ratings were unspectacular, though certainly not bottom-barrel.

"Today a network would kill for those kind of numbers," said Ilson. Thicke added, "It was a marginal hit; by today's standards it would certainly be on."

Even before the announcement, people on the set realized things weren't clicking, and there was some tension when new ideas were brought up. Dick Bakalyan recalls that he and Darin favored scrapping the show's format entirely and making it one half music, one half "Carmine and Angie."

"Bobby was anxious to do 'The Neighborhood' for a half hour," said Bakalyan, who has no doubt the sketch could have successfully been expanded. "We had great ideas the producers didn't want to do."

One unusual, bizarre item that Darin did get past Ilson and Chambers' objections was a chess segment, in which he would make chess moves against a computer. It was hardly the stuff of riveting television.

"NBC was violently against it," Ilson recalled. "They thought it was boring. They thought it was kind of an esoteric thing that never belonged, but he wanted to do it. I guess he felt that it would give him a little more dignity, class him up a little bit. We did it until one day the network said 'No more; that's it.'"

A more serious problem re-occurred as the weeks went by: Darin's health declined dramatically. His heart fibrillations increased, the oxygen mask was ever-present, and Darin's energy level was precarious. Looking back sixteen years after the show ended, those working with Darin at the time have differing recollections as to how obvious—and how much a point of controversy—Darin's health was.

Alan Thicke: "It was only during the end that we became aware of it. He didn't like to talk about it. He intimated to me a couple of times that he didn't quite have the energy and he was going to have some tests."

Geoff Edwards: "I'd go into his dressing room to rehearse and he'd be breathing oxygen. He'd have to take the mask off to laugh, then he'd put it right back on. Bobby was really sick, but the producers didn't believe that. They thought it was his temperament. They didn't treat him well."

Dick Bakalyan: "He was fighting with the producers. They thought he was faking it. I went into their office and told them 'This is for real. The man is really sick, guys. Lighten up.'"

Ernest Chambers: "As I recall, it [Darin's health] wasn't a big factor. He was a hard worker, volatile, and all that. I don't recall that it was a factor."

Saul Ilson: "He was quite ill toward the end. I didn't know how serious it was. None of us did at the time. I remember the last couple of shows, it was very sad. He could hardly get through them."

Another old friend, Quitman Dennis, paid Darin a visit on the set. "He just sat there slumped," Dennis recalled. "It was terribly uncomfortable; I couldn't even get a conversation going with an old friend."

Nevertheless, the show-business trouper made it through, though Darin appeared in fewer comedy sketches as the series wound down. Whatever was happening in Darin's dressing room, the public saw the usual finger-snapping, hard-working entertainer.

"I spent an awful lot of time with him on the last three or four shows," Saul Ilson said. "Sometimes, I thought he would never, ever get up to do those shows.

"I remember the second to last show, he was in his dressing room and he was quite ill," said Ilson. "I didn't know what to do, we just blocked around him. The time came for him to go out, and usually he would warm up the audiences; he would talk to them. And in this case, I told him 'You don't have to do that.' But he went out anyway. They started to applaud and the man just grew and came to life. I don't know how he did it."

"He found it somewhere," recalled Bakalyan. "He reached way inside and came up with the smile on his face and the whole deal. No matter how bad he felt, he never laid it on other people."

At one point, an exhausted Darin told Saul Ilson "It's getting tougher and tougher to get up every morning and look in the mirror and become Bobby Darin."

Darin was not about to let the series go down without a bang. The final show would be a spectacular, in-concert show featuring Darin and special guest Peggy Lee.

"He knew the series was over," said Chambers, "and his attitude was 'screw the world, I want to do one show just the way I want to do it.' If he had his druthers, he would have done nothing but sixty minutes of music every week."

Despite the fact that there were no production numbers to be staged, Darin's health and attitude made the taping less than smooth. Unable to even come out for rehearsal, the music was piped into his dressing room. When Darin did go before the cameras, he was displeased with the sound, and irritable with the crew, in one of the few times he lashed out at the people he worked with. (Darin's anger was usually reserved for those "above" him, such as the producers and the network.)

"The crew was very upset with him," Ilson recalled. "We were running long and we got into a situation where we had to take a mandatory break. All we had to do was one more number. One song to go and Bobby could have gone home.

"The only way we could waive the break was to poll every member of the crew, and they all had to agree to it. Somebody in the crew said no, so we had to take the break and he had to hang around. It was sad."

As usual, the public saw nothing of the problems, health or otherwise. What they saw, on April 27, 1973, was the episode generally regarded as the high point of the Darin series.

"The final show of the series was the best," Alan Thicke said. "In hindsight, you wonder if you would have been better had you started at that point."

Peggy Lee performed two songs solo, and joined Darin for five duets. The remainder of the show was prime Darin in the setting he loved—the concert stage. The unedited tape of the entire final performance, which does not include the Peggy Lee numbers but does include songs excised from the broadcast for time reasons, shows that Darin treated the performance not as a television show, but as a nightclub appearance at which cameras just happened to be present.

Throughout, he made no remarks about the series and no reference to a "final show." When, in the middle of "Bridge Over Troubled Water," Darin picked up the wrong harmonica—and did not realize it until a few sour notes had been blown—there was no yelling "cut" and no re-doing the number. Darin simply joked his way out of it after the song was over.

This attitude was most evident in Darin's patented introduction to "If I Were A Carpenter." As he did in his concert act, he relayed the comically twisted Koppelman and Rubin pitch to him. To explain his turn down of "Younger Girl," Darin cracked, "I can't do a song about a younger girl, they'll throw my ass in jail."

Then, acknowledging the fact that you couldn't say "ass" on television in 1973, he remarked "Get out the scissors!" This, combined with the monologue's length and the fact that Darin had already performed "Carpenter" in earlier episodes, probably factored in to the decision not to include this number in the aired version of the show.

The set list for the final taping was typical of late Darin. Though he abandoned any pretense of sympathizing with the hip rock crowd, and also gave up trying to present himself as a (serious or otherwise) songwriter, it's still hard to find critical fault with a set that included songs by Paul Simon, Leadbelly, Tim Hardin, Hank Williams and Bo Diddley.

Among the show's many highlights was Darin's performance of "Bridge Over Troubled Water" in his restrained folk voice. It made one wish that he'd have taken one more crack at the interpretive contemporary style he showed on the '66-'67 LPs. With this song, the Neil Diamond material performed on earlier shows, and a few others, another strong album could have resulted.

Darin took off suit and tie for "Midnight Special," then strapped on a guitar for Hank Williams' "(I Heard That) Lonesome Whistle." Darin could still joke about his hairpiece; patting his head, he told the audience to notice how carefully he put on the guitar.

The encore/finale, while no surprise to anyone who had caught Darin's at-the-piano r&b encores in concert since 1968, was still a delight for those who might have justifiably thought that Darin had repudiated his rock'n'roll roots.

It began with a bit of "You Are My Sunshine," sung Ray Charles-style. Darin then sat down at the piano for "Bo Diddley." Finally, after a long instrumental passage during which the band was introduced and Darin played harmonica, he tore into "Splish Splash," playing rock'n'roll piano, Jerry Lee-style. It was a driving, intense rendition, and Darin was obviously enjoying the release. He showed that look of complete musical contentment, the same look he had when performing "Simple Song Of Freedom" on the Canadian TV special three years earlier.

Fittingly, perhaps surprisingly, the last line Bobby Darin ever sang on his prime-time network TV variety show was "Roll over Beethoven, dig these rhythm and blues." It is impossible to view this number and still contend that Darin did not like rock'n'roll.

Darin went out his way and he went out spectacularly. But that could not obscure the fact that the series failed.

"I think Bobby was a real competitive guy," observed Thicke, "and I think he took any form of failure personally."

"I'm positive he was hurt by it," Ilson said.

Despite the fact that the short-lived series never really got off the ground, those who worked on the show retain fond memories of that time, and of Darin the person. Darin would often join the staff for softball games, or invite them to his home's screening room to watch a movie. During the show's run, he held the first annual Bobby Darin picnic for the crew and their families.

"Remember the character The Godmother?," said Ilson. "Well, Bobby liked to think of himself as The Godfather. After every show, he would choose a restaurant and the staff would join him, so he could hold court. He'd sit at the head of the table. So there was a part of him that loved that role of being in control, of being that Godfather figure."

As opposed to Thicke and Edwards, who looked up to Darin, or Bakalyan, an old friend, producers Saul Ilson and Ernest Chambers have personal recollections about Darin forged only from those twenty weeks of hard, occasionally trying work. The team made television shows with stars like Sinatra, The Smothers Brothers, Carol Channing, Doris Day, Tony Orlando, Pearl Bailey, Leslie Uggams and Danny Kaye. But even after more than a dozen years, both producers retained vivid recollections of Darin's talent and personality.

Ernest Chambers: "I found him a fascinating character. He was a very contradictory character. He was a very tough kid who came up really rough. And he loved great music, drama and literature, and had tremendous respect for the finer things in life. So he was this kind of schizoid character. On the one hand, he was a real back-alley street fighter, a survivor. On the other hand, a guy of tremendous dignity, great aspiration and artistic gifts. On the set, he was extremely courteous with people. He'd lose his temper with us, the bosses. But he would never pick on the little guy. I liked him very much and felt a lot of affection and respect toward him."

Saul Ilson: "If you didn't know him, he came across as a very cocky individual. I got to know him, and there was that side to him. But I got to really like him a lot. We didn't always see eye-to-eye. My philosophy was, when I felt he was wrong, I would tell him. I think he respected me. He wasn't the easiest, but none of them are. We've done a lot of entertainers, a lot of shows. As an entertainer, he was right up there."

Bobby Darin
sings "Happy"
(The Love Theme
from Lady Sings
The Blues)
Music by Michel LeGrand
Lyrics by Smokey Robinson
Produced by Bob Crewe
Four of music's most important personalities combine their talents to create one of the year's most important singles—from one of the year's most important motion pictures. Listen.
Listen to what's happening at Motown.
You'll hear the times change.
©1972 MOTOWN RECORD CORPORATION
MOTOWN

Chapter 26

"The Curtain Falls"

The Final Days

In addition to being back on television, Bobby Darin was also back on the charts—for the first time in four years—as 1973 opened. In late 1972, Darin recorded "Happy," a song written by Michel LeGrand and Smokey Robinson for the film "Lady Sings The Blues."

To work with Darin on this track, Motown brought in producer Bob Crewe, who had produced all of the Four Seasons classics of the 1960s, as well as hits by Mitch Ryder and others. Darin and Crewe had known each other since the early sixties, so the pairing seemed ideal.

"He was terrific, very easy to work with, the consummate professional," Crewe said of Darin. "A lot of people thought he was temperamental. I never did. He wanted things right."

"Happy" was an orchestrated MOR ballad. It was cut in New York with a forty-six-piece orchestra, and, at Darin's insistence, it was recorded live, with no overdubbing. Though Darin had to sing over a powerful arrangement, he came through with his best show-stopper voice. Like the Motown album, the single was aimed at an older audience, but Crewe said Darin had not explicitly set out to pursue the MOR path at Motown.

"I don't think he thought in those terms at that time in his life," Crew said, recalling that Darin was still "very interested in what was going on in the world; very socially involved."

Darin and Crewe thought they had a hit on their hands, but Motown then had little experience with a white MOR record.

"Motown had not had this kind of record ever—mainstream, white, big orchestration," Crewe said. "The promotion department didn't quite know what to do with it. I personally went out on the old proverbial road to help break the record."

"Happy" stalled on the pop charts at #67 after eight weeks. It fared better, though still not spectacularly, on the Easy Listening chart, reaching #32. "We all thought it was going to be bigger," Crewe said. "I think it could have done a lot more if there had been a concentrated effort behind it."

In January 1973, Darin extended his reach into another area he loved—chess. As other entertainers sponsored golf tournaments, Darin saw no reason why he shouldn't be the first celebrity to have his name attached to a chess tournament. The Bobby Darin International Chess Classic was planned for October and described as the "richest tournament ever," with $25,000 at stake.

While Darin was presenting himself as the slick, old-fashioned show-biz pro on his weekly television series, he showed another side during an appearance on "The Midnight Special" in March.

Appearing in a casual jacket and no tie, and accompanied only by his four-piece band (which still included Quitman Dennis and Tommy Amato, along with pianist Bob Rozario and guitarist Terry Kellman), Darin opened his segment with "If I Were A Carpenter."

He then sat down at the piano and began a song curiously absent from his nightclub act for years: "Dream Lover." After a couple of verses, Darin shifted into an uninhibited rendition of "Splish Splash." Here was Darin the rock'n'roll revivalist, and it was a sheer delight.

The band rocked with abandon, while Darin tore into Jerry Lee-style piano breaks and wailing harmonica solos. Terry Kellman took an absolutely blistering electric guitar solo. The studio audience loved Bobby Darin, rock'n'roll bandleader, and Darin appeared much more into this performance than anything he'd done on the TV show. Again, any conception that Darin could not rock, or did not like rock'n'roll, was emphatically, undeniably refuted by this performance. In many respects, it was Bobby Darin at his very best.

In one way, it was a simple matter of Darin knowing his audience: rock'n'roll was what the younger, hipper "Midnight Special" viewers wanted. Darin was aware that there was a revival in interest in fifties rock, and he correctly believed that his contributions should not be forgotten.

"I think it's a kick to have somebody include me in a revival of the oldies and talk about one of the grand old men," he told *Melody Maker*. "It's much nicer to be included as time goes by than to be excluded."

With the TV show cancelled, Darin had some time for personal matters in the spring of 1973. On June 25, Darin and Andrea Yaeger finally made their marriage official, with a ceremony held in Walnut Grove, California. The union didn't last, however, as the couple was divorced by November.

Also in the legal arena, Darin tried to recoup some money from his failed sale of T.M. Music to Commonwealth United Corp., and to get out of his songwriting contract with that firm. That June, Darin filed a breach of contract suit against Commonwealth United, five related firms, and Charles Koppelman, asking for the 1968 contract to be rescinded, and for all T.M. assets to be returned to him.

Darin was also back on the big screen that summer in his first movie in almost four years. He received third billing in the film "Happy Mother's Day...Love, George," also featuring Patricia Neal, Cloris Leachman, and a young Ron Howard. While *Variety* called it Darin's "first good role since 'Captain Newman, M.D.'," his part, and the film itself, was edited heavily.

By the time Darin opened his Hilton engagement on July 18, it was apparent to many of his friends and associates that time was running out. Before his wedding, Darin spent six weeks in the hospital with blood poisoning. The ailment was reported to have resulted from Darin not receiving proper antibiotics prior to having dental work done, an essential precaution against infection for patients who have had heart surgery or rheumatic fever.

Darin's heart was again beating out of rhythm, he was having difficulty breathing, and he began losing weight. Word spread among Darin's friends that the end might be near.

"I got a phone call from a friend who said that Bobby was really ill and probably didn't have long to go," recalled Darin's high school bandmate and Capitol arranger Walter Raim. "I went out to his house in Las Vegas and spent a couple of days with him. He was so thin and weak that he spent his days lying on a raft in his swimming pool all day long."

Darin on stage at The Hilton, July 1973.
(Las Vegas News Bureau)

But at the Hilton, it was a different Darin. "We saw him do an hour-and-a-half of the most fevered, energetic, unbelievable performance," Raim said. "You couldn't believe that he could do it. He was a demon."

Just as he hid his sickness on the TV show, Vegas audiences never knew how ill Bobby Darin was. Reviews noted his usual energetic showmanship. But it was killing him.

"I know why he was doing it," Raim observed. "That's what he loved. One of his great fantasies as a kid was that he was going to die on stage."

Darin played three weeks at the Hilton, took a break for Elvis Presley's engagement there, then returned for ten days in late August. His last performance was on August 26.

Darin was experiencing heart fibrillations again, and in early October he was treated for congestive heart failure. Darin was in bad shape, but he tried to keep reasonably active. Geoff Edwards visited him in the hospital and remembered that Darin had an appointment each day to play chess with a seventy-year-old woman.

Again on December 10, Darin re-entered Cedars of Lebanon Hospital. The two artificial valves he received in the 1971 operation were malfunctioning. A second open-heart surgery was the only option, and on December 19, Darin underwent an eight-hour surgery. Finally, his heart gave way. The four-surgeon team said he was "just too weak to recover."

Bobby Darin died in the early morning of December 20, 1973, at Cedars of Lebanon, at the age of thirty-seven.

Chapter 27
"Something To Remember You By"
Post-Mortem

There was no funeral or memorial service for Bobby Darin. His will directed that his body be donated to medical science, and it was taken to the UCLA medical school for use in research.

Because Darin's death occurred so close to Christmas, combined with the fact that his career was in a down cycle, news and reaction to his passing were somewhat buried. Some Top 40 stations spun "Mack The Knife" as a tribute, and that was it.

His death was front-page news in the *L.A. Times*, where celebrity passings at Cedars are treated as a local story, and in the *New York Post*, which had always regarded Darin's comings and goings as big news.

In an uncharacteristic and mysteriously vengeful move, *Time* magazine felt it had to get in one last shot at Darin while noting his death. A one-paragraph item citing the passing of "Walden Robert Cassotto, the crooner known as Bobby Darin" brought up Darin's old comment about wanting to be a legend by twenty-five. "He never made it" was the *Time* obit's last line. The knock made one wonder what Darin had done to annoy the anonymous *Time* writer. Celebrities much more obnoxious than Darin, not to mention ones who had made far less a contribution to their chosen fields, generally received better treatment in death.

Surprisingly, the publication which noted Darin's death with the most dignity and accuracy was *Rolling Stone*, which ignored Darin while he was alive. In 1969, the publication failed to even notice **Born Walden Robert Cassotto** and

Commitment, albums aimed straight at the magazine's constituency. But the *Rolling Stone* obituary treated Darin's career with the respect and importance it deserved.

Referring to Darin as "the brash and ambitious pop singer" (if one has to slap only two adjectives on Darin, those aren't bad choices), the article was accompanied by a series of photos tracing different phases of Darin's career. Steve Blauner and Dave Gershenson (who acted as Darin's publicist and was once Sandra Dee's manager) were quoted, with Gershenson going public with the story of the dentistry foul-up for the first time. Blauner also dropped the news that Darin had received release from his Motown contract and was planning to record an album with hot producer Richard Perry.

Another fine tribute to Darin came in *Down Beat*, the respected jazz-oriented magazine which had put Darin on its cover in 1960. Writer Michael Cuscuna unabashedly stood up for Darin's critical merits in retort to "cynics of his talent," specifically in the jazz community.

"Darin was an unusually talented singer and a consistent songwriter," Cuscuna wrote. "He phrased beautifully, singing lyrics with the freedom, understanding and sincerity of the best jazz singers. Each record was professionally and tastefully arranged, using top jazz studio musicians and continually illustrating Darin's talent as a sensitive and interpretive singer."

Though Darin's career and his contributions to pop history have been largely overlooked or underestimated since his death, he has not been forgotten. Darin's name has popped up every now and again in musical/entertainment circles in the years following his death.

Motown was first to jump in with the February 1974 release of **Darin 1936-1973**, an album assembled by Bob Crewe.

"Someone from Motown had me go in and cull whatever I could find to put together an album," Crewe recalled. "There wasn't much that was around. I put together an album of what was available."

After recording "Happy" (which made its album debut posthumously), Crewe and Darin had talked about further work together, and two tracks had been recorded in Los Angeles: Darin and Tommy Amato's "Another Song On My Mind" and the Carpenters' hit "I Won't Last A Day Without You."

Both were included on **1936-1973**, along with a few Darin-produced tracks which sounded like demos—covers of "Blue Monday," "The Letter" and Dylan's "Don't Think Twice." Two tracks planned for the scrapped Desert Inn live album also surfaced: "Mack The Knife" and "If I Were A Carpenter."

Darin's name has also been brought up in a couple of noteworthy records. He is among the dead rock stars mentioned in the Righteous Brothers' morbid 1974 hit "Rock'n'Roll Heaven." The song paid a strange kind of tribute to mostly hip sixties icons such as Janis Joplin, Jimi Hendrix, Jim Morrison and Otis Redding, but perhaps in an effort to make the song timely, two 1973 deaths—Darin's and Jim Croce's—were acknowledged.

Frank Sinatra recorded "Mack The Knife" for his 1984 album **L.A. Is My Lady**, adding a lyric verse mentioning previous "Mack" hitmakers: "Satchmo Louis Armstrong, Bobby Darin,... Lady Ella, too," after which the Chairman of the Board modestly claimed "Old Blue Eyes can add nothing new." This action led to further doubts about any rumored feud between Darin and Sinatra. As late as 1991, Sinatra still included "Mack The Knife" in his concert repertoire.

In 1982, Darin took his place alongside numerous other show-biz greats, with the dedication of his star on the Hollywood Walk Of Fame. The ceremony occurred on May 26, 1982, and Darin's star was placed at 1735 North Vine Street, in front of the Palace Theatre, and across the street from Capitol Records.

Darin's star, the 1,749th placed on the Walk Of Fame, was sponsored by Dick Clark, who spoke at the ceremony, and Dave Gershenson. Darin's star lies between those honoring Jim Backus and Roy Rogers.

Nina Cassotto, by then publicly acknowledged as Darin's mother, and Dodd Darin attended the ceremony.

In May 1988, Atlantic Records celebrated its fortieth anniversary with a concert and party held at Madison Square Garden (and telecast live nationally by HBO). A segment of the concert paid tribute to two of Atlantic's biggest, most important stars who had passed away—Otis Redding and Bobby Darin.

The tribute to Darin—a performance of "Mack The Knife" by a 1980s Atlantic star—was originally supposed to have been handled by Bette Midler. When Midler pulled out at the last minute, singers Tim Hauser and Alan Paul—the male half of the Grammy-winning jazz-pop vocal group The Manhattan Transfer—were asked to step in. As Darin fans, they gladly accepted.

"Alan and I were influenced by Darin," Tim Hauser said. "When 'Mack The Knife' came out, I was completely floored by that record. I thought it was one of the best things I had ever heard in my life."

The Transfer incorporates elements of doo-wop and early rock vocalizing into its sound, but Hauser's admiration of Darin came from the standards and jazz standpoint. Hauser hosted a radio show called "Sunday Sings Jazz" on National Public Radio affiliate KCRW, Santa Monica, from 1983-1989, and spun a lot of Darin records.

"I got a lot of requests for Darin," he said. "One of my favorite cuts is 'That's All.' I was into 'legit' singers as a kid. I was into Darin's phrasing. I think he always wanted to be another Sinatra. And it's very evident in listening to **Darin At The Copa**."

Hauser and Paul—who only had time for one rehearsal with concert bandleader Paul Shaffer—pulled off "Mack The Knife" admirably. "We just got up and did it and it worked," Hauser recalled. "We did it from how we had always felt about the song."

Darin's place among rock immortals again came up in deliberations about the Rock'n'Roll Hall Of Fame. During the Hall's fifth annual ballot, in 1989, Darin gained entrance, along with The Who, The Four Seasons, Simon & Garfunkel, The Kinks, The Four Tops, The Platters, and Hank Ballard.

Darin's nomination was greeted with some of the same cynicism about his "rock credentials" that he met during his career. As usual, Dick Clark stood up for Darin in a *Rolling Stone* interview, bluntly saying that those who criticized Darin's induction made him want to throw up. "The man was one of the most multi-talented individuals I ever met," Clark said.

Complaints aside, the results showed that Darin did have the backing of a sizeable number of voters, including long-time fan Robert Hilburn of the *Los Angeles Times*, who had no trouble placing Darin among rock'n'roll greats.

"He started off in rock," Hilburn said. "I liked all the components—folk, country, r&b. As long as he could make interesting records in each of those styles, it didn't bother me which way he was going. He had that kind of questioning attitude and defiance. There was individuality in what he said. To me, that added up to rock'n'roll."

One of the most enjoyable elements of the Rock'n'Roll Hall Of Fame induction ceremonies each year had been the choices of, and speeches by, "inductors" who would offer tributes to the inductees. Bruce Springsteen had paid eloquent tribute to Roy Orbison. Lou Reed memorably toasted Dion. Tributes from John Fogerty, Brian Wilson, Pete Townsend, Phil Spector and other greats brought class to the induction of numerous Hall of Famers.

Choice of inductors had often been made on the basis of the presenter being obviously influenced by, or an outspoken fan of, the artist being celebrated. And inductors were often present or future Hall of Famers themselves. So, in Darin's case, the choice was tough: There really was no seventies or eighties rocker or pop star who had been obviously indebted to Darin.

The 1990 induction ceremony occurred on January 17, 1990 at the Waldorf-Astoria Hotel in New York.

The choice of Darin's old friend, Paul Anka, to make the induction speech was a bit disappointing to those who had hoped that the Hall of Fame recognition would provide the definitive legitimization of Darin in rock circles. Though Anka and Darin were friends and contemporaries, it is extremely doubtful that Anka will ever even be considered for the Hall himself, and his presence only seemed to reinforce the perception that Darin belonged in a decidedly non-rock world.

But, given the dearth of Darin influencees, who would have been an appropriate alternative? Robert Hilburn did suggest one.

"I called the Rock'n'Roll Hall of Fame and recommended that they get Neil Young to induct Darin," Hilburn said, noting Young's praise of Darin in an *L.A. Times* piece. "That would have been a good statement to show that Darin was admired by really critically-acclaimed people.

"To me, Paul Anka's talk was nice," Hilburn continued. "But most people didn't hear the talk. They just heard that

Paul Anka inducted him, so that made it sound even worse for Darin."

It is not known whether the Hall acted on Hilburn's advice. Young did not attend the ceremony.

Another more appropriate choice may have been Dion DiMucci, himself an inductee two years earlier. Dion was chosen by *Rolling Stone* to provide the tribute to Darin in the magazine's own Hall of Fame section, and he eloquently summed up Darin's genius: "Bobby's act at the Copa was just unreal...He was up there doing jazz and folk and rock and anything else he wanted...Singles like 'Splish Splash' were great, because Bobby knew how to rock, but he also knew how to have fun with it."

Dodd Darin accepted the Hall of Fame award and thanked "everyone who voted on my dad's induction. I'm very proud; this is something I'll never forget," he said.

* * * * * * * *

The CD boom of the mid-eighties finally saw some new or different Darin product hit the marketplace. Warner Special Products checked in with **The Ultimate Bobby Darin**, a seventeen-track collection of Darin's pre-Capitol Atco hits. No "second phase" Atlantic hits ("Mame," "Carpenter," *et al*) appeared.

Motown finally got around to releasing its shelved 1971 Darin live album on CD. The 1987 release **Live At The Desert Inn** contained Darin's entire Desert Inn show. The CD's versions of "Mack," "Carpenter" and "Simple Song Of Freedom" are superior to versions Motown had released earlier on the **1936-1973** album (for the first two) or radio-only promotional single (for the latter), which were taken from different shows recorded during the Desert Inn stand.

By the late eighties, Darin's Capitol recordings had been out of print for nearly twenty years, making even hit singles like "You're The Reason I'm Living" and "18 Yellow Roses" very hard to find. After years of sitting on Darin's catalog, the label finally got a Darin collection on the market in 1989, and the Bobby Darin "Capitol Collectors Series" CD was everything a Darin fan and collector could have hoped for.

Expertly compiled by Ron Furmanek and Steve Kolanjian,

the CD presented—in pristine sound—Darin's Capitol single A and B sides. Thus tracks such as "Treat My Baby Good," "As Long As I'm Singing," "When I Get Home," and many others which had never appeared on a Darin LP became available for the first time since their original 45 rpm release. The album presented more of Darin's MOR side than the Warner compilation, but it also more accurately displayed Darin's versatility with folk, country, and folk-rock.

Also in 1989, Capitol released a Wayne Newton "Collectors Series" CD which contained tracks produced by T.M. Music. Again, many of these Darin-involved tracks had been unavailable for decades. The CD booklet revealed publicly, perhaps for the first time, just how active Darin was in Newton's early Capitol tracks.

Atlantic released two "best of" compilations in 1991: **Splish Splash: The Best Of Bobby Darin, Volume One** concentrated on the pop-rock material, while **Mack The Knife: The Best Of Bobby Darin, Volume Two** focused on standards.

At twenty-one tracks each, these releases certainly expanded the amount of Darin's Atco material on the market, but curiously absent were obvious classics such as "Bullmoose" and "That's All." The Top 40 hits "If I Were A Carpenter" and "Lovin' You" were the only representatives of Darin's 1965-1968 association with the label, leaving standouts such as "Mame," "We Didn't Ask To Be Brought Here" and "Talk To The Animals" out in the cold.

Though there was no excuse for the extreme dearth of Darin records on the market in the pre-CD seventies and eighties (both Atlantic and Capitol were negligent), there was not a large demand for more Darin product. Unlike the out-of-print catalogs of some other fifties and sixties stars, most of Darin's older records (his debut LP and Christmas album being exceptions) were not priced sky-high in used record stores or collectors shops, which became the only options for a fan who did not catch all of Darin's discs the first go-round.

Nevertheless, there was enough of a market for "unreleased" Darin that two apparently unauthorized, yet very fascinating discs of rare tracks have been released, indicating that the labels have underestimated Darin's lingering popularity.

The first, **As Long As I'm Singin'**, released on the R'n'D

(Rare'n'Darin) label in 1986, focused mostly on Darin the standard-singer. Live television performances of "Mack The Knife," "Beyond The Sea" and "Clementine" are of only slightly better than bootleg quality. A tape of "Dream Lover" from the "Ed Sullivan Show" is sub-par, sound-wise.

Yet, certain tracks such as "Just In Time," Rodgers & Hammerstein's "This Nearly Was Mine" and Richard Rodgers' "The Sweetest Sounds," apparently taken from radio broadcasts, are of near-studio quality and they are eye-opening, dramatic performances, alone worth the price of the CD. **As Long As** also includes some of the rarer, non-LP Atlantic single sides, such as "Minnie The Moocher," "The Breaking Point" and "Silver Dollar."

The compilers of **Rare Performances** on Tye, a 1990 CD release again weighted heavily toward the MOR Darin, display their utter lack of rock/r&b knowledge by mis-titling Ray Charles' "What'd I Say" as "Alright." Prior to listening, one might also be wary of this effort because the label couldn't even spell Tahoe (Taho) and Vegas (Veges?) correctly.

However, the CD itself is again a treat for those wanting a taste of previously unheard Darin. More than half the collection is a live Darin Lake Tahoe gig from early 1967. Eleven tracks in length, this segment is probably an entire nightclub show, *sans* Darin's celebrity impression routine. Audio appears to be picked up from Darin's microphone, so the music is a little thin, particularly the strings and horns, but it is above-average bootleg quality.

Another four tracks of lesser quality come from radio broadcasts. The CD is rounded out by five numbers from the 1966 British-only **Something Special** live album. On these, both audio quality and Darin's performances are superb. The inclusion of the previously-unreleased-in-America "About A Quarter To Nine" and "I Wish I Were In Love Again" again make the CD a must for the serious Darin aficionado.

These releases not withstanding, for an artist of his stature, Darin remains woefully unrepresented on CD as of 1993, largely due to the lack of activity on the part of Atlantic Records. At the very least, **That's All**, **This Is Darin**, and **Live At The Copa** should be out.

Likewise, only two tracks from Darin's 1968-1968 Atlantic

stint are available on CD as of this writing. This era not only produced the outstanding **Carpenter** LP, but **In A Broadway Bag** and **The Shadow Of Your Smile**, arguably two of the best MOR albums of his career. Darin recorded sixty-three tracks during his "second phase" at the label; at minimum, a "best of" compilation should be available.

CHAPTER 28

"If"

What Might Have Been

The death of any artist always leads to the inevitable "What might have been if he had lived" questions. While answers about any deceased artist are at best speculative, in Darin's case, even speculation is difficult. As he died at so young an age, one must answer that question with another question—Had he lived how long? Three years? Ten years? Twenty years?

Consider the long and strange, but ultimately triumphant comebacks that Darin contemporaries like The Everly Brothers or Dion made well into the eighties. Or consider how completely irrelevant to the music scene the traditional "Las Vegas entertainer" became in the seventies and eighties.

Speculating about Darin is also more difficult because unlike almost all of the pop greats who were lost before their time, Darin was alone in knowing his time was short. By most accounts, Darin's decisions about the directions his career and music were going to take were made with consideration to the fact he would not be around too long.

Consider that in eight years, Darin moved from Broadway show tunes to gentle folk; from four-piece band protest rock back to Vegas and network TV variety. Again, it's speculation, but some of these "phases" might have been explored at more length, or some might never have occurred at all, if Darin himself figured on a long and full life.

Still, the exercise of speculating what might have happened is so inviting that it shouldn't be passed upon after examining Darin's career so closely. First, its quite likely that Bobby Darin would have had another hit. In the early seventies, the public and radio became kinder to acts who had started in the fifties (most of whom The Beatles had swept under the rug).

If the Darin-Richard Perry pairing would have come to fruition, it is highly likely that some measure of commercial success would have resulted. Perry was just a few years ahead of himself when he tried to revive Fats Domino on the charts in 1968, but by 1973, he was the hottest producer in the business, the first "star" producer since Phil Spector. Barbra Streisand, Carly Simon and Ringo Starr had all achieved Top 10 success with Perry-produced releases.

Even though Darin's voice seemed to have lost a little power on the Bob Crewe sessions, its hard to believe that a Perry-Darin combination wouldn't have struck a little gold. Perhaps only six more months would have given us one more Bobby Darin album, and a Top 10 swan song.

To mount his comeback, Darin probably would have had to pick up the songwriting bag he seemed to drop upon the Motown contract. Not that his hit would necessarily have to have been self-written. But part of Darin's "comeback" build up would likely have been how well "Dream Lover," "Splish Splash," "Queen Of The Hop" and "Early In The Morning" stood the test of time—and how, with "Mack The Knife" and subsequent MOR standards, Darin's reputation as a songwriter got buried.

Keep in mind the big comebacks that two Darin contemporaries (and friends), Neil Sedaka and Paul Anka, made within a year of Darin's death. Their reputations as songwriters saved them from teen-idol/oldies relic oblivion. While they would never exactly be embraced by the *Rolling Stone* crowd, neither would they be vilified (*a la* Fabian and Frankie Avalon).

While neither Anka nor Sedaka had gone as far into Sinatra/Vegas territory as Darin, neither were any of their rock'n'roll hits as fondly remembered as Darin's. Therefore, "Hello Dolly" and the like not withstanding, Darin still retained some instant rock'n'roll credibility—Whatever had happened since, the guy once genuinely rocked. With quality material, Darin might have been welcomed back with more open arms—and with a wider audience—than either Anka or Sedaka.

A case could be made that Darin was heading back to rock'n'roll based on the 1973 "Midnight Special" performance. With the rock'n'roll revival in full bloom, Darin probably saw the value of aligning himself with his high quality fifties hits, not only as a singer, but as a songwriter and musician. It's hard to imagine that Darin would have gone all the way in this direction—Richard Nader's oldies shows, etc.—but he went through twenty episodes of his TV show without singing "Dream Lover," then surprised observers by dusting it off on "The Midnight Special." Maybe Darin was about to proudly rescue his rock'n'roll oldies from the closet. With Paul Revere & The Raiders, Sonny & Cher and others moving into the showrooms, Las Vegas was finally ready for fifties-sixties rock'n'roll by the mid-seventies, so Darin would not have had to alter a more rock-oriented repertoire if he continued to play there.

Would Darin have been happy as an oldies act? Probably not in the long term, but in the short term, he may have thrown himself into it with the same verve as he did the protest phase or the TV variety show phase. He might have seen it as a shot to secure his place in the music's history. And if he would have had the chance to do that before he died, he might be more acknowledged in rock circles today.

More than fifteen years after Darin's death, two of his closest musical associates—Bobby Scott and Nik Venet—pondered the question of what would have become of Darin. Neither saw Darin as aging rocker or Vegas remnant.

"Had he lived today," Scott opined, "he would probably be doing what a guy like Tony Bennett is doing: Doing a lot of things that are considered jazzier. And he would bring interpretive things to songs, and a different look at them, so that people would happily pay their money to hear him."

Venet saw Darin as rising to the upper echelons of the non-performing end of the business: "He'd probably have his own film company and his own record company, and he'd be the executive like Francis Ford Coppola."

Probably the safest prediction is that Darin would have continued to keep everyone guessing, just as he did throughout his career. His death deprived the entertainment world of one of its most fascinating professionals, and denied younger audiences the chance to see a performer whose repertoire could encompass nearly a century of music and show business tradition—from vaudeville and the Broadway musical to rock'n'roll and folk songs.

The supreme combination of versatility, professionalism, taste and artistry exhibited by Bobby Darin has been all too rare in the history of American popular music. His eighteen-year body of work, on records, on film, on television, and on the concert stage, is a legacy of quality that few performers of any age can match.

Appendix A

"Some Of These Days"

Chronology

A Summary of Important Dates
in the Life and Career of Bobby Darin

1936

May 14: Walden Robert Cassotto (Bobby Darin) born.

1956

January 17: Bobby Darin and Don Kirshner copyright their first song.

March: Darin makes TV debut on the "Dorsey Brothers' Stage Show," singing "Rock Island Line."

1957

May: Darin records first two Atco Records singles in Nashville.

July 19: Darin appears (with Chuck Berry, Frankie Lymon and Andy Williams) on Alan Freed's TV show, "The Big Beat."

October: Darin appears at the Apollo Theatre.

December 16: Darin makes debut on "American Bandstand," singing "Don't Call My Name," chatting with Dick Clark.

1958

April 10: Darin records "Splish Splash" and "Queen Of The Hop" in New York.

August 4: "Splish Splash" reaches #3 on the *Billboard* chart.

September: Darin's composition, "This Little Girl's Gone Rockin'," written with Mann Curtis, becomes a pop/r&b hit for Ruth Brown.

December 19-24: Darin records tracks for his **That's All** album, including "Mack The Knife."

1959

March 5: Darin records "Dream Lover" in New York.

May 7-17: Darin opens for George Burns at Harrah's, Lake Tahoe.

July: "Dream Lover" hits #2 nationally.

August 7: Darin debuts in Hollywood at The Cloister; George Burns introduces him.

September 25: Darin guests on Jimmy Durante's TV special, singing "Mack The Knife," two duets with Durante.

October 5: "Mack The Knife" hits #1, stays there for 9 weeks.

That's All enters *Billboard*'s LP chart, eventually reaching #7, charting for fifty-two weeks.

Darin appears on CBS' "Hennesey."

October 6: Darin becomes youngest artist ever to headline at The Sands, Las Vegas.

November 17: Darin guests on George Burns' TV special, "The Big Time."

November 29: Darin wins two Grammy Awards. "Mack The Knife" is named Record of the Year, and Darin is chosen as Best New Artist.

November 30: Infamous UPI story appears, quoting Darin as saying he hopes "to surpass Sinatra in everything he's done."

December 2: Darin appears on TV's "This Is Your Life."

December 4: Darin is questioned about payola and his radio appearances on Alan Freed's show by the New York District Attorney. He denies paying Freed.

December 26: *TV Guide* profiles Darin ("Hottest Singer Since Elvis").

1960

January 3: Darin and Connie Francis sing together ("You're The Top") on the "Ed Sullivan Show."

January 11: Darin profiled by Shana Alexander in *Life* magazine.

March: Darin plays Britain with Duane Eddy, Clyde McPhatter; some audience members boo Darin's non-rock 'n' roll material.

March 7: **This Is Darin** enters LP chart; will eventually reach #6.

May 12: Darin featured in a cover story in the jazz magazine *Down Beat* ("Bobby Darin And The Turn From Junk Music").

June: Darin debuts at the Copacabana; records **Darin At The Copa** LP June 15-16.

October 3: Darin sings "Lazy River" on Bob Hope's TV special; duets with Hope and Patti Page on "Mack The Knife."

October 17: **Darin At The Copa** LP enters chart; will eventually reach #9.

December 1: Darin (twenty-four) marries actress Sandra Dee (nineteen) at 3:00 a.m. at Don Kirshner's house.

December: Darin appears (briefly) in his first movie, "Pepe."

1961

January 31: "Bobby Darin And Friends" special airs on NBC.

August 9: "Come September," starring Darin and Dee, opens.

December 16: Dodd Mitchell Darin born at Cedars of Lebanon Hospital, Hollywood.

1962

April 4: "State Fair," starring Darin, Pat Boone, and Ann-Margret, opens.

May: Darin introduces "folk" segment into his act; accompanying himself on guitar on "Cottonfields" at the Copa.

July: Darin signs with Capitol Records.

August 25: "Things" hits #3 on the *Billboard* charts.

September 19: "Pressure Point," starring Darin and Sidney Poitier, opens.

November 29: Darin guests on Bob Hope's TV special with Ethel Merman, Jack Benny.

1963

February: Darin purchases T.M. Music for $500,000.

March 23: "You're The Reason I'm Living" hits #3.

July: Wayne Newton's "Danke Schöen," produced by Darin, enters chart.

October: Darin announces decision to leave nightclub performing to devote more time to T.M. Music, movies;

opens last Vegas performance October 24 at the Flamingo.

December 25: "Captain Newman, M.D." opens.

December 29: Darin guests on Judy Garland's TV show; performs folk material and duets with Garland.

1964

February 24: Academy Awards nominations announced. Darin nominated for Best Supporting Actor for his role in "Captain Newman, M.D."

April 13: Academy Awards ceremony held; Melvyn Douglas wins Best Supporting Actor Award.

October 9: Darin and Janet Leigh star in sixty-minute TV drama "Murder In The First."

1965

March 24: Darin participates in demonstration protesting voting discrimination in Montgomery, Alabama (with Dick Gregory, Harry Belafonte, Peter, Paul & Mary).

August 25: "That Funny Feeling," third and final Darin/Dee film, opens.

1966

January: Darin returns to nightclub performing after two- and-a-half-year hiatus; appears at the Flamingo in Vegas.

March 7: Darin appears on TV's "Run For Your Life" in a pilot for a projected fall series, "It's A Sweet Life" (with Eve Arden).

April: Darin returns to the Copa for the first time since May 1963.

August 12: Sandra Dee sues for divorce, asking for custody of Dodd (five).

August 15: Darin records "If I Were A Carpenter" in Los Angeles.

August 16: Darin appears with Richard Pryor (making his Vegas debut) at the Flamingo, Vegas.

October 8: "If I Were A Carpenter" enters Top 40.

1967

March 2: "Rodgers & Hart Today" airs on ABC, with Darin, Petula Clark, The Supremes, The Mamas & The Papas, Count Basie.

March 7: Sandra Dee awarded a default divorce from Darin.

August 25: Darin performs at Princess Grace's annual Red Cross Gala in Monte Carlo.

October 4: Darin stars in Kraft Music Hall's "Give My Regards To Broadway," playing George M. Cohan.

1968

January 10: Darin hosts Kraft Music Hall's "A Grand Night For Swinging."

May: Darin campaigns for Robert F. Kennedy.

May 30: Darin is first performer at new San Francisco supper club, Mr. D's. Here he receives news that RFK is shot, June 4.

June 8-9: Darin attends RFK memorial service in New York, and funeral at Arlington Cemetery.

July: Darin announces formation of his own label, Direction Records.

August: Commonwealth United Corp. buys Darin's T.M. Music.

October 30: Darin debuts new protest song, "Long Line Rider," at the Cocoanut Grove; changes from tuxedo to denim jacket mid-show.

1969

January 2: Darin returns to the Copacabana with a four-piece rock band; performs "Long Line Rider."

January 31: Darin prohibited from singing "Long Line Rider" on Jackie Gleason TV show; walks off set.

May 13-18: Sporting moustache, Darin plays Troubadour, L.A., with four-piece band; sings songs from Direction LPs and debuts "Simple Song Of Freedom."

July 16: "Bob" Darin appears at Bonanza, Las Vegas, performing protest material and "Simple Song Of Freedom" solo on guitar.

August 2: Tim Hardin's recording of "Simple Song Of Freedom" enters *Billboard* chart; will peak at #50.

October 2: "Bob" Darin makes TV debut; sings "Distractions" on Tom Jones' TV show.
December 2: "Bob" Darin plays Sahara in Las Vegas, turns down requests for "Mack The Knife."

1970

May: Darin takes out newspaper ads denouncing U.S. invasion of Cambodia.
May 12: At an anti-war demonstration, Darin addresses a crowd (of mostly USC students) at City Hall in Los Angeles. He announces "Phone For Peace," urges crowd to phone White House.
May 21: "Bobby" Darin back at the Landmark, Las Vegas; returns "Mack The Knife" into show.
June 17: Darin performs concert at London's Albert Hall.
July 27-31: Darin co-hosts on "The Mike Douglas Show."

1971

February 6: Darin records Desert Inn act for a possible live album.
February 9: Darin enters hospital for heart operation.
April: "Melodie," Darin's first single for Motown, released.
September 1: Darin performs for the first time since heart surgery, opening at Harrah's in Reno.
October 5: Darin appears on TV's "Ironsides."

1972

January 13: Darin sings "Mack The Knife" and "Simple Song Of Freedom" on "Flip Wilson Show."
February 7: Darin returns to Desert Inn, Las Vegas.
February 9: Darin appears on "Night Gallery."
July: Darin performs concert in Central Park.
July 27: "The Bobby Darin Amusement Company" debuts for seven-week run on NBC; Burt Reynolds, George Burns guest on debut.
August: **Bobby Darin** (first Motown LP) released.
November: NBC announces that Darin's TV show will return in January.
"Happy," Darin's last single, released.

1973

January 16: Plans for "Bobby Darin International Chess Classic" announced in New York; to be "richest chess tournament ever."

January 19: "The Bobby Darin Show" debuts on NBC.

April 3: NBC announces cancellation of Darin's show.

April 27: Last episode of Darin's show airs; "concert" show with Peggy Lee.

June 25: Darin marries Andrea Joy Yaeger in Walnut Grove, California.

July 18: Darin opens at the Hilton, Las Vegas. His August 26 performance there will be his last concert.

August: "Happy Mother's Day...Love, George," Darin's final film, opens.

December 11: Darin enters Cedars of Lebanon Hospital, L.A., to repair two artificial heart valves received in a previous operation.

December 20: After eight hours on operating table, Bobby Darin dies at the age of thirty-seven.

1990

January 17: Darin inducted into the Rock 'n' Roll Hall Of Fame.

APPENDIX B

"The Sweetest Sounds"

Discography

Albums

BOBBY DARIN Atco 33-102

(Released July 1958)

Produced by: Herb Abramson & Ahmet Ertegun

Tracks: Splish Splash; Just In Case You Change Your Mind; Pretty Betty; Talk To Me Something; Judy, Don't Be Moody; (Since You're Gone) I Can't Go On; I Found A Million Dollar Baby (In A Five And Ten Cent Store); Wear My Ring; So Mean; Don't Call My Name; Brand New House; Actions Speak Louder Than Words

THAT'S ALL Atco 33-104

(Released March 1959)

Produced by: Ahmet Ertegun, Nesuhi Ertegun, Jerry Wexler

Arrangements by: Richard Wess

Tracks: Mack The Knife; Beyond The Sea; Through A Long And Sleepless Night; Softly As In A Morning Sunrise; She Needs Me; It Ain't Necessarily So; I'll Remember April; That's The Way Love Is; Was There A Call For Me; Some Of These Days; Where Is The One; That's All

Recorded: December 19, 22, 24, 1958

THIS IS DARIN Atco 33-115

(Released January 1960)

Produced by: Ahmet Ertegun & Nesuhi Ertegun

Arrangements by: Richard Wess, Buddy Bregman

Tracks: Clementine; Have You Got Any Castles Baby; Don't Dream Of Anybody But Me; My Gal Sal; Black Coffee; Caravan; Guys And Dolls; Down With Love; Pete Kelly's Blues; All Nite Long; The Gal That Got Away; I Can't Give You Anything But Love

Recorded: May 19-21, 1959

DARIN AT THE COPA Atco 33-122

(Released July 1960)

Produced by: Ahmet Ertegun & Nesuhi Ertegun

Arrangements by: Richard Behrke, Buddy Bregman; Bobby Scott; Richard Wess

Tracks: Swing Low Sweet Chariot/Lonesome Road; Some Of These Days; Mack The Knife; Love For Sale; Clementine; You'd Be So Nice To Come Home To; Dream Lover; Bill Bailey; I Have Dreamed; I Can't Give You Anything But Love; Alright, O.K., You Win; By Myself/ When Your Lover Has Gone; I Got A Woman; That's All

Recorded: June 15-16, 1960

FOR TEENAGERS ONLY Atco SP-1001

(Released September 1960)

Produced by: Ahmet Ertegun & Jerry Wexler

Tracks: I Want You With Me; Keep A Walkin'; You Know How; Somebody To Love; I Ain't Sharin' Sharon; Pity Miss Kitty; That Lucky Old Sun; All The Way Home; You Never Called; A Picture No Artist Could Paint; Hush, Somebody's Calling My Name; Here I'll Stay

THE 25TH DAY OF DECEMBER Atco 33-125

(Released October 1960)

Produced by: Ahmet Ertegun

Arrangements by: Bobby Scott

Tracks: Oh Come All Ye Faithful; Poor Little Jesus; Child Of God; Baby Born Today; Holy Holy Holy; Ave Maria; Go Tell It On The Mountain; While The Shepherds Watched Their Flocks; Jehovah Hallelujah; Mary, Where Is Your Baby; Silent Night; Dona Nobis Pacem; Amen

Recorded: June 19-21, 1960

BOBBY DARIN & JOHNNY MERCER: TWO OF A KIND Atco 33-126

(Released February 1961)

Produced by: Ahmet Ertegun

Arrangements by: Billy May

Tracks: Two Of A Kind; Indiana; Bob White; Ace In The

Hole; East Of The Rockies; If I Had My Druthers; I Ain't Gonna Give Nobody None Of My Jellyroll; Lonesome Polecat; My Cutey's Due At Two-To-Two Today; Medley: Paddlin' Madelin' Home/Row Row Row; Who Takes Care Of The Caretaker's Daughter; Mississippi Mud; Two Of A Kind

Recorded: August 13-22, 1960

LOVE SWINGS Atco 33-134

(Released July 1961)

Produced by: Ahmet Ertegun

Arrangements by: Torrie Zito

Tracks: Long Ago And Far Away; I Didn't Know What Time It Was; How About You; The More I See; It Had To Be You; No Greater Love; In Love In Vain; Just Friends; Something To Remember You By; Skylark; Spring Is Here; I Guess I'll Have To Change My Plan

Recorded: March 21-23, 1961

TWIST WITH BOBBY DARIN Atco 33-138

(Released December 1961)

Produced by: Ahmet Ertegun & Jerry Wexler

Tracks: Bullmoose; Early In The Morning; Mighty Mighty Man; You Know How; Somebody To Love; Multiplication; Irresistible You; Queen Of The Hop; You Must Have Been A Beautiful Baby; Keep A Walkin'; Pity Miss Kitty; I Ain't Sharin' Sharon

BOBBY DARIN SINGS RAY CHARLES Atco 33-140

(Released March 1962)

Produced by: Ahmet Ertegun

Arrangements by: Jimmy Haskell

Tracks: What'd I Say; I Got A Woman; Tell All The World About You; Tell Me How You Feel; My Bonnie; The Right Time; Hallelujah I Love Her So; Leave My Woman Alone; Ain't That Love; Drown In My Own Tears; That's Enough

Recorded: November 7, 8, 10, 14, 1961

THINGS AND OTHER THINGS Atco 33-146

(Released July 1962)

Produced by: Ahmet Ertegun

Tracks: Things; I'll Be There; Lost Love; Look For My True Love; Beachcomber; Now We're One; You're Mine; Oo-Ee-Train; Jailer Bring Me Water; Nature Boy; Theme From "Come September"; Sorrow Tomorrow

OH! LOOK AT ME NOW Capitol 1791

(Released October 1962)

Produced by: Tom Morgan

Arrangements by: Billy May

Tracks: All By Myself; My Buddy; There's A Rainbow 'Round My Shoulder; Roses Of Picardy; You'll Never Know; Blue Skies; Always; You Made Me Love You; A Nightingale Sang In Berkeley Square; I'm Beginning To See The Light; Oh! Look At Me Now; The Party's Over

Recorded: July 1962

YOU'RE THE REASON I'M LIVING Capitol 1866

(Released February 1963)

Produced by: Nik Venet

Arrangements by: Shorty Rogers, Gerald Wilson, Jimmy Haskell

Tracks: Sally Was A Good Old Girl; Be Honest With Me; Oh Lonesome Me; (I Heard That) Lonesome Whistle; It Keeps Right On A-Hurtin'; You're The Reason I'm Living; Please Help Me, I'm Falling; Under Your Spell Again; Here I Am; Who Can I Count On; Now You're Gone; Release Me

Recorded: January, 1963

IT'S YOU OR NO ONE Atco 33-124

(Released June 1963)

Arrangements by: Torrie Zito, Bobby Scott

Tracks: It's You Or No One; I Hadn't Anyone Till You; Not Mine; I Can't Believe That You're In Love With Me; I've Never Been In Love Before; All Or Nothing At All; Only One Little Item; Don't Get Around Much Anymore; How About Me; I'll Be Around; All I Do Is Cry; I Guess I'm

Good For Nothing But The Blues
Recorded: January 25-27, 1960

18 YELLOW ROSES Capitol 1942
(Released July 1963)
Produced by: Nik Venet
Arrangements by: Jack Nitzsche, Bobby Scott, Bert Keyes, Walter Raim
Tracks: 18 Yellow Roses; On Broadway; Ruby Baby; Reverend Mr. Black; End Of The World; Not For Me; Walk Right In; From A Jack To A King; I Will Follow Her; Our Day Will Come; Can't Get Used To Losing You; Rhythm Of The Rain

EARTHY! Capitol 1826
(Released July 1963)
Produced by: Tom Morgan
Arrangements by: Walter Raim
Tracks: Long Time Man; Work Song; La Bamba; I'm On My Way Great God; The Sermon Of Samson; Strange Rain; Why Don't You Swing Down; Everything's Okay; Guantanamera; When Their Mama Is Gone; Fay-O; The Er-i-ee Was A'Rising
Recorded: July, 1962

GOLDEN FOLK HITS Capitol 2007
(Released November 1963)
Produced by: Nik Venet
Arrangements by: Walter Raim
Tracks: Mary Don't You Weep; Where Have All The Flowers Gone?; If I Had A Hammer; Don't Think Twice; Greenback Dollar; Why Daddy Why; Michael Row The Boat Ashore; Abilene; Green, Green; Settle Down (Goin' Down That Highway); Blowin' In The Wind; Train To The Sky

WINNERS Atco 33-167
(Released June 1964)
Produced by: Ahmet Ertegun & Nesuhi Ertegun

Arrangements by: Bobby Scott
Tracks: Milord; Between The Devil And The Deep Blue Sea; Anything Goes; Do Nothin' Till You Hear From Me; Golden Earrings; When Day Is Done; I've Found A New Baby; What A Difference A Day Made; What Can I Say After I Say I'm Sorry; Hard Hearted Hannah; Easy Living; They All Laughed
Recorded: February 1-2, 1960

FROM HELLO DOLLY TO GOODBYE CHARLIE Capitol 2194
(Released November 1964)
Produced by: Jim Economides
Arrangements by: Richard Wess
Tracks: Hello, Dolly!; Call Me Irresponsible; The Days Of Wine And Roses; More; The End Of Never; Charade; Once In A Lifetime (Only Once); Sunday In New York; Where Love Has Gone; Look At Me; Goodbye, Charlie

VENICE BLUE Capitol 2322
(Released May 1965)
Produced by: Steve Douglas
Arrangements by: Richard Wess, Ernie Freeman
Tracks: Venice Blue; I Wanna Be Around; Somewhere; The Good Life; Dear Heart; Softly, As I Leave You; You Just Don't Know; There Ain't No Sweet Gal That's Worth The Salt Of My Tears; Who Can I Turn To?; A Taste Of Honey; In A World Without You

BOBBY DARIN SINGS THE SHADOW OF YOUR SMILE Atlantic 8121
(Released April 1966)
Arrangements by: Richard Wess, Shorty Rogers
Tracks: The Shadow Of Your Smile; The Sweetheart Tree; I Will Wait For You; The Ballad Of Cat Ballou; What's New Pussycat?; Rainin'; Lover Come Back To Me; Cute; After You've Gone; It's Only A Paper Moon; Liza
Recorded: December 1965, March 1966

IN A BROADWAY BAG Atlantic 8126
(Released June 1966)
Arrangements by: Shorty Rogers; Perry Botkin, Jr.
Tracks: Mame; I Believe In You; It's Today; Everybody Has The Right To Be Wrong; Feeling Good; Don't Rain On My Parade; The Other Half Of Me; Once Upon A Time; Try To Remember; I'll Only Miss Her When I Think Of Her; Night Song
Recorded: May 10, 1966

IF I WERE A CARPENTER Atlantic 8135
(Released December 1966)
Produced by: Charles Koppelman & Don Rubin
Arrangements by: Donald Peake, Bob Halley
Tracks: If I Were A Carpenter; Reason To Believe; Sittin' Here Lovin' You; Misty Roses; Until It's Time For You To Go; For Baby; The Girl That Stood Beside Me; Red Balloon; Amy; Don't Make Promises; Daydream
Recorded: August 15, October 31, November 1, 1966

INSIDE OUT Atlantic 8142
(Released May 1967)
Produced by: Charles Koppelman & Don Rubin
Tracks: The Lady Came From Baltimore; Darling Be Home Soon; Bes' Friends; I Am; About You; I Think It's Gonna Rain Today; Whatever Happened To Happy; Black Sheep Boy; Hello Sunshine; Lady Fingers; Back Street Girl
Recorded: March 7, 10, 1967

BOBBY DARIN SINGS DOCTOR DOLITTLE Atlantic 8154
(Released August 1967)
Produced by: Ahmet Ertegun
Arrangements by: Roger Kellaway
Tracks: At The Crossroads; When I Look In Your Eyes; I Think I Like You; Where Are The Words; Something In Your Smile; Fabulous Places; My Friend, The Doctor; Beautiful Things; After Today; Talk To The Animals
Recorded: July 25, 1967

BOBBY DARIN BORN WALDEN ROBERT CASSOTTO Direction 1936
(Released September 1968)
Produced by: Bobby Darin
Arrangements by: Bobby Darin
Tracks: Questions; Jingle Jangle Jungle; The Proper Gander; Bullfrog; Long Line Rider; Change; I Can See The Wind; Sunday; In Memoriam

COMMITMENT Direction 1937
(Released July 1969)
Produced by: Bob Darin
Arrangements by: Bob Darin
Tracks: Me & Mr. Hohner; Sugar-Man; Sausalito (The Governors Song); Song For A Dollar; The Harvest; Distractions (Part 1); Water Color Canvas; Jive; Hey Magic Man; Light Blue

BOBBY DARIN Motown M753L
(Released August 1972)
Produced by: Joe Porter
Arrangements by: Jimmy Haskell, Michael O'Martian
Tracks: Sail Away; I've Already Stayed Too Long; Something In Her Love; Who Turned The World Around; Shipmates in Cheyenne; Let It Be Me; Hard Headed Woman; Average People; I Used To Think It Was Easy; My First Night Alone Without You

DARIN 1936-1973 Motown 813V1
(Released February 1974)
Produced by: Bob Crewe, Bobby Darin, Joe Porter, Jerry Marcellino & Mel Larson
Arrangements by: Charles Fox, Dave Watkins, Bill Holman, Jimmy Haskell, Ben Lanzarone, Art Freeman, Quitman Dennis
Tracks: I Won't Last A Day Without You; Wonderin' Where It's Gonna End; Sail Away; Another Song On My Mind; Happy (Love Theme From "Lady Sings The Blues"); Blue Monday; Don't Think Twice, It's All Right; The Letter; If I Were A Carpenter; Moritat (Mack The Knife)

LIVE AT THE DESERT INN Motown MCD09070MD
(Released 1987)
Produced by: Jerry Marcellino and Mel Larson
Arrangements by: Quitman Dennis
Tracks: Save The Country; Moritat (Mack The Knife); Fire And Rain; Hi-De-Ho (That Old Sweet Roll); Beatles Medley: Hey Jude/Eleanor Rigby/Blackbird/A Day In The Life/Something; (Your Love Keeps Lifting Me) Higher And Higher; I'll Be Your Baby Tonight; Simple Song Of Freedom; Encore Medley: Chain Of Fools/Respect/Splish Splash/Johnny B. Goode
Recorded: February 6, 1971

Compilation Albums

Darin's recordings have appeared in numerous compilation collections, "greatest hits" and otherwise. Most noteworthy are the following:

THE BOBBY DARIN STORY (Atco 33-131, 1961)
THE BEST OF BOBBY DARIN (Capitol 2571, 1966)
THE ULTIMATE BOBBY DARIN (CD) Warner Special Products 9-27606-2, 1986)
THE CAPITOL COLLECTORS SERIES (CD) (Capitol CDP 791625 2, 1989)
SPLISH SPLASH: THE BEST OF BOBBY DARIN: VOLUME ONE (CD) (Atco 91794-2, 1991)
MACK THE KNIFE: THE BEST OF BOBBY DARIN: VOLUME TWO (CD) (Atco 91793-2, 1991)

"Bootlegs"

"Unauthorized" Darin recordings (mostly live cuts) have surfaced on two noteworthy collections:

AS LONG AS I'M SINGIN' (r 'n' d 1, 1986)
RARE PERFORMANCES (Tyrecords TCD-101, 1990)

ATCO RECORDS

Singles

1956

Rock Island Line / Timber	Decca 9-29883
Silly Willy / Blue Eyed Mermaid	Decca 9-29922
Hear Them Bells / The Greatest Builder	Decca 9-30031

1957

Dealer In Dreams / Help Me	Decca 9-30225
I Found A Million Dollar Baby/ Talk To Me Something	Atco 6092
Don't Call My Name / Pretty Betty	Atco 6103

1958

Just In Case You Change Your Mind / So Mean	Atco 6109
Splish Splash / Judy, Don't Be Moody	Atco 6117
Early In The Morning / Now We're One	Atco 6121
Queen Of The Hop / Lost Love	Atco 6127
Mighty Mighty Man / You're Mine	Atco 6128

1959

Plain Jane / While I'm Gone	Atco 6133
Dream Lover / Bullmoose	Atco 6140
Mack The Knife / Was There A Call For Me	Atco 6147

1960

Beyond The Sea / That's The Way Love Is	Atco 6158
Clementine / Tall Story	Atco 6161
Moment Of Love / She's Tanfastic	Atco SPD
Bill Bailey / I'll Be There	Atco 6167
Beachcomber / Autumn Blues	Atco 6173
Artificial Flowers / Somebody To Love	Atco 6179
Christmas Auld Lang Syne / Child Of God	Atco 6183
That's How It Went All Right / (non-Darin flip)	Colpix CP1

1961

Lazy River / Oo-Ee-Train	Atco 6188
Nature Boy / Look For My True Love	Atco 6196
Come September / Walk Back To Me	Atco 6200

You Must Have Been A Beautiful Baby/ Sorrow Tomorrow	Atco 6206
Ave Maria / Oh Come All Ye Faithful	Atco 6211
Irresistible You / Multiplication	Atco 6214

1962

What'd I Say (Part 1) / What'd I Say (Part 2)	Atco 6211
Things / Jailer, Bring Me Water	Atco 6229
If A Man Answers / A True True Love	Capitol 4837
Baby Face / You Know How	Atco 6236
I Found A New Baby / Keep A Walkin'	Atco 6244

1963

You're The Reason I'm Living / Now You're Gone	Capitol 4897
18 Yellow Roses / Not For Me	Capitol 4970
Treat My Baby Good / Down So Long	Capitol 5019
Be Mad Little Girl / Since You've Been Gone	Capitol 5079

1964

I Wonder Who's Kissing Her Now/ As Long As I'm Singing	Capitol 5126
Milord / Golden Earrings	Atco 6297
Swing Low Sweet Chariot / Similau	Atco 6316
The Things In This House / Wait By The Water	Capitol 5257

1965

Hello Dolly! / Goodbye Charlie	Capitol 5359
Venice Blue / In A World Without You	Capitol 5399
When I Get Home / Lonely Road	Capitol 5443
That Funny Feeling / Gyp The Cat	Capitol 5481
Minnie The Moocher / Hard Hearted Hannah	Atco 6334
We Didn't Ask To Be Brought Here/ Funny What Love Can Do	Atlantic 2305

1966

The Breaking Point / Silver Dollar	Atlantic 2317
Mame / Walking In The Shadows Of Love	Atlantic 2329
Who's Afraid Of Virginia Wolf / Merci Cherie	Atlantic 2341
If I Were A Carpenter / Rainin'	Atlantic 2350

In his hit-making
"Carpenter" groove!

BOBBY DARIN

THE LADY CAME FROM BALTIMORE

ATLANTIC #2395

Written by TIM HARDIN
Produced by KOPPELMAN & RUBIN

The Girl That Stood Beside Me/ Reason To Believe	Atlantic 2367

1967

Lovin' You / Amy	Atlantic 2376
The Lady Came From Baltimore / I Am	Atlantic 2395
Darling Be Home Soon / Hello Sunshine	Atlantic 2420
She Knows / Talk To The Animals	Atlantic 2433

1969

Long Line Rider / Change	Direction 350
Me & Mr. Hohner / Song For A Dollar	Direction 351
Jive / Distractions (Part 1)	Direction 352
Baby May / Sweet Reasons	Direction 4001

1970

Maybe We Can Get It Together / Rx-Pyro (Prescription: Fire)	Direction 4002

1971

Melodie / Someday We'll Be Together	Motown 1183

1972

Sail Away / Hard Headed Woman	Motown 1203
Average People / Something In Her Love	Motown 1212
Happy / Something In Her Love	Motown 1217

1974

Mack The Knife (Live) / If I Were A Carpenter (Live)	Motown Y572F

APPENDIX C
"Oh! Look At Me Now"
Bobby Darin On Film

From 1960 through 1973, Bobby Darin appeared in thirteen motion pictures. He held significant roles in eleven of them, and was the star or co-star of six movies. He received an Academy Award nomination for Best Supporting Actor for his role in "Captain Newman, M.D." Below is a list of Darin's movies, in chronological order. Information on opening dates and locations is taken from the *American Film Institute Catalog*.

"PEPE"
Opening: December, 1960
Darin's billing: Cameo
Cast: Cantinflas, Don Dailey, Shirley Jones, Carlos Montalban
Darin's role: himself
Director: George Sidney
Producer: George Sidney

"COME SEPTEMBER"
Opening: August 9, 1961, Minneapolis
Darin's billing: Fourth
Cast: Rock Hudson, Gina Lollobrigida, Sandra Dee, Bobby Darin, Walter Slezak, Joel Grey
Darin's role: Tony
Director: Robert Mulligan
Producer: Robert Arthur

"TOO LATE BLUES"
Opening: January, 1962, Detroit
Darin's billing: First
Cast: Bobby Darin, Stella Stevens, Everett Chambers, Cliff Carnell, Seymour Cassel
Darin's Character: John "Ghost" Wakefield
Director: John Cassavetes
Producer: John Cassavetes

Darin in "Pressure Point."
(United Artists publicity photo)

"STATE FAIR"
Opening: April 4, 1962, Dallas
Darin's billing: Second
Cast: Pat Boone, Bobby Darin, Pamela Tiffin, Ann-Margret, Tom Ewell, Alice Faye
Darin's character: Jerry Dundee
Director: Jose Ferrer
Producer: Charles Brackett

"HELL IS FOR HEROES"
Opening: May 30, 1962, Los Angeles
Darin's billing: Second
Cast: Steve McQueen, Bobby Darin, Fess Parker, Harry Guardino, Bob Newhart, James Coburn
Darin's character: Private Corby
Director: Don Siegel
Producer: Henry Blanke

"PRESSURE POINT"
Opening: September 19, 1962, Los Angeles
Darin's billing: Co-top billing (with Sidney Poitier)
Cast: Sidney Poitier, Bobby Darin, Peter Falk, Carl Benton Reid, Mary Munday
Darin's character: The Patient
Director: Hubert Cornfield
Producer: Stanley Kramer

"IF A MAN ANSWERS"
Opening: October 10, 1962, Chicago
Darin's billing: Co-top billing (with Sandra Dee)
Cast: Sandra Dee, Bobby Darin, Michelle Presle, John Lund, Cesar Romero, Stefanie Powers
Darin's character: Eugene Wright
Director: Henry Levin
Producer: Ross Hunter

"CAPTAIN NEWMAN, M.D."
Opening: December 25, 1963, Los Angeles
Darin's billing: "Co-starring"
Cast: Gregory Peck, Tony Curtis, Bobby Darin, Eddie Albert,

Angie Dickinson, Robert Duvall, Dick Sargent
Darin's character: Corporal Jim Tompkins
Director: David Miller
Producer: Robert Arthur

"THAT FUNNY FEELING"
Opening: August 25, 1965, Los Angeles
Darin's billing: Co-top billing (with Sandra Dee)
Cast: Sandra Dee, Bobby Darin, Donald O'Connor, Nina Talbot, Larry Storch
Darin's character: Tom Milford
Director: Richard Thorpe
Producer: Harry Keller

"GUNFIGHT IN ABILENE"
Opening: May 1967
Darin's billing: First
Cast: Bobby Darin, Emily Banks, Leslie Nielsen, Donelly Rhodes, Don Galloway, Michael Sarrazin
Darin's character: Cal Wayne
Director: William Hale
Producer: Howard Christie

"COP-OUT"
Opening: January 5, 1968, New Orleans (Released in Great Britain with the title "Stranger In The House," July 1967)
Darin's billing: Third
Cast: James Mason, Geraldine Chaplin, Bobby Darin, Paul Bertoya, Ian Ogilvy
Darin's character: Barney Teale
Director: Pierre Rouve
Producer: Dimitri De Grunwald

"THE HAPPY ENDING"
Opening: December 21, 1969, New York
Darin's billing: Seventh (as "Robert Darin")
Cast: Jean Simmons, John Forsythe, Lloyd Bridges, Teresa Wright, Dick Shawn, Nanette Fabray, Robert Darin, Tina Louise

Darin's character: Franco
Director: Richard Brooks
Producer: Richard Brooks

"HAPPY MOTHER'S DAY...LOVE, GEORGE"
Opening: August 1973
Darin's billing: Third
Cast: Patricia Neal, Cloris Leachman, Bobby Darin, Tessa Dahl, Ron Howard
Darin's character: Eddie
Director: Darren McGavin
Producer: Darren McGavin

Darin with singer Helen O'Connell.

Appendix D

"Someone To Watch Over Me"

Television Appearances

This section chronicles Bobby Darin's appearances on television, including his own 1972-73 variety series, his two specials, and his guest appearances on musical, variety and drama programs. The majority of the information on air dates, guests and musical numbers has been gathered from *TV Guide*. The listing of guest appearances, based on information gathered during the author's research, is not intended to be comprehensive.

Bobby Darin's Own Variety Series (1972-73)

"The Bobby Darin Amusement Company" aired as a summer replacement for the "Dean Martin Show" for seven weeks in the summer of 1972. It returned, as "The Bobby Darin Show," for thirteen weeks in early 1973.

The information on songs and guests was gathered from *TV Guide*, with the exceptions of six shows (numbers 9, 11, 14, 16, 18, and 19) which were viewed by the author. It is quite likely that song lists are incomplete for some episodes and that additional songs were performed.

The seven 1972 episodes aired Thursdays at 10:00 p.m. The thirteen 1973 episodes aired Fridays at 10:00 p.m.

Each show closed with Darin performing "Mack The Knife" as the credits rolled.

"The Bobby Darin Amusement Company"

Show #1

Air Date: July 27, 1972

Guests: George Burns, Burt Reynolds, Bobbie Gentry

Darin's Songs: "Can't Take My Eyes Off You," "You Are My Sunshine/Got My Mojo Working," "Medley: Niki Hoeky/ Proud Mary/Polk Salad Annie/Never Ending Song Of Love" (duet with Bobbie Gentry)

Show #2
Air Date: August 3, 1972
Guests: Debbie Reynolds, Charles Nelson Reilly
Darin's Songs: "Charade," "Beyond The Sea," "You And Me Babe" (duet with Debbie Reynolds)

Show #3
Air Date: August 10, 1972
Guests: Pat Paulsen, Joan Rivers, Dusty Springfield
Darin's Songs: "I'll Be Your Baby Tonight," "You've Got A Friend" (duet with Dusty Springfield)

Show #4
Air Date: August 17, 1972
Guests: Donald O'Connor, Dionne Warwick, Phil Ford & Mimi Hines
Darin's Songs: "If I Were A Carpenter," "Spinning Wheel," "Bridge Over Troubled Water" (duet with Dionne Warwick), "I'll Never Fall In Love Again" (duet with Donald O'Connor)

Show #5
Air Date: August 24, 1972
Guests: Carl Reiner, Claudine Longet
Darin's Songs: No information available

Show #6
Air Date: August 31, 1972
Guests: Florence Henderson, Pat Paulsen
Darin's Songs: "That's All," "Artificial Flowers," "Work Song," "Happy Together" (duet with Florence Henderson)

Show #7
Air Date: September 7, 1972
Guests: The Smothers Brothers, Joanie Sommers
Darin's Songs: "Brother Can You Spare A Dime?," "Talk To The Animals," "Side By Side By Side" (with the Smothers Brothers)

"The Bobby Darin Show"

Show #8
Air Date: January 19, 1973
Guests: Burl Ives, Dyan Cannon, Mimi Hines
Darin's Songs: "Once In A Lifetime," "Sweet Caroline," "About A Quarter To Nine," "Happy," "Something" (duet with Dyan Cannon)

Show #9
Air Date: January 26, 1973
Guests: Helen Reddy, David Steinberg
Darin's Songs: "Born Free," "Caravan," "Bridge Over Troubled Water," "I'll Be Your Baby Tonight," "St. Louis Blues," "If Not For You" (duet with Helen Reddy), "Meet Me In St. Louis" (with Helen Reddy and ensemble)

Show #10
Air Date: February 2, 1973
Guests: Flip Wilson, Petula Clark
Darin's Songs: "Hello Young Lovers," "In The Midnight Hour" (duet with Petula Clark)

Show #11
Air Date: February 9, 1973
Guests: Redd Foxx, Nancy Sinatra, Seals & Crofts
Darin's Songs: "Lover Come Back To Me," "King Of The Road," "Lonesome Road," "If," "Light My Fire" (duet with Nancy Sinatra), "My Kind Of Town" (duet with Nancy Sinatra)

Show #12
Air Date: February 16, 1973
Guests: Joey Heatherton, Charles Nelson Reilly, Taj Mahal
Darin's Songs: "Sixteen Tons"

Show #13
Air Date: February 23, 1973
Guests: Cloris Leachman, Tim Conway
Darin's Songs: "Don't Rain On My Parade," "A Nightingale

Sang In Berkeley Square," "Song Sung Blue," "Alone Again (Naturally)," "Never My Love" (duet with Cloris Leachman)

Show #14
Air Date: March 2, 1973
Guests: Elke Sommer, Donald O'Connor
Darin's Songs: "It's Today," "Mame," "Once Upon A Time," "Two Of A Kind" (duet with Donald O'Connor), "Let's Fall In Love" (duet with Elke Sommer), "Give A Little Whistle" (duet with Charlene Wong)

Show #15
Air Date: March 23, 1973
Guests: Sid Caesar, Dusty Springfield, Jackie Joseph, The Persuasions
Darin's Songs: "Some People," "Help Me Make It Through The Night," I Get A Kick Out Of You," "Climb Every Mountain," "Baby I Need Your Lovin'" (duet with Dusty Springfield)

Show #16
Air Date: March 30, 1973
Guests: Andy Griffith, Connie Stevens, Eric Weissberg & Steve Mandel
Darin's Songs: "As Long As I'm Singing," "Brooklyn Roads," "I've Got You Under My Skin," "If I Were A Carpenter," "You've Got A Friend" (duet with Connie Stevens)

Show #17
Air Date: April 6, 1973
Guests: Phyllis Diller, Leslie Uggams, David Bromberg
Darin's Songs: "Charade," "I'll Remember April," "Here's That Rainy Day," "I'll Be Seeing You," "Happy Together" (duet with Leslie Uggams)

Show #18
Air Date: April 13, 1973
Guests: Artie Johnson, Freda Payne, Bread
Darin's Songs: "There's A Rainbow 'Round My Shoulder,"

"Let The Good Times Roll," "Cry Me A River"

Show #19
Air Date: April 20, 1973
Guests: Carol Lawrence, Pat Buttram, Bill Withers
Darin's Songs: "Get Me To The Church On Time," "Shilo," "Guys And Dolls," "Come Rain Or Come Shine," "Volare," "Words" (duet with Carol Lawrence), "There's A Hole In The Bucket" (duet with Carol Lawrence), "It's De-Lovely" (duet with Carol Lawrence), "High Hopes" (duet with Charlene Wong)

Show #20
Air Date: April 27, 1973
Guests: All-music show featuring Bobby Darin and Peggy Lee in concert
Songs Performed By Darin: "For Once In My Life/Once In A Lifetime," "Help Me Make It Through The Night," "Can't Take My Eyes Off You," "Bridge Over Troubled Water," "Midnight Special," "(I Heard That) Lonesome Whistle," "Medley: You Are My Sunshine/Bo Diddley/Splish Splash"
Songs Performed By Darin and Peggy Lee: "Just Friends," "Something To Remember You By," "Skylark," "Spring Is Here," "Long Ago And Far Away"

Bobby Darin's Own TV Specials

"BOBBY DARIN & FRIENDS"
Air Date: January 31, 1961
Host/Star: Bobby Darin
Guests: Joanie Sommers, Bob Hope,
Darin's Songs: "I Got Rhythm/I Got Plenty Of Nothing," "I Have Dreamed," "Some People," "Lucky Pierre," "I've Had It," "I Wish I Were In Love Again" (duet with Joanie Sommers), "Bill Bailey" (with Joanie Sommers and Bob Hope)

"THE DARIN INVASION"
Air Date: (Syndicated; Aired in New York in October 1971)

Host/Star: Bobby Darin
Guests: George Burns, Pat Carroll, Linda Ronstadt, The Poppy Family
Darin's Songs: "Higher And Higher," "Reviewing The Situation," "Hi-De-Ho," "If I Were A Carpenter," "Simple Song Of Freedom"

Darin Guest Appearances On Musical/Variety Programs

"STAGE SHOW" (series episode)
Air Date: March 10, 1956
Host/Star: The Dorsey Brothers
Darin's Songs: "Rock Island Line"

"THE BIG BEAT" (series episode)
Air Date: July 19, 1957
Host/Star: Alan Freed
Guests: Chuck Berry, Frankie Lymon, Andy Williams, Bobby Darin
Darin's Songs: "Talk To Me Something"

"DICK CLARK BEECHNUT SHOW" (series episode)
Air Date: July 19, 1958
Host/Star: Dick Clark
Guests: Bobby Darin, George Hamilton IV, Jack Scott
Darin's Songs: "Splish Splash"

"BOB CROSBY SHOW" (series episode)
Air Date: August 23, 1958
Host/Star: Bob Crosby
Guests: Bobby Darin, Allen & DeWood, The Modernaires
Darin's Songs: "Splish Splash"

"DICK CLARK BEECHNUT SHOW" (series episode)
Air Date: November 1, 1958
Host/Star: Dick Clark
Guests: Bobby Darin, The Everly Brothers, The Olympics, The Elegants

Darin's Songs: "Queen Of The Hop"

"DICK CLARK BEECHNUT SHOW" (series episode)
Air Date: January 10, 1959
Host/Star: Dick Clark
Guests: Bobby Darin, LaVern Baker, Morton Downey, Jr.
Darin's Songs: unknown

"PERRY COMO SHOW" (series episode)
Air Date: April 18, 1959
Host/Star: Perry Como
Guests: Julie London, Bobby Darin, Lou Carter, Art Wall, Jr.
Darin's Songs: unknown

"DICK CLARK BEECHNUT SHOW" (series episode)
Air Date: May 2, 1959
Host/Star: Dick Clark
Guests: Bobby Darin, Connie Francis, Wilbert Harrison, The Crests
Darin's Songs: "Dream Lover"

"ED SULLIVAN SHOW" (series episode)
Air Date: May 31, 1959
Host/Star: Ed Sullivan
Guests: Bobby Darin, Edith Piaf, Wayne & Shuster, Trude Adams, Rex Ramer
Darin's Songs: "Mack The Knife," "Dream Lover"

"DICK CLARK BEECHNUT SHOW" (series episode)
Air Date: August 22, 1959
Host/Star: Dick Clark
Guests: Bobby Darin, Fabian, Dodie Stevens
Darin's Songs: "Mack The Knife," "Dream Lover"

"ED SULLIVAN SHOW" (series episode)
Air Date: September 6, 1959
Host/Star: Ed Sullivan
Guests: Bobby Darin, others

Darin's Songs: "Clementine," "By Myself"

"AN EVENING WITH JIMMY DURANTE" (Special)
Air Date: September 25, 1959
Host/Star: Jimmy Durante
Guests: Lawrence Welk, Sal Mineo, Bobby Darin, Gisele MacKenzie
Darin's Songs: "Mack The Knife," "That's All," "Bill Bailey" (with Durante), "Personality" (with Durante)

"THE LOUIS JOURDAN TIMEX SPECIAL" (Special)
Air Date: November 11, 1959
Host/Star: Louis Jordan
Guests: Jerry Lewis, Abbe Lane, Xavier Cugat, Bobby Darin, Jane Morgan
Darin's Songs: unknown

"GEORGE BURNS IN THE BIG TIME" (Special)
Air Date: November 17, 1959
Host/Star: George Burns
Guests: Jack Benny, Eddie Cantor, George Jessel, Bobby Darin, The Kingston Trio
Darin's Songs: "Clementine," "I Ain't Got Nobody" (with Burns)

"THE BIG PARTY" (series episode)
Air Date: December 3, 1959
Host/Star: Douglas Fairbanks, Jr.
Guests: Danny Thomas, Mike Nichols & Elaine May, Chuck Connors, Bobby Darin, Harold Arlen & Johnny Mercer
Darin's Songs: unknown

"ED SULLIVAN SHOW" (series episode)
Air Date: January 3, 1960
Host/Star: Ed Sullivan
Guests: Bobby Darin, Connie Francis, Edgar Bergen
Darin's Songs: "You're The Top" (with Connie Francis)

"ED SULLIVAN SHOW" (series episode)
Air Date: February 28, 1960

Host/Star: Ed Sullivan
Guests: Bobby Darin, Connie Francis, Della Reese, Senor Wences
Darin's Songs: unknown

"DICK CLARK BEECHNUT SHOW" (series episode)
Air Date: March 19, 1960
Host/Star: Dick Clark
Guests: Bobby Darin, Freddy Cannon, Dorsey Burnette, The Coasters
Darin's Songs: "Beyond The Sea"

"DICK CLARK BEECHNUT SHOW" (series episode)
Air Date: June 11, 1960
Host/Star: Dick Clark
Guests: Bobby Darin, The Skyliners, The Crests
Darin's Songs: "I'll Be There," "Bill Bailey"

"COKE TIME" (Special)
Air Date: June 27, 1960
Host/Star: Pat Boone
Guests: Frankie Avalon, Bobby Darin, Annette Funicello, Paul Anka, Edward Byrnes, Bob Denver, Anita Bryant
Darin's Songs: unknown

"BOB HOPE" (Special)
Air Date: October 3, 1960
Host/Star: Bob Hope
Guests: Patti Page, Bobby Darin, Joan Crawford
Darin's Songs: "Artificial Flowers," "Lazy River," "Two Different Worlds" (with Patti Page), "Medley: Thanks For The Memory/Mack The Knife/Two Sleepy People" (with Bob Hope)

"JACKIE GLEASON" (series episode)
Air Date: March 17, 1961
Host/Star: Jackie Gleason
Guests: Bobby Darin
Darin's Songs: unknown

"AT THIS VERY MOMENT" (Special)
Air Date: April 1, 1962
Host/Star: Burt Lancaster
Guests: Harry Belafonte, Bobby Darin, Jimmy Durante, Connie Francis, Charlton Heston, Bob Hope, Dinah Shore, Lena Horne, The Kingston Trio
Darin's Songs: "Bill Bailey" (with Jimmy Durante)

"ED SULLIVAN SHOW" (series episode)
Air Date: May 6, 1962
Host/Star: Ed Sullivan
Guests: Diahann Carroll, Bobby Darin, The Amazing Ballantine
Darin's Songs: unknown

"MERV GRIFFIN SHOW" (series episode)
Air Date: October 4, 1962
Host/Star: Merv Griffin
Guests: Bobby Darin
Darin's Songs: unknown

"BOB HOPE" (Special)
Air Date: November 29, 1962
Host/Star: Bob Hope
Guests: Ethel Merman, Jack Benny, Bobby Darin
Darin's Songs: "All Of Me"

"JUDY GARLAND SHOW" (series episode)
Air Date: December 29, 1963
Host/Star: Judy Garland
Guests: Bobby Darin, Bob Newhart
Darin's Songs: "I'm On My Way," "Michael Row The Boat Ashore," "Railroad Medley" (with Judy Garland)

"JACK BENNY SHOW" (series episode)
Air Date: January 28, 1964
Host/Star: Jack Benny
Guests: Bobby Darin
Darin's Songs: "As Long As I'm Singing"

"EDIE ADAMS SHOW" (series episode)
Air Date: February 6, 1964
Host/Star: Edie Adams
Guests: Bobby Darin
Darin's Songs: "This Nearly Was Mine," "Kurt Weill Medley: Mack The Knife/Moon-Faced And Starry-Eyed/ Surghaya Johnny/Here I'll Stay/Bilbao Song/Alabama Song" (duet with Edie Adams)

"ANDY WILLIAMS SHOW" (series episode)
Air Date: January 11, 1965
Host/Star: Andy Williams
Guests: Bobby Darin, Vic Damone, Henry Mancini
Darin's Songs: "Once In A Lifetime," "To Be A Performer/ Three Of A Kind/Broadway Medley" (with Andy Williams and Vic Damone), "Leader Of The Pack" (with Vic Damone and The Osmonds

"RED SKELTON SHOW" (series episode)
Air Date: September 21, 1965
Host/Star: Red Skelton
Guests: Bobby Darin, Jackie and Gayle
Darin's Songs: unknown

"STEVE LAWRENCE SHOW" (series episode)
Air Date: October 11, 1965
Host/Star: Steve Lawrence
Darin's Songs: unknown

"ANDY WILLIAMS SHOW" (series episode)
Air Date: January 10, 1966
Host/Star: Andy Williams
Guests: Bobby Darin, Eddie Fisher, Herb Alpert & The Tijuana Brass
Darin's Songs: unknown

"AND DEBBIE MAKES SIX" (Special)
Air Date: January 19, 1967
Host/Star: Debbie Reynolds
Guests: Bobby Darin, Bob Hope, Jim Nabors, Donald

O'Connor, Frank Gorshin
Darin's Songs: unknown

"RODGERS & HART TODAY" (Special)
Air Date: March 2, 1967
Host/Star: none
Guests: Bobby Darin, The Supremes, Petula Clark, The Mamas & The Papas, Count Basie
Darin's Songs: "The Lady Is A Tramp," I Wish I Were In Love Again" (with the Basie Band), "Any Old Place" (with Petula Clark), "Falling In Love With Love" (with The Supremes and the Basie Band), "Mountain Greenery" (with Petula Clark, The Supremes and the Basie Band)

KRAFT MUSIC HALL: "GIVE MY REGARDS TO BROADWAY" (Special)
Air Date: October 4, 1967
Host/Star: Bobby Darin
Guests: Liza Minnelli, Kaye Stevens, Dennis Day, Max Morath, Jack Benny
Darin's Songs: "Yankee Doodle Dandy," "Always Leave 'Em Laughing"

KRAFT MUSIC HALL: "A GRAND NIGHT FOR SWINGING" (Special)
Air Date: January 10, 1968
Host/Star: Bobby Darin
Guests: Bobbie Gentry, Bobby Van, George Kirby
Darin's Songs: "Talk To The Animals," "Mack The Knife," "Drowning In My Tears," "Long Time Movin'" (with Bobbie Gentry), "Nothing Can Stop Us Now" (with Bobbie Gentry and Bobby Van)

"ROWAN & MARTIN'S LAUGH-IN" (series episode)
Air Date: October 14, 1968
Host/Star: Rowan & Martin
Guests: Bobby Darin
Darin's Songs: "Mack The Knife" (parody) (duet with Artie Johnson)

"TOM JONES SHOW" (series episode)
Air Date: October 2, 1969
Host/Star: Tom Jones
Guests: Bob Darin, others
Darin's Songs: "Distractions," "Aquarius/Let The Sunshine In" (with Tom Jones)

"THE MIKE DOUGLAS SHOW" (Daily talk show)
Air Date: Week of July 27, 1970 (July 27-31)
Host/Star: Mike Douglas
Guest Host: Bobby Darin
Darin's Songs: unknown

"FLIP WILSON SHOW" (series episode)
Air Date: September 24, 1970
Host/Star: Flip Wilson
Guests: Bobby Darin, Denise Nichols, Roy Clark
Darin's Songs: "Melodie," "Who Takes Care Of The Caretaker's Daughter" (with Flip Wilson and Roy Clark)

"FLIP WILSON SHOW" (series episode)
Air Date: November 20, 1970
Host/Star: Flip Wilson
Guests: Ella Fitzgerald, Bobby Darin, Charlie Pride
Darin's Songs: "Higher And Higher," "Country-Western Medley" (with Flip Wilson and Charlie Pride)

"FLIP WILSON SHOW" (series episode)
Air Date: December 17, 1970
Host/Star: Flip Wilson
Guests: Bobby Darin, Sid Caesar, B.B. King
Darin's Songs: "Gabriel," "Paddlin' Madelin' Home/Row Row Row" (with Flip Wilson), "Noises In The Street" (with Flip Wilson and Sid Caesar)

"FLIP WILSON SHOW" (series episode)
Air Date: January 21, 1971
Host/Star: Flip Wilson
Guests: Muhammad Ali, Bobby Darin, Lily Tomlin
Darin's Songs: "Lazy River," "If I Were A Carpenter," "Toot

Toot Tootsie" (with Flip Wilson)

"FLIP WILSON SHOW" (series episode)
Air Date: January 13, 1972
Host/Star: Flip Wilson
Guests: Bobby Darin, others
Darin's Songs: "Mack The Knife," "Simple Song Of Freedom," "One Of Those Songs" (with Flip Wilson)

"SONNY & CHER COMEDY HOUR" (series episode)
Air Date: November 10, 1972
Host/Star: Sonny & Cher
Guests: Bobby Darin
Darin's Songs: "Sail Away"

"THE MIDNIGHT SPECIAL" (series episode)
Air Date: March 16, 1973
Host/Star: Paul Anka
Guests: Bobby Darin, Tammy Wynette, George Jones, Doobie Brothers, Fanny, Edwin Hawkins Singers
Darin's Songs: "If I Were A Carpenter," "Medley: Dream Lover/Splish Splash"

Darin Appearances On Drama Programs

"HENNESEY"
Air Date: October 5, 1959
Episode Title: "Hennessey Meets Honeyboy"
Darin's Character: Honeyboy Jones

"DAN RAVEN"
Air Date: September 23, 1960
Episode Title: "The High Cost Of Fame"
Darin's Character: Bobby Darin

"WAGON TRAIN"
Air Date: October 4, 1964
Episode Title: "The John Gillman Story"
Darin's Character: John Gillman

"BOB HOPE CHRYSLER THEATRE"
Air Date: October 9, 1964
Episode Title: "Murder In The First"
Stars: Janet Leigh, Bobby Darin
Darin's Character: Brad Kubec

"RUN FOR YOUR LIFE"
Air Date: March 7, 1966
Episode Title: "Who's Watching The Fleshpot"
Stars: Bobby Darin, Eve Arden
Darin's Character: Mark Shepherd

"DANNY THOMAS SHOW"
Air Date: January 15, 1968
Episode Title: "The Cage"
Stars: Bobby Darin, Dean Stockwell, Sugar Ray Robinson

"IRONSIDES"
Air Date: October 5, 1971
Episode Title: "The Gambling Game"

"CADES COUNTY"
Air Date: November 28, 1971
Episode Title: "A Gun For Billy"
Stars: Bobby Darin, Glenn Ford
Darin's Character: Billy Dobbs

"NIGHT GALLERY"
Air Date: February 9, 1972
Episode Title: "Dead Weight"
Stars: Bobby Darin, Jack Albertson

Darin Guest Appearances On Game Shows

"PASSWORD"
Air Date: January 6, 1963
Host: Allen Ludden
Guests: Bobby Darin, Rosemary Clooney

"I'VE GOT A SECRET"
Air Date: February 17, 1964
Host: Gary Moore
Guests: Bobby Darin

"MATCH GAME"
Air Date: February 1-5, 1965
Host: Gene Rayburn
Guests: Bobby Darin, Joan Fontaine

APPENDIX E

"The Harvest"

Songs Written By Bobby Darin

The following list, derived from an examination of copyright records at the Library Of Congress, consists of songs written or co-written by Bobby Darin. The majority of these compositions are copyrighted under the name Bobby Darin, although some are credited to "Bob Darin," a few others to "Bob Cassotto."

Arranged Alphabetically By Song Title

Song Title	Collaborator	Copyright Date
After School Rock And Roll	Don Kirshner-George M. Shaw	Mar. 21, 1956
All Your Friends Are Here		Apr. 14, 1967
Amy		Jan. 27, 1967
Another Song On My Mind	Tommy Amato	Mar. 11, 1974
As Long As I'm Singing		Aug. 28, 1962
Autumn Blues		Aug. 9, 1960
Baby I Miss You		Sep. 15, 1965
Baby May		Dec. 29, 1969
Bad Girl		Apr. 4, 1963
Ballet Dance		Apr. 14, 1967
Barb'ry Ann	Claire Kaufman	Apr. 2, 1958
Be Mad Little Girl		Sep. 18, 1963
Beachcomber		Aug. 9, 1960
Bi-aza-ku-sasa	Rudi Trailor	July 11, 1958
Boss Barracuda	Terry Melcher	May 22, 1964
Brand New House	Woody Harris	July 30, 1958
Broken Up Inside	David Hill	Mar. 17, 1960
Bubble Gum Pop	Don Kirshner	Jan. 17, 1956
Bullfrog		Sep. 10, 1968
Bullmoose		Apr. 9, 1958
By My Side	Don Kirshner	July 22, 1957
Can't You See Me		Apr. 14, 1967

Song Title	Collaborator	Copyright Date
Casey, Wake Up!		Mar. 12, 1964
Change		Aug. 9, 1968
Chantal's Theme		June 21, 1962
Coffee Perkin' Time		Oct. 7, 1964
Come		Apr. 14, 1967
Come September (Instrumental Theme)		June 1, 1961
Come September (with added lyric)	Cy Coben	Nov. 2, 1966
Comin' Down With A Heartache	Rudy Clark	Apr. 15, 1963
Daydreamer	Jimmy Boyd	May 1, 1962
Dealer In Dreams	Don Kirshner	Apr. 24, 1956
Delia	Don Kirshner	Apr. 3, 1957
Distractions		June 6, 1969
Don't Call My Name	Don Kirshner	Oct. 21, 1957
Down So Long		July 25, 1963
Dream Baby	Arthur Resnick	Sep. 25, 1963
Dream Lover		Apr. 9, 1959
Early In The Morning	Woody Harris	Jun. 9, 1958
Eighteen Yellow Roses		Apr. 22, 1963
Elizabeth		Dec. 13, 1963
The End Of Never	Francine Forest	July 31, 1964
Everywhere I Go		Jan. 18, 1968
Face To Face		Apr. 14, 1967
The Feelin'	David Hill	Mar. 17, 1960
Fourteen Pairs Of Shoes	Russell Alquist	Apr. 9, 1965
Freedom To Love	Arthur Resnick	Feb. 12, 1964
Funny What Love Can Do		Sep. 15, 1965
Gone		Dec. 26, 1962
The Great Society		Feb. 3, 1965
The Greatest Lover In The World		Apr. 14, 1967
Gyp The Cat	Don Wolf	July 29, 1965
The Harvest		June 6, 1969
Hello Sunshine		Apr. 7, 1967
Hey Magic Man		June 6, 1969

Song Title	Collaborator	Copyright Date
Hot Rod U.S.A.	Terry Melcher	Apr. 13, 1964
I Am		Apr. 7, 1967
I Can See The Wind		Aug. 9, 1968
I Can't Believe A Word You Say	Rudy Clark	Apr. 15, 1963
I Want To Spend Christ -mas With Elvis	Don Kirshner	Nov. 29, 1956
I Got My Own Thing Going	Rudy Clark	July 29, 1965
I'll Be There		Oct. 20, 1959
I'm Gonna Love You		Jan. 18, 1968
If You Love Him		Mar. 12,1964
If A Man Answers		June 21, 1962
In Memoriam		Aug. 9, 1968
It's Him I Wanna Go With Mama	Arthur Resnick	Apr. 20, 1964
It's What's Happening Baby		June 14, 1965
Jailer, Bring Me Water		June 12, 1962
Jingle Jangle Jungle		Aug. 9, 1968
Jive		June 6, 1969
Keep A-Movin' Mama	Don Kirshner	Feb. 11, 1957
Light Blue		June 6, 1969
The Lively Set		Mar. 23, 1964
Long Time Movin'		Jan. 18, 1968
Long Line Rider		Aug. 9, 1968
Look At Me	Randy Newman	June 25, 1964
Look For My True Love		June 24, 1960
Los Angeles	Francine Forest	Aug. 4, 1966
Lost Love	Don Kirshner	Aug. 6, 1958
Love Me Right	Don Kirshner	July 23, 1957
Made In The Shade		May 1, 1962
Maybe We Can Get It Together		Mar. 2, 1970
Me & Mr. Hohner		May 12, 1969
Mighty Mighty Man		Oct. 24, 1958
Moment Of Love		Oct. 8, 1959
Monkey	Rudy Clark	June 18, 1963
Mountain Of Love	Don Kirshner	Feb. 7, 1958

Song Title	Collaborator	Copyright Date
Multiplication		Aug. 15, 1961
My First Real Love	Don Kirshner-George M. Shaw	Feb. 15, 1956
My Dog Got A Tag On Her		Nov. 19, 1964
My Mom	Terry Melcher	Aug. 22, 1964
Not For Me		Apr. 22, 1963
Now We're One		June 9, 1958
O.K. Girl (aka "O.K. Boy")	Russell Alquist	Apr. 26, 1965
Oo-ee Train		Feb. 2, 1962
Peck-A-Cheek	Cy Coben	Mar. 17, 1958
Prescription Fire (Rx-Pyro)		Mar. 2, 1970
Pretty Betty	Don Kirshner	Oct. 21, 1957
Prison Of Your Love		Jan. 18, 1968
The Proper Gander		Aug. 9, 1968
Queen Of The Hop	Woody Harris	Aug. 29, 1958
Questions		Aug. 9, 1968
Rainin'		Apr. 7, 1966
Real Love	Woody Harris	June 11, 1958
The Rest Of My Life		Apr. 2, 1958
Revolution Of The Goats	Norman Strass-berg	Aug. 6, 1958
Rock Pile	Don Kirshner-George M. Shaw	Mar. 14, 1956
The Rogers Cha Cha	Don Kirshner	Feb. 6, 1956
Run, Little Rabbit		Apr. 13, 1964
Sausalito (The Governors Song)		June 6, 1969
Save A Sinking Heart	Al Byron	Jan. 26, 1961
School's Out	Woody Harris	June 11, 1958
She's Tanfastic		May 6, 1960
Shirl Girl	Rudy Clark	Sep. 25, 1963
Silly Willy	Don Kirshner-George M. Shaw	Mar. 14, 1956
Simple Song Of Freedom		June 12, 1969
So Mean	Don Kirshner	July 3, 1957

Song Title	Collaborator	Copyright Date
Somebody To Love		Oct. 20, 1959
Something In Her Love	Tommy Amato	Oct. 31, 1972
Somewhere Out There		Apr. 14, 1967
Song For A Dollar		May 12, 1969
Soul City		Aug. 7, 1964
Splish Splash	Jean Murray	June 6, 1958
Sugar Man		Dec. 5, 1966
Sugar Man		June 6, 1969
Summertime Symphony		June 22, 1959
Sunday		Aug. 9, 1968
Sweet Reasons		Dec. 29, 1969
Talk To Me Something	Don Kirshner	Feb. 14, 1957
That Funny Feeling		Oct. 12, 1964
That's The Way Love Is		Apr. 2, 1958
Things		Sep. 8, 1961
The Things In This House		Aug. 26, 1964
This Little Girl's Gone Rockin'	Mann Curtis	Apr. 25, 1958
Three To Get Ready		Mar. 23, 1961
Timber	Don Kirshner-George M. Shaw	Mar. 12, 1956
Treat My Baby Good		July 25, 1963
A True True Love		Aug. 28, 1962
Turbine Montage		Oct. 7, 1964
Turned Down Theme		Mar. 2, 1964
Two Of A Kind	Johnny Mercer	Dec. 8, 1960
Two Tickets		Oct. 12, 1964
Wait A Minute	Don Kirshner	Jan. 12, 1961
Wait By The Water		Aug. 26, 1964
Walk Back To Me		July 11, 1961
Water Color Canvas		June 6, 1969
We Didn't Ask To Be Brought Here		Sep. 15, 1965
Wear My Ring	Don Kirshner	Apr. 30, 1957
Wendy		Dec. 3, 1964
Wha'ch You Mean	Rudi Trailor	July 11, 1958
When I Get Home	Russell Alquist	May 12, 1965
While I'm Gone		Feb. 18, 1963

Song Title	Collaborator	Copyright Date
Whomp Be Omp Bomp		June 13, 1958
Why Oh You	Don Kirshner	Feb. 21, 1957
Wilco Jingle	Don Kirshner	Feb. 6, 1956
A World Without You	Rudy Clark	Mar. 22, 1965
You Just Don't Know		Mar. 22, 1965
You Know How		Oct. 8, 1959
You Got Me		Apr. 14, 1967
You're The Reason I'm Living		Dec. 26, 1962
You're Mine		Oct. 24, 1958
Zoom-A-Roo	Arthur Resnick	Mar. 9, 1964

Appendix F

"Everybody Has The Right"
Covers

Below is a partial listing of songs written (or co-written) by Bobby Darin which have been recorded by other artists.

Song	**Artist**
Brand New House	Otis Spann
By My Side	Davy Hill
Come September	John Severson
Delia	Bobby Short
Dream Baby	Wayne Newton
Dream Lover	Susie Brading
	Glen Campbell & Tanya Tucker
	Billy "Crash" Craddock
	Dion
	Peter McCann
	Don McLean
	Johnny Nash
	Rick Nelson
	Tony Orlando
	Paris Sisters
Early In The Morning	Mac Curtis
	Buddy Holly
	Tommy Roe
Eighteen Yellow Roses	C.L. Goodson
Hot Rod USA	Rip Chords
I Want To Spend Christmas with Elvis	Little Lambsie Penn
I'll Be There	Gerry & The Pacemakers
	Clint Holmes
Love Me Right	LaVern Baker
Multiplication	Johnny Rivers
	Showaddywaddy
My First Real Love	Connie Francis
My Mom	Osmond Brothers
Now We're One	Buddy Holly
Queen Of The Hop	Dave Edmunds

Song	Artist
Real Love	Jaye Sisters
School's Out	Jaye Sisters
Shirl Girl	Wayne Newton
Simple Song Of Freedom	Tim Hardin
	Mystic Moods Orchestra
Splish Splash	Johnny Cash
	Charlie Drake
	Loggins & Messina
	Barbra Streisand
	Wonderland Singers & Orchestra
Sweat Reasons	Judy Mayhan
Things	Buddy Alan
	Ronnie Dove
	Dean Martin & Nancy Sinatra
	Anne Murray
This Little Girl's Gone Rockin'	Ruth Brown
Wait A Minute	Coasters
Wear My Ring	Gene Vincent
When I Get Home	Searchers
You Just Don't Know	Mary K. Miller
	Wayne Newton
You're The Reason I'm Living	Price Mitchell
	Lamar Morris

APPENDIX G

"Release Me"

Unreleased Tracks

This list consists of never-released tracks recorded by Bobby Darin during his stints at Atco (1957-62) and Atlantic (1965-67). Information was gathered from *Atlantic Records: A Discography* by Michel Ruppli. "Session Notes" are included when the unreleased track was recorded at the same session as a released Darin single or LP.

Although additional unreleased material is reported to exist from Darin's Capitol and Motown periods, specific information regarding unreleased tracks recorded for these labels was unavailable.

Song Title	Session Date	Session Notes
Some Of These Days (early version)	10/29/58	----------------------
Didn't It Feel Good	12/05/58	----------------------
The Breeze And I	05/19/59	**This Is Darin** LP
Sunday Kind Of Love	05/20/59	**This Is Darin** LP
Since My Love Was Gone	05/20/59	**This Is Darin** LP
The Lamp Is Low	05/21/59	**This Is Darin** LP
A Game Of Poker	02/01/60	**Winners** LP
I Got A Woman	02/02/60	**Winners** LP
Birth Of The Blues (Live)	06/15-16/60	**Darin At Copa** LP
My Funny Valentine (Live)	06/15-16/60	**Darin At Copa** LP
Splish Splash (Live)	06/15-16/60	**Darin At Copa** LP
Lily Of Laguna	08/14/60	**Johnny Mercer** LP
Back In Your Own Backyard	08/17/60	**Johnny Mercer** LP
Cecilia	08/22/60	**Johnny Mercer** LP
Bobby's Blues	03/25/61	----------------------
Special Someone	06/06/61	Come September (45)
Teenage Theme	06/06/61	Come September (45)
Movin' On	06/06/61	Come September (45)

Sweet Memories Of You	08/19/65	We Didn't Ask...(45)
Ain't That A Bunch Of Nonsense	08/19/65	We Didn't Ask...(45)
Baby I Miss You So	08/23/65	----------------------
Ace In The Hole	12/13/65	**Shadow Of...** LP
The Best Is Yet To Come	12/13/65	**Shadow Of...** LP
The Sheik Of Araby	12/14/65	**Shadow Of...** LP
This Could Be The Start Of Something	12/14/65	**Shadow Of...** LP
I Got Plenty Of Nothing	12/15/65	**Shadow Of...** LP
Baby Won't You Please Come Home	12/15/65	**Shadow Of...** LP
Weeping Willow	02/04/66	"Rainin' " (45)
Strangers In The Night	03/23/66	**Shadow Of...** LP
True Love Are Blessing	04/21/66	----------------------
Merry Go Round In The Rain	06/21/66	----------------------
LA	08/01/66	Unreleased LP
I Can Live On Love	08/01/66	Unreleased LP
Manhattan In My Heart	08/01/66	Unreleased LP
Lulu's Back In Town	08/01/66	Unreleased LP
Mountain Greenery	08/01/66	Unreleased LP
For You	08/01/66	Unreleased LP
What Now My Love	08/01/66	Unreleased LP
It's Magic	08/01/66	Unreleased LP
Danke Schöen	08/01/66	Unreleased LP
My Own True Love	08/01/66	Unreleased LP
On A Clear Day	08/01/66	Unreleased LP
Quarter To Nine	08/01/66	Unreleased LP
Seventeen	08/01/66	Unreleased LP
Funny What Love Can Do (alt.version)	11/01/66	**Carpenter** LP
Good Day Sunshine	11/01/66	**Carpenter** LP
Younger Girl	11/01/66	**Carpenter** LP
Saginaw Michigan	03/28/67	----------------------

Biggest Night Of Her Life	07/19/67	"She Knows" (45)
My Baby Needs Me	11/13/67	----------------------
All Strung Out	11/13/67	----------------------
Tupelo Mississippi Flash	11/18/67	----------------------
Natural Soul Loving Big City Countryfied Man	11/19/67	----------------------
When I'm Gone	11/19/67	----------------------

Darin at The Landmark Hotel, September 1970.
(Las Vegas News Bureau)

APPENDIX H

"More"

Songs Performed Live, But Not Recorded By Bobby Darin

The following is a partial list of songs which were never recorded by Bobby Darin, but which he performed live. The list includes numbers from his concert and TV appearances; duets are not included. Songs included on the "official" live albums **Darin At The Copa**, **Live At The Desert Inn**, and the British **Something Special** are not listed here, even if Darin never recorded a studio version. However, songs appearing on the "bootleg" live compilations **As Long As I'm Singin** and **Rare Performances** are listed. The list clearly exhibits the wide range of popular music embraced by Bobby Darin.

After I've Gone Away
All Of Me
Alone Again (Naturally)
Always Leave 'Em Laughing
Bo Diddley
Boil That Cabbage Down
Born Free
Bridge Over Troubled Water
Brooklyn Roads
Brother, Can You Spare A Dime?
Can't Take My Eyes Off You
Climb Every Mountain
Come A Rum Rum
Come Rain Or Come Shine
Cottonfields
Cry Me A River
The Curtain Falls
Danny Boy
Don't Worry 'Bout Me
The Erie Canal
Everybody's Talkin'
For Once In My Life
Gabriel
Get Me To The Church On Time
Got My Mojo Working
Hello Young Lovers
Help Me Make It Through The Night
Here's That Rainy Day
He's Got The Whole World In His Hands
I Ain't Nobody
I Got A Kick Out Of You
I Got Plenty Of Nothing
I Got Rhythm
If
I'll Be Seeing You
I'm A Fool To Want You
I've Got The World On A String
I've Got You Under My Skin
Just In Time
King Of The Road
The Lady Is A Tramp
Lady Madonna

Let The Good Times Roll
Meditation
Midnight Special
My Funny Valentine
My Kind Of Town
My Tears
One For My Baby
One Of Those Songs
Pass Me By
Reviewing The Situation
Shilo
Short Fat Fannie
Sing Sing Song
(Sittin' On) The Dock Of The Bay
Sixteen Tons
Some People
Someone To Watch Over Me
Song Sung Blue
Spinning Wheel
Spirit In The Dark
St. Louis Blues
Sweet Caroline
The Sweetest Sounds
This Could Be The Start Of Something Big
This Is The Life
This Nearly Was Mine
Too Good To Be True
Toot Toot Tootsie
Travel On
Try A Little Tenderness
Volare
When The Saints Go Marching In
When You Wore A Tulip
Yankee Doodle Dandy
Yesterday
You Are My Sunshine
You're Nobody Till Somebody Loves You
You've Lost That Lovin' Feelin'

APPENDIX I

"As Long As I'm Singing"

Bobby Darin's "Favorite" Songwriters

This section lists the songwriters whose compositions were most frequently recorded by Bobby Darin. The list is compiled only from Darin's recorded output. Songs performed live or on television are not included. Of course, Darin himself is not counted.

For the purpose of this list, songs from three of Darin's "theme" albums revolving around specific songwriters are not included: **Two Of A Kind** (with Johnny Mercer), **Bobby Darin Sings Ray Charles**, and **Dr. Dolittle** (featuring Leslie Bricusse's entire score). Other Mercer, Charles and Bricusse songs recorded by Darin elsewhere were counted.

Here are the outside songwriters and their songs which Bobby Darin turned to most often:

1) JOHNNY MERCER (eight songs)
   You Must Have Been A Beautiful Baby (Mercer-Warren)
   Have You Got Any Castles Baby (Mercer-Whiting)
   Skylark (Mercer-Carmichael)
   Not Mine (Mercer-Schertzinger)
   The Days Of Wine And Roses (Mercer-Mancini)
   Charade (Mercer-Mancini)
   I Wanna Be Around (Mercer-Vimmerstedt)
   The Sweetheart Tree (Mercer-Mancini)

2) TIM HARDIN (seven songs)
   If I Were A Carpenter
   Reason To Believe
   Misty Roses
   Red Balloon
   Don't Make Promises
   Lady Came From Baltimore
   Black Sheep Boy

3) SAMMY CAHN (six songs)
   Pete Kelly's Blues (Cahn-Heindorf)

It's You Or No One (Cahn-Styne)
Call Me Irresponsible (Cahn-Van Heusen)
Where Love Has Gone (Cahn-Van Heusen)
Everybody Has The Right To Be Wrong (Cahn-Van Heusen)
I'll Only Miss Her When I Think Of Her (Cahn-Van Heusen)

4) DOC POMUS & MORT SHUMAN (five songs)
Plain Jane
(Since You're Gone) I Can't Go On
I Ain't Sharin' Sharon
Sorrow Tomorrow
Can't Get Used To Losing You

5) IRA GERSHWIN (five songs)
The Gal That Got Away (I. Gershwin-H. Arlen)
It Ain't Necessarily So (I. Gershwin-G. Gershwin)
Long Ago And Far Away (I. Gershwin-J. Kern)
They All Laughed (I. Gershwin-G. Gershwin)
Liza (I. Gershwin-G. Kahn)

6) IRVING BERLIN (four songs)
All By Myself
Blue Skies
Always
How About Me

7) JOHN SEBASTIAN (four songs)
Daydream
Lovin' You
Darling Be Home Soon
Bes' Friends

8) GARY BONNER & ALAN GORDON (four songs)
About You
Whatever Happened To Happy
Lady Fingers
She Knows

9) DUKE ELLINGTON (four songs)
Caravan (Ellington-Mills-Tizol)

I'm Beginning To See The Light (Ellington-James-Hodges-George)
Don't Get Around Much Anymore (Ellington-Russell)
Do Nothin' Till You Hear From Me (Ellington-Russell)

10) HENRY MANCINI (four songs)
The Sweetheart Tree (Mancini-Mercer)
Dear Heart (Mancini-Livingston-Evans)
The Days Of Wine And Roses (Mancini-Mercer)
Charade (Mancini-Mercer)

11) RICHARD RODGERS (four songs)
I Didn't Know What Time It Was (Rodgers-Hart)
Spring Is Here (Rodgers-Hart)
I Have Dreamed (Rodgers-Hammerstein)
This Isn't Heaven

12) ANDRE PREVIN (four songs)
Tall Story (Previn-Langdon-Manne)
That's How It Went All Right (Previn-Langdon)
Goodbye, Charlie (Previn-Langdon)
Once Upon A Time (Previn-Comden)

Four Darin songs co-written by Jimmy Van Heusen are noted under Sammy Cahn.

Darin recorded three songs by each of the following writers:
Harold Arlen
Leslie Bricusse & Anthony Newley
Howard Dietz & Arthur Schwartz
Bob Dylan
George Gershwin
Jerry Herman
Libby Holden
Frank Loesser
Cole Porter
Jule Styne

(Las Vegas News Bureau)

APPENDIX J

Bibliography

The following list consists of books and articles consulted during research for this book. Numerous concert and movie reviews, mostly from *Billboard*, *Variety*, and the *New York Times*, are not listed.

Books

Bianco, David. *Heat Wave: The Motown Fact Book*. Ann Arbor, MI: Popular Culture, Ink., 1988.

Bronson, Fred. *The Billboard Book Of Number One Hits*. New York: Billboard Publications, Inc., 1985.

Brooks, Tim and Earle Marsh. *The Complete Directory To Prime Time Network TV Shows 1946-Present*. New York: Ballantine Books, 1981.

DiMucci, Dion and Davin Seay. *The Wanderer: Dion's Story*. New York: Beech Tree Books, 1988.

DiOrio, Al. *Borrowed Time: The 37 Years Of Bobby Darin*. Philadelphia: Running Press, 1986.

Francis, Connie. *Who's Sorry Now?* New York: St. Martin's Press, Inc., 1984.

Gillett, Charlie. *Making Tracks: Atlantic Records And The Growth Of A Multi-Billion-Dollar Industry*. London: W.H. Allen, 1975.

Kaplan, Mike (editor). *Variety International Showbusiness Reference*. New York: Garland Publishing Inc., 1981.

Katz, Ephraim. *The Film Encyclopedia*. New York: Thomas Y. Crowell Publishers, 1979.

Lee, Peggy. *Miss Peggy Lee: An Autobiography*. New York: Donald I. Fine, Inc., 1989.

Munden, Kenneth W. (executive editor). *The American Film Institute Catalog Of Motion Pictures Produced In The United States*. New York: R.R. Bowker, 1971

Nash, Jay Robert and Stanley Ralph Ross. *The Motion Picture Guide*. Chicago: Cinebooks, 1985.

Newfield, Jack. *Robert Kennedy: A Memoir*. New York: E.P Dutton & Co., Inc., 1969.

Newton, Wayne with Dick Maurice. *Once Before I Go*. New

York: William Morrow and Company, Inc., 1989.

Parish, James Robert. *Actors Television Credits 1950-1972.* Metuchen, NJ: The Scarecrow Press, Inc., 1973

Ribowsky, Mark. *He's A Rebel.* New York: E.P. Dutton, 1989

Rice, Joe (compiled by). *The Guinness Book Of British Hit Singles.* Enfield: Guinness Superlatives, 1979.

Ruppli, Michel (compiled by). *Atlantic Records: A Discography.* Westport, CT: Greenwood Press, 1979

Sedaka, Neil. *Laughter In The Rain: My Own Story.* New York: Putman's, 1982.

Shale, Richard. *Academy Awards.* New York: Frederick Ungar Publishing Co., 1978.

Shore, Michael with Dick Clark. *The History Of American Bandstand.* New York: Ballantine Books, 1985.

Smith, Joe. *Off The Record: An Oral History Of Popular Music.* New York: Warner Books, 1988.

Terrace, Vincent. *Encyclopedia Of Television Series, Pilots And Specials 1937-1973.* New York: New York Zoetrope, 1986.

Whitburn, Joel. *Top 1000 Singles 1955-1987.* Milwaukee: Hal Leonard Books, 1988.

------------. *Top Country Singles 1944-1988.* Menomonee Falls, WI: Record Research Inc., 1989.

------------. *Top Easy Listening Records 1961-1974.* Menomonee Falls, WI: Record Research Inc., 1975.

------------. *Top Pop 1955-1982.* Menomonee Falls, WI: Record Research Inc., 1983.

------------. *Top Pop Albums 1955-1985.* Menomonee Falls, WI: Record Research Inc., 1985.

Articles

Alexander, Shana. "Hit Singer Bobby Darin Has Big Ambitions, Prospects To Match." *Life*, January 11, 1960.

Alpert, Don. "Bobby Darin Shuns Run-Of-Mill Targets." *Los Angeles Times*, July 26, 1959.

Alterman, Loraine. "Darin—Back With A Splash." *Melody Maker*, April 15, 1972.

Aronowitz, Alfred G. "Brash Bobby Darin In Las Vegas." *New*

York Post, December 18, 1969.
------------. "The Copa's Bobby Darin" (four-part series). *New York Post*, March 2-7, 1972.
Aronowitz, Alfred G. with Jack D. Fox. "Bobby Darin" (six-part series). *New York Post*, September 19-25, 1960.
Barry, Bernard. "This Is Why Darin Had To Do His Own Thing..." *Melody Maker*, June 13, 1970.
"Bobby Darin: Hottest Singer Since Elvis." *TV Guide*, December 26, 1959.
Changas, Estelle. "The Real Bobby Darin Fights For A Fresh Start." *Los Angeles Times*, April 16, 1972.
"Darin Bounces Back—Thanks To 'The Younger Guys.'" *Melody Maker*, November 15, 1966.
"Darin Exits Nitery Field To 'Widen His Music Biz Scope.'" *Variety*, October 23, 1963.
Ehrman, Anita. "The Darin' Young Man (three-part series). *New York Journal-American*, September 18-20, 1960.
Gehman, Richard. "The Astoundingly Brash Character Of Darin." *TV Guide*, January 28, 1961.
Grevatt, Ren. "On The Beat." *Billboard*, September 1, 1958.
------------. "The New Sinatra?" *Melody Maker*, March 12, 1960.
Hammond, Sally. "Bobby Darin's Regards To Broadway." *New York Post*, September 30, 1967.
Hilburn, Robert. "Crises, Rewards—Darin's Daily Diet." *Los Angeles Times*, July 22, 1972.
------------. "Darin Touches All The Music Bases." *Los Angeles Times*, July 20, 1969.
Lees, Gene. "Bobby Darin And The Turn From Junk Music." *Down Beat*, May 12, 1960.
"Look At Me." *Newsweek*, April 9, 1962.
Lorenzo, Richard J. "Bobby Darin: Doing His Thing And Other Things." *Goldmine*, April 7, 1989.
"'New' Darin Forms Own Label To 'Speak Out' Via Songs." *Billboard*, August 3, 1968.
"Nightclubs: 2 1/2 Months To Go." *Time*, March 10, 1961.
O'Haire, Patricia. "Bobby Strikes Back." *New York Daily News*, March 1, 1972.
Price, Joe X. "Darin Sounds Off In Marking 10th Anni in ShowBiz." *Variety*, April 27, 1966.
Raddatz, Leslie. "Bobby Darin—15 Years Later." *TV Guide*,

August 26, 1972.
"Splish Becomes Splash." *Newsweek*, October 19, 1959.
Van Gelder, Lawrence. "Purse Of $25,000 Offered In Chess." *New York Times*, January 16, 1973.
Wiener, Allen J. "Bobby Darin: The Available Recordings." *Goldmine*, April 7, 1989.
Wilson, Earl. "Bobby Darin, Primarily A Citizen." *New York Post*, March 20, 1968.
------------. "Censored Darin Sings A Song Of Protest." *New York Post*, February 1, 1969.
------------. "Darin Had 'Revelation' At RFK Grave." *New York Post*, January 8, 1969.
Wilson, John S. "Showmanship In Some Pop Singers." *New York Times*, February 21, 1960.

General Index

D

H

W